A Guide to
Learning
Independently

A Guide to
Learning
Independently

Lorraine Marshall • Frances Rowland

MURDOCH UNIVERSITY

Open University Press

BUCKINGHAM

Published in Great Britain by
Open University Press
Celtic Court
22 Ballmoor
Buckingham
MK18 1XW

A catalogue record of this book is available from the British Library.

ISBN 0 335 19171 1 (pb)

Printed in Malaysia – VVP

Contents

List of Tables

Thanks

We would like to thank the people who have given us encouragement and advice, especially those who put time into reading the manuscript—Simon Avenell, Michael Booth, Mary Dale, Patsy Hallen, Richard Jakob-Hoff, Jim Macbeth, John Raser and John Webb. For comments on the section on using libraries, thanks to Tricia Cawley, Nancy Lane and Hugh Malcolm. We would also like to thank our typists/secretaries Anne Francis, Leonie Pimm, Annette Ritchie, and especially Meredith Wills for burning the midnight oil.

Thanks to my parents for their encouragement—to my father who gave so much and would have been so proud to have his copy of this book, and to my mother for her continuing support. Thanks to Al for the spark that led to this book. And last, but in fact first, special thanks to Jim for his patience and support throughout, for his endless reading of the drafts and for saving my sanity at sea. And for the second edition, thanks again to Jim and also to Suzannah who although not involved in the first edition has helped with this one.

Lorraine Marshall

My personal thanks to John Holt, who reminded me of what I believe about teaching; to Ann, who taught me about learning; and to Ann's babysitters, without whom I wouldn't have written this book. And to John—thank you.

Frances Rowland

Preface to the Second Edition

The revision of **A Guide to Learning Independently** has worked towards three main objectives. First, we have corrected deficiencies in the first edition while, second, adding new information and techniques. Third, we have integrated new material which springs from other (and newer) philosophical and theoretical bases.

- Some major technological changes of the 1980s which affect learning have been accounted for. For example, libraries now access information electronically, and word processors are commonly used by students for their written work.
- Some sections of the book have been updated, such as the chapter on conventions and the further reading lists at the end of each chapter.
- Material has been modified in the light of experience. For example, as a result of extensive use by students and tutors at Murdoch University, the section on 'Analysing a topic' has been streamlined in ways that work better for students

It is over ten years since the first edition of **A Guide to Learning Independently** was published and the ideas it contains were formulated and written in the 1970s, a time when educationally it seemed possible for any motivated individual to achieve whatever level of education they desired and when access to higher education had expanded in western societies. It was a time of focus on individual growth and **A Guide to Learning Independently** with its emphasis on 'you' grew out of that time.

Today the emphasis is different—it is now recognised that for some groups in our society all the determination and effort they can muster is unlikely to get them where they would like to be educationally. There is increasing recognition of what it means to live in a culturally diverse society and of the influence of gender, race and class on people's opportunities.

However, **A Guide to Learning Independently** still rests on the premise that it is possible for a person to change the way they approach their learning; and it is directed to the individual student because it is the individual who must write the essays and reports, pass the exams and organise themselves appropriately in order to be successful in the tertiary education system. The book still offers techniques to help you do what is expected of you by your teachers. But rather than providing a guide which only sets out to help you jump successfully through the hoops held by other people, we still would argue that your learning should be centred on you and on your purposes for learning. To some academics (and possibly some students), this approach may seem out-of-touch with the realities of budget cuts and institutional 'rationalisations'—and this second edition of the **Guide** takes account of current factors such as worsening staff-student ratios. But we claim that it is even more important in such times for students to try to take charge of their own learning as much as possible; and any help that this book can give with this is worthwhile.

So the philosophical basis of the book in both editions is the same, but the content takes into account some of the developments in educational theory in the last decade. Some examples follow.

- The role of culture and society in shaping learning is explored in Chapters 1 and 5; and the need for students to learn to operate in the culture of a tertiary institution is discussed in Chapters 1 and 3. In particular, throughout the book we have taken into consideration the diverse learning experiences of students from a range of different ethnic backgrounds.
- The challenges posed by feminist methodologies to the fundamental paradigms of a range of disciplines is reflected in material such as that on subjectivity and objectivity.
- The chapters on writing, especially Chapters 11 and 12, follow what is commonly called the process approach to teaching writing. Students are led from analysing a topic to research, to writing and rewriting a

piece of work. While the demands of different disciplines and genres in which students are writing are accounted for, the writing chapters rest on the conviction that the process approach works and students' writing benefits from it. This conviction is based on extensive experience helping students with their research and writing.

- In the first edition of the book, students were urged to link content with process—that is, to link what they are learning with how they learn it. The past ten years of research into student learning have strengthened this basic premise, and it is reinforced in the second edition.

Many of the techniques we describe have not changed, although we have introduced some new ones. What is different is the nature of the awareness that we suggest you bring to your learning. Our thanks to the many people who have taken the time to tell us that they have found the first edition of the **Guide** helpful and to make suggestions for improvements. We hope that the second edition of the book will prove as useful.

Read this first!

If you are looking for a book which does more than describe techniques to help you succeed in your formal education, **A Guide to Learning Independently** is the book for you. It will help you with learning tasks such as writing assignments, reading textbooks, taking notes and concentrating when you study, and it does present a range of techniques to help you meet the requirements of your teachers and courses. However, **A Guide to Learning Independently** is also designed to help you discover your own learning purposes and style. It doesn't set out to prescribe how you should learn, but offers a range of ideas and techniques from which you can choose. These alternatives are presented in the context of encouraging you to use tertiary institutions for your own purposes. To set the ideas and techniques in a broader framework, the book also discusses learning in general and tertiary education in particular.

This book focuses on you—who you are and what you bring to your learning. Throughout the book you are encouraged to examine your purposes and what you want to learn. You are also encouraged to look at how you learn informally, and to build on this self-knowledge in your formal learning. Implicit in this approach are the beliefs that there is no single way of learning which suits everyone and that it is your right and responsibility to shape your own learning.

So the *first five chapters* of the book concentrate on you—those aspects of your self and your lifestyle which affect your learning, when and how you study, and the decisions and adjustments you make when beginning tertiary studies. The importance of asking your own questions in your learning is emphasised, as is learning in ways that suit you so that you remember what you learn. The *next four chapters* look at how you can find, take in and evaluate information and ideas when pursuing your own and other people's questions. These chapters deal with analysing and researching a topic, finding and using a range of information sources, reading and listening to lectures. The *last six chapters* look at communicating, using and evaluating what you learn. They deal with tutorials, seminars and informal discussion groups, with developing your writing, and with writing and presenting assignments and reports.

Within each chapter you will find questions and ideas about you as a learner. These are intended to centre the book on you and to help you discover your own purposes and methods for learning. Because the questions are based on the premise that only you can answer them, we don't prescribe one 'best' way of learning, but instead suggest alternative study techniques. We give reasons for these techniques so you can decide how useful they are for your purposes, and we encourage you to try them as you actually learn and study to find those which suit you. Often these techniques are presented in the framework of 'before', 'during' and 'after' stages of a learning activity, such as researching a topic and reading.

This book contains frequent *cross references* to other sections of the book. These direct you to another section within the chapter you are using to a section within another chapter, or to another whole chapter.

In case you wish to go into a topic in greater depth, we suggest *further reading* at the end of some chapters and the general bibliography. We also use *quotations* from a wide variety of sources to offer different perspectives, to reinforce what we say, and to entertain you.

Each chapter in **A Guide to Learning Independently** *has a particular focus.* However, the ideas and techniques mentioned in any one chapter cannot be neatly separated from those in any other chapter, any more than your learning can be segmented. Use this introduction and the 'What to do now' section to familiarise yourself with the whole book. Use the Contents list to become familiar with the theme of each chapter. When working with a chapter, use the Index and cross references to move backwards and forwards through the book, to think about the ideas and techniques in different contexts.

This book is intended primarily as *a guide and reference* for people who have some opportunity for independent learning. It is intended for students who are past the age of compulsory schooling, and for people who want to learn how to use the resources of formal tertiary education for their own purposes in learning. However, the learning techniques presented in the book can be used in structured classes, and sections of the book can be used by people who need help with activities such as journal writing, producing business reports and running discussion groups.

You are likely to find the book valuable if you are a student at university or college, especially in first or second year. You will find it useful if you are in the final years of high school, whether or not you are going on to tertiary study. If you have left school and are taking technical or training courses, the book can help you with basic learning skills. If you are a student who has little contact with teachers, perhaps because you belong to a large institution or because you are studying part-time or at a distance, the book offers information otherwise available from frequent face-to-face contact with teachers. If you are a student straight from a highly structured school situation, the book will help you adjust to taking responsibility for your studies. If you are returning to study after an absence from it, you can use our suggestions to help you gain confidence in yourself as a learner.

A Guide to Learning Independently can be used in several different ways, each of which involves actively trying the ideas and techniques in your learning and studying. Don't simply read the book. Acquaint yourself with its contents, and then use it as a guide and reference when the need arises. *Firstly*, you can use the book on your own. Refer to it, for example, when you need help with how to use the library or write an essay. Read chapters such as 'Becoming an Independent Student', 'Learning and Remembering' and 'Learning from Evaluation' if you are thinking about the nature of formal tertiary education. *Secondly*, the book can be used when studying and learning with other people. You might, for example, use the chapter on 'Developing Your Writing', to work on your writing with other students. The process of learning with other students can enrich your education and make it less solitary. You can also use the book when working on your learning skills with a teacher, so you can both relate our suggestions to your particular learning activity. For example, refer to the chapters on 'Analysing and Researching a Topic' and 'Writing Essays' when working on how to prepare and write an essay. *Thirdly*, teachers can use this book too. A teacher within a subject area can refer students to sections of the book which would be most helpful to the particular individual or group. Study skills teachers and counsellors can also use the book in their classes or with individual students.

However, all the ideas, information, techniques and suggestions we offer are of little value to you as a student unless you are reading, writing, listening, talking, asking questions, experimenting, stretching your mind—unless you are engaged in learning. Exploring and practising alternative approaches to learning and study provides a basis from which you can choose those approaches which are most effective and satisfying for you. This experience with alternative ways of learning is also essential if you are to change habits which no longer suit you. Such changes take time and practice, and suggestions which are easy for us to make may take courage and persistence for you to apply. But defining your purposes, building on your strengths, and working on your weaknesses as a student are all crucial to learning independently. This book is intended to help you discover these challenges and pleasures.

ﺓ ﺓ ﺓ

'Students' minds are like containers to be filled.'
'Education is to sharpen that tool which is the mind.'
'Knowledge is to be built up, block by block.'

These are a few of the metaphors commonly used to describe formal education. But such metaphors describe learning as essentially confined and defined, rather than as a process of growing and changing.

Each of us is born with a great curiosity, and this curiosity is essential for us to survive and learn. We learn as we ask and think about what we need and want to know. We are learning all the time, whether or not we realise it. We learn from what we do, from what happens to us, from our jobs and our pastimes ... the list is endless. And we learn more easily when actively involved and when using what we learn in doing or talking, thinking or dreaming.

Learning is often thought of largely as an approved activity which happens in certain places (schools, universities and colleges) at certain ages (usually between five and twenty one) and in certain ways (in classrooms, according to a curriculum taught by teachers). But this formal study is only one part of our learning, and is designed to achieve only particular objectives. At the heart of all of our significant learning, formal and informal, are the questions we ask because of who we are and what we need to know.

Formal educational institutions can help you ask and pursue your own questions. There are teachers in these institutions who care about learning and about you as a learner, who can convey to you the fierce and gentle pleasures of the mind. Having teachers who help you ask your own questions, who share their knowledge and experience and who are also questioning and learning for themselves is an invaluable part of formal education. There are also students to talk and argue with, to theorise and fantasise with.

However, formal education can be one of the most effective methods for squashing curiosity or channelling it in artificial and unnecessary directions. And without curiosity, you are limited to learning what is presented to you rather than discovering how to learn, how to ask your own questions and communicate and exchange ideas. Knowing how to learn makes it possible for you to continue learning after you finish formal education. Otherwise you are restricted to learning a particular body of knowledge, which may soon become outdated.

Using the resources of an educational institution for your own purposes entails thinking about what is expected of you—and why. Who decides what you should learn, and how and when this should be taught? Who decides when and how you should be required to prove what you have learned? These decisions, made partly by teachers, reflect what many others see as the purposes of a university or college in our society. These 'others' include government bodies, academic committees, administrators, professional organisations, employers, and individuals who hold power in our society. If you want to use formal education as part of your purposes for learning rather than simply following other people's goals, try to identify and examine and question the assumptions and purposes of the people who shape tertiary education. Will you accept what these people expect, what they require? If not, think about your options.

Formal educational institutions expect a lot of you. As with most work, sometimes you will be involved and enthusiastic, and sometimes you will have other priorities in your life which detract from your study. Learning is a personal process, not simply a commodity or a meal ticket which you will acquire after a set programme of study, so keep your questions and your purposes in mind. Play with ideas—speculate, hypothesise, fantasise. Do the ideas offered excite you or make sense to you? If so, grab them with both halves of your brain. Read, write, draw, experiment, for the sake of your own learning and for the pleasure and discovery of a craft. Learn how to communicate your own questions and ideas, and try hard to understand what others are communicating. Don't reject an idea or a topic or a course out of hand because of your biases or lazinesses or fears. Be willing to take a risk, to reach a little further than you are sure you can reach. Don't expect to understand all you read or hear or say.

Real, active learning of your own isn't easy—it's hard work. But the hard work is not that of a dutiful conscience, it arises from the joy of intense involvement. One of the most challenging things you can do is to attempt to be aware of your purposes for learning, to question profoundly what and how you learn, to communicate your ideas clearly and to understand the thoughts of others. This process of learning is one of growing and changing, and that is more exciting than filling bins or sharpening tools or building with blocks.

What to do now

1 Read through the Contents list.
2 Flick through the book and choose a chapter which would be especially useful to you now, or start with Chapter 1 'You' or Chapter 5 'Becoming an Independent Student'. Read thoroughly the chapter you have chosen.
3 Choose a topic which interests you, look it up in the Index, and read the relevant pages of the book.
4 Turn to Table 8. 1, 'The anatomy of a book', and apply the questions in this table to **A Guide to Learning Independently**.
5 Look back over 'Read This First!'
6 Any questions or ideas? Ask someone else—another student, a teacher, or a friend, for their thoughts on your questions and ideas.

1

You

This book begins with you. It begins with you because asking questions and thinking about yourself, your lifestyle and your background, can give you insights into your individual learning style. You can then use these insights to make your learning and study more effective and satisfying.

Your body and your emotions, your cultural background and your beliefs, who you live with and where you study—all these affect your learning. Your physical state and your emotions influence your ability to learn, and too little sleep or exercise may affect your enthusiasm for and ability to study. A belief in the value of hard work may make you a conscientious student. An argument with the people in your household can create difficulties when you try to concentrate on study, and moving house or changing jobs can leave little time and energy for formal learning.

As people and as students we are all different. If you are slow and deliberate, a study task may take you longer. This may leave you feeling inadequate, or you may enjoy the leisurely savouring of new ideas. At the other extreme, if you have a high energy level and live at a fast pace, you might wish you could occasionally slow down enough to integrate in more depth what you learn, or you might enjoy the speed with which new insights come to you. There is no one way of learning and studying that suits everyone. And because you change daily, weekly and monthly, there is no one way of studying which always suits you. So you need to get to know more about yourself and examine how you live.

This chapter contains three parts—your physical and emotional self, your cultural and social self, and your surroundings. Each section of the chapter gives you information, asks questions and makes suggestions. It is a chapter to work with, to take time with. Consider the questions and suggestions carefully. Here are some ideas on how to use them.

- Read each set of questions in turn and write down your answers or ideas on them, perhaps in a special notebook or a journal (see 'Keeping a journal', Chapter 11). When you have read and thought about the whole chapter, look back over it and revise any notes.
- Read through the whole chapter and think about those questions and suggestions which are relevant to you at present. Later re-read the chapter and focus on other questions. Re-think your responses if you or your lifestyle have changed significantly.
- Discuss the questions with one or two friends or with a group of people.
- If you want to read more on a topic, check the further reading at the end of the chapter or in the reference books.

Your physical and emotional self

This section looks at aspects of your physical and emotional self that directly affect your learning and your study. As a first step to thinking about your self, centre your attention on your body. Stop for a few minutes. Centre your attention on your face—your forehead, eyes, nose, mouth, jaw. Are they relaxed? strong? tired? tense? Move your awareness down to your neck, shoulders, spine. Focus on each part of your body —down to your toes. How does your whole body feel now?

What do you like most about your body?
What do you like least?
How does your body feel now?

Now **stop**. Did you actually spend time thinking about and answering these questions, or did you just read them? If you didn't answer them, go back and think about them seriously. Get in touch with your body before you go on to the next set of questions. This chapter centres on you, but can only be effective if you become actively involved with the questions and ideas it contains.

Body rhythms

Mental preferences

> Certainly people show consistent, life-long predilections for morning or night activity. Physiological differences may be found in the circadian rhythms of the so-called lark people, who are most alive by morning, and the owls, who perform at their best late in the day, yet the owls are generally penalised by the usual scheduling of school hours.
>
> *Gay Gaer Luce*

Your body has many rhythms and cycles. Each day, for example, your temperature and pulse rate fluctuate slightly, and you pass through the same pattern of dreaming several times each night. Monthly cycles apparently occur for males as well as females. Perhaps you go through cycles where your desire for physical activity alternates with your desire for mental activity. One of the difficulties in studying for final exams in the southern hemisphere is that you often need to be mentally active during the first bright spring days when you would prefer to be outside and physically active after the hibernation of winter. If you are a night person you may be unwilling to leave your bed for an early lecture on a gloomy winter morning, or if you are a day person you may find it difficult to concentrate during an evening class. A cup of coffee may revive you for that evening class, but regularly using stimulants to help you cope with study is self-defeating in the long run. Discovering your individual body rhythms can help you plan study times when you are more mentally active.

Are you a lark or an owl? owl

Are you aware of patterns in your body's needs for sleep? for exercise? for food? for sex? no

How is your study related to these patterns? I study when I have to

- Determine when during the day you are usually most alert mentally and when you feel physically ready to study.
- Try to schedule your classes and your study during your alert times. If it is necessary to study when your energy level is low, plan to do work which demands less intense concentration.

Sleep

> I haven't been to sleep for over a year. That's why I go to bed early. One needs more rest if one doesn't sleep.
>
> *Evelyn Waugh*

Sleep needs vary for different people. If you are frequently irritable and can't cope as well as usual with minor problems, you are possibly getting too little sleep. How well you concentrate on study is influenced by how much sleep you have.

Do you often sleep so much that your mind feels drugged? yes

What effect does a late or interrupted night's sleep have on your concentration next day? a big effect

Can you think clearly after a nap? Does a brief nap or a couple of hours' sleep refresh you for long periods of study? No .

When do your sleep needs vary—when you are emotionally upset or physically active, for example? Do you often have to change your sleep times—because of shift work or a restless baby, for example? How do these changes affect your study?

- Think about your sleep patterns for the past two weeks. Determine your minimum sleep needs and the amount of sleep you think you need for a good night's rest.
- Try to work out how your sleep patterns help or interfere with your learning.
- Try to plan your most demanding study periods for times when you are not short of sleep.
- On a night when you can't fall asleep, try deep breathing exercises and relaxing your body completely (see 'Tension and relaxation'). If this doesn't work, get up and do something rather than lying in bed and worrying about not sleeping.
- If you often have difficulty getting enough sleep, allow time to wind down before going to bed, and don't drink a lot of tea and coffee during the evening. Give yourself two or three periods of deep relaxation during the day. Relaxing your body fully from head to toe is different from sleeping, but can be almost as refreshing.

Food and drink

> One cannot think well, love well, sleep well, if one has not dined well.
> *Virginia Woolf*

A breakfast which is more nourishing than tea and toast, or a lunch which is more than a bag of chips, a doughnut or a bowl of rice, helps you concentrate during class or private study. A light evening meal instead of a large dinner makes it easier to focus on your study or during an evening class. If you generally feel tired and irritable because of poor eating or heavy drinking, studying is difficult at any time.

Do you prefer to eat one large meal a day or frequent small meals? Do you try to study after a large meal?

When settling to study, does preparing something to eat or drink help or hinder you?

Do you often drink so much alcohol that you cannot think clearly next day?

- Make sure your diet is well balanced, and includes protein, carbo-hydrates, and plenty of fruit and vegetables. Essential protein is available from complex carbohydrates such as beans or rice as well as from meat and dairy products, but refined carbohydrates such as ice cream, alcohol and soft drinks add little to your diet except kilojoules. If you generally lack energy, check that your diet isn't deficient in minerals and vitamins, particularly iron and the vitamin B complex. If you don't have much money, eating properly takes more planning and a knowledge of nutrition, but it can be done.
- Avoid studying after a heavy meal.
- If you feel the need for food during a study session have a small amount of protein food, such as a piece of cheese, a glass of soy milk, or a handful of peanuts. Sugary food gives you a temporary lift then leaves you more tired than before.
- A judiciously chosen treat can help you when you settle to work or reward you when you finish.

Physical exercise

> Not taking care of your body is like not paying the rent; you end up with no place to live.
>
> *Gayle Olinekova*

Physical exercise can provide a welcome break from mental activity. It helps you study because it reduces tension, increases the oxygen supply to your brain, improves your digestion and helps you sleep more sound-ly. Long periods without exercising your body can make it difficult to exercise your mind effectively. However, immediately after strenuous physical exercise some people find it difficult to settle down to study.

What form of physical exercise do you enjoy?—for example a team sport, cycling, swimming, sailing, yoga, sex, dancing, walking, skating?
If you are a physically active person, do you find it difficult to sit still for long periods to read, write or listen to a lecture?
Does exercise usually refresh or fatigue you for learning?
Do you renew your concentration during a study session by taking a short break to move about?

- Choose exercise that feels good to you and do it regularly. Include activity that exercises your whole body, including your heart and lungs, and activity which stretches your body and helps you loosen up.
- Plan to study and exercise when these two activities help rather than conflict with each other.
- If your work is physically tiring, allow yourself time to relax and eat something nourishing before you try to study.
- At times when you need to be especially mentally alert, such as during

exams, regular physical exercise helps increase your alertness and concentration.

Senses

All creative activity, as well as much of your pleasure in life, depends on your sensory awareness. Even your ability to absorb and use second-hand information depends on your ability to relate it to your own first-hand observations. Yet, constantly exposed to second-hand information, you may forget to use your senses and may become, to some degree, cut off from the world immediately around you.

Fred Morgan

Your earliest learning is through your senses, but as you come to rely more on abstract reasoning it is easy to forget how vital your senses are to your learning.

Stop for a moment. Shut your eyes. What can you smell? What can you hear? What tastes do you have in your mouth? What sensations do you feel on your skin? Now open your eyes. What can you see?

- At the end of each day ask yourself what you remember most vividly— which sight, sound, taste or touch comes instantly to your mind? Conjure up these sense impressions as you drift off to sleep or write a description of them in a daily journal.
- When you feel like relaxing, take a few minutes to become deeply aware of the smells, sounds, tastes, touch and sights you are experiencing.
- In your study utilise as many of your senses as you can. For example, when trying to learn something you find difficult don't just read it silently and use only your sense of sight. Speak it out loud so that you hear it, and make notes using patterns and colours so that you use your sense of sight more fully. The act of writing also uses the kinesthetic sense of touch.

Tension and relaxation

'How did I live to be a hundred years old? Well, when I moves I moves slow. When I sits, I sits loose. And when I worries, I goes to sleep.'

Liz Carpenter

If you are reasonably relaxed you can learn more effectively. To relax, you may need to put aside problems for a while, exercise more often, or learn how to relax your body consciously from head to toe.

Where in your body do you usually feel anxiety or tension?
Do you feel relaxed now? If so, why? If not, why not?
Can you study when you feel tense? If not, do you know how to relax?
While you are studying or listening to a lecture, do you occasionally check to see if any parts of your body are tense?

After a period of study do you suffer from eye strain, headaches, or tension in your shoulder muscles?

- Learn and practise relaxation techniques which help your whole body relax fully: for example deep breathing, yoga, gentle exercise, massage.
- If you think your tension is due to physical causes such as eyestrain, seek appropriate help.
- When reading or writing or using a computer, stretch and change positions occasionally, rest your eyes by focusing on a distant object, and yawn and take several deep breaths to ease any tension around your mouth and jaw.

Your emotions

> Last night I was seized by a fit of despair that found utterance in moans, and that finally drove me to throw the dining room clock into the sea.
>
> *Marie Bashkirtseff*

The ups and downs of your emotions influence your learning. If you are feeling cheerful you probably find it easy to study; if you are feeling depressed you may have difficulty concentrating or absorbing new ideas. Most students have emotional problems at one time or another—including anxiety or guilt about study.

What are the most positive aspects in your life at present? List these. Lee parents Tracy
What are the most positive aspects of your studies?
What are you most worried about? List these worries.
Which aspects of your studies worry you the most?

- Write down what is worrying you before you begin studying or if you continue to be distracted as you study. Ask yourself if it is more urgent to go on studying or to tackle your worries. Plan another time to deal with whichever is less urgent.
- Spend five to ten minutes before you are fully awake each morning remembering your dreams. This becomes easier with practice, and reflecting on your dreams can help you understand your emotions.
- Allow yourself a set time during the day to think about your problems and try to put them aside for the rest of the day. Talk to a friend about them or write them out.
- Practise physical relaxation techniques or activities which help you deal with your emotions.
- Reading for pleasure can give you a respite from your worries.
- Spend some time away from the place where you seem to worry most. Going for a walk or visiting friends can make problems seem less important.
- If you have a persistent problem, discuss it with a close friend, a sympathetic 'outsider' or a trained counsellor.

- If your difficulties are connected with your learning or lack of it, do some work. A few hours of concentrated study often works wonders if you are feeling overwhelmed with study demands. If you are stuck on a problem, discuss it with your teacher or with other students— often other people have the same problem. Read the relevant sections in this guide for some useful suggestions.
- If you are anxious about a responsibility such as taking an exam or giving a seminar paper, find out as precisely as possible what you want to know about your subject, and study it as thoroughly as you can. Talk to someone with experience in the techniques of exams or seminars, or read the relevant sections in this book.

Your cultural and social self

This section encourages you to consider the impact of your cultural and social background on your thinking and learning, your beliefs and values and your relationships with others and how this affects your study.

Stop for a moment and think about your cultural background in your wider society and then within your tertiary institution.

Which cultural groups have been influential in shaping who you are? Do you identify with a strong cultural group in your country?
Were you born here or are you a migrant or an overseas student? If you were born here, for how many generations has your family been in this country?
To what socio-economic class does your family belong?
Are you from a group whose numbers in this society are small: for example, a recent migrant or an aboriginal group?
Are you from the 'bush', a country town, or the city?

For many years, most tertiary education communities in Australia and some other countries consisted of school leavers from affluent families. This has changed, and university and college communities are now more varied. There has been an influx of students from overseas, and tertiary study now attracts students from different backgrounds, including mature-age people, migrants, minority ethnic groups, and people from lower socio-economic groups.

Ways of thinking and learning

All of us are living and thinking subjects ... Everybody both acts and thinks. The way people act or react is linked to a way of thinking, and of course thinking is related to tradition.

Michel Foucault

It is valuable to spend some time thinking about how your cultural and social background might influence your thinking and how you go about your learning.

Do the cultural groups with which you identify value learning?
How has your background helped or hindered you in your desire for a tertiary education?
With which cultural groups in the university or college community do you identify?
How does your background affect your view of the world? How has this world view affected your study? For example, how is your interpretation of what you read and hear different from that of other students?
How does your background give you particular strengths in your learning? Do you ever feel that there are gaps in your learning because of your background?

- If you are studying because it is a cultural or social expectation and not because you want to, think about your alternatives. If you are to continue with a formal education, you need to work out your own purposes for your learning so that the time and effort you invest does not seem like a waste of time (see 'Choices and decisions', Chapter 3). If you want a tertiary education but in pursuing this are at odds with others in your cultural or social group, consider how you can handle this opposition and look for support from within your university or college (see 'Becoming an independent student', Chapter 3).
- Try to identify how your background might contribute strengths to your learning at university or college, and how it might leave you with areas on which you need to work. For example, if you come from a family with experience of books and academic learning, you may have an understanding of the approaches to study expected of university students but you may also have to handle pressures from others for you to achieve at a high level. If you come from a society where teachers are highly respected and where questioning the teacher is not acceptable, it may take you time to become accustomed to more informal teacher–student interactions, but your respect for teachers perhaps means that you are more ready to listen carefully in lectures. If you are a student from a developing country, your formal education may have suffered because of large classes and limited books and resources, but your learning is enriched by the cross-cultural comparisons you can make.
- Once you become involved in your studies, you will find that your way of interpreting what you read and what is discussed in tutorials sometimes differs noticeably from that of other students, and that this difference reflects your background, your experiences and your previous schooling. You are entitled to your own interpretation, which should be supported by evidence, examples and reasons. If you are a

lone voice presenting a particular point of view, you need to think through your interpretation as fully as possible, and you may have to work harder to have your ideas considered or accepted. Remember, however, that diversity of opinions is an important part of the intellectual debate in a university, and that everyone has a contribution to make.

Beliefs and values

Ideally, our choices will be made on the basis of the values we hold; but frequently, we are not clear about our own values.

Sidney B. Simon et al.

What you believe and value directly affects your learning. It can affect your choice of courses, your work within courses, your open-mindedness and how you relate to other students and to teachers. For example, if you are from a religious family and you don't believe in genetic engineering you may find yourself in conflict with teachers in a biology course who see no harm in this area of research; if you are concerned about the environment you might write your assignments on topics related to this area.

At times your beliefs and values conflict with your learning. For example, a course on Eastern religious philosophy may affect your belief in a Western ethic which is goal-oriented. You may find yourself disillusioned with the studies required for a long dreamed-of profession, or with the realities of formal education. Perhaps you are confronted with a challenge to a cherished prejudice about the superiority of the male sex or of white-skinned races. A new insight into personal relationships can create dissatisfaction with your belief in the nuclear family.

How would you complete the sentences:
'I believe that humans are essentially ...'
'I believe that our society should be organised so that ...'?
How does what you believe and value affect what and how you learn?

- Try to work out which beliefs and values are most important to you, and try to identify their source, that is those which are embedded in your upbringing.
- If a conflict of beliefs and values is seriously affecting your study, talk it over with a close friend or a counsellor. If this conflict is related to a course, talk to a teacher in that course if possible.
- Think about the beliefs and values of the other people with whom you have frequent contact—your friends, a partner, your teachers, fellow students. Try to work out why they differ from or are similiar to your own.

Your relationship with others

It isn't the work that is going to be hard in college. It's the play. Half the time I don't know what the girls are talking about; their jokes seem to relate to a past that everyone but me has shared. I'm a foreigner in the world and I don't understand the language. It's a miserable feeling. I've had it all my life. At the high school the girls would stand in groups and just look at me. I was queer and different and everyone knew it ...

Jean Webster

Think back for a moment to times in your life when you have been the only different person in a group; for example, if you were the only young person in a group of older people, or when you were with others who all spoke a different language, or when the others all had different beliefs from yours.

- If you feel different and isolated from other students, find others with a similiar background who understand how you feel and share with them your experiences and your problems with learning. At the same time remember that you have much to offer to other students, and contribute your perspectives in formal and informal discussions.
- If you have rarely thought about what it is like to be on the outside, the chances are that you are a part of a particular majority group.
- Take advantage of the richness and variety of experience available in the diverse cultural and social groups within the student body. Being open to new ideas, approaches and perspectives is an important part of your formal learning within the classroom, but is also available to you through informal social interactions with other students.

Your surroundings

The environment in which you work and play and eat and sleep influences your learning. If you are a full-time student and your friends frequently drop by, your approach to studying will differ from that of a parent with young children who is studying part-time and taking evening classes, or an external student who lives and works on a farm. If you have a room of your own, you will organise study sessions differently from a person who works at the kitchen table or in a library. It is not essential to have ideal surroundings before you can study effectively, but often you can make changes which improve your study situations.

This section looks at two aspects of your surroundings which directly affect your learning—the people you live with and the places where you study—and suggests alternatives which can make study easier.

Who you live with

On Mondays mum has a tutorial, so I have to go around to Grandma's place for tea. That's all right. She lets me watch television.

8 year-old girl

The time and energy you have for study can be dramatically increased if you manage to work out a satisfactory living pattern with the other people in your home. This usually takes time, and even if you have a comfortable arrangement, there will be difficult periods as you all adapt to the inevitable changes in your lives. But any time and effort in this direction is well spent to increase your enjoyment of formal learning. If the people you live with co-operate in making your study effective, you will have more energy and enthusiasm for study.

Do you live on your own, or with others—parents, relatives, friends, other students, a partner/spouse, children?
Do your working hours coincide with those of the other people in your house? Are the others also studying or do they have some idea of the demands of being a student? Are they considerate of your study needs? Do they resent the time you spend studying? How do you arrange time with them and time to study? Do you have responsibilities in your household, such as domestic chores, financial burdens, or caring for young children or a sick relative? Do these responsibilities leave you little time and energy for study? How might they be reallocated?
Are you under pressure from people such as your partner or your parents to succeed in your studies? Why? Are their criteria for success the same as yours?

- If there is a persistent or major problem in your living arrangements which makes it difficult for you to study, talk about it as soon as possible with the person or people you live with. Describe how you feel about the problem and suggest ways it might be handled, particularly what you can do about it. Listen to suggestions from others concerned and see if you can come to a workable compromise. If compromise doesn't seem possible, think seriously about the priority that formal learning has in your life (see 'All work and no play...', Chapter 2).

Where you study

If you are deeply involved with what you are learning, you can concentrate just about anywhere for short periods of time. However, in formal learning you also need to concentrate for sustained periods and to study subjects which aren't of immediate importance to you. It is then that your surroundings become important.

Location

Where do you prefer to study? Why? Does a relatively impersonal environment such as a library help you study?
Are the books and references you need readily available where you study? Are there other people around where you study? Are they also studying? Do they help or hinder your learning? Why?

- Decide whether you study more effectively at home or elsewhere. if necessary, try to reorganise your time so that you can study in the location where you learn most effectively.

Study spots

> You say I'm well read.
> Thank you but—
> I owe my deep and liberal knowledge
> To the 100 watt bulb
> in the loo
> And not college
> > *Margaret Norton*

If you don't have a quiet study place at home where you can leave your work spread out, can you arrange one? How?
What objects on your work space help you study—a box of file cards, a dictionary, photographs, a collection of shells, a bunch of flowers? Why?
Can you study effectively outdoors?

The association of one place with a particular study activity helps you settle down to study more quickly and also enables you to leave it behind when you finish. You might choose a comfortable chair to read a book, but prefer a library desk when organising essay notes.

- If possible, find or create one or two places where you can regularly study—a desk in your bedroom at home, a corner table in a library or a chair in a quiet room at a friend's house. You may be able to screen off a corner of a room or to move a table into one corner of a backyard workshop.
- Create a work space which includes objects which prompt you to study and is organised according to your needs for space and order. Having your own work space, no matter how small, is much preferable to packing away your papers and books each time after you use them.

Comfort

You concentrate better on studying if you are physically relaxed (but not too relaxed!)—if you are sitting in a comfortable position, with lighting that cuts down eye strain, and without distracting noise.

Are you more comfortable when studying at a table or desk, or when sitting on a couch or bed? Do any of these positions help you study for a sustained period? If your study places are too warm, too cold or too stuffy, how can you alter this?
What type of noise distracts you? How long can you concentrate fully with 'background' music playing?

- Prevent eye strain by avoiding glare or uneven lighting on your book or work surface. Try to use adequate direct and indirect light or an appropriate desk light. Light the whole room as evenly as possible, and position yourself so that light falls over the shoulder opposite your writing arm to avoid a shadow on your work space. Prop up your book at a constant angle so that your eyes don't have to accommodate to different distances.
- To reduce noise distraction, avoid irregular noise and exciting music, use ear plugs or headphones, or study when your household is at its quietest.
- If you are cold, put on an extra layer of clothes, wrap yourself in a blanket, or turn a heater on at a low setting rather than attempting to study in a stuffy overheated room. If the weather is hot, study at the cooler times of day.
- If you use a computer ensure that the screen is placed so that you avoid eye strain and that you are sitting correctly. Make sure that you look away from the screen frequently and that you get up and loosen up from time to time.
- There is appropriate study furniture available for sale; for example, ergonomic chairs, special word processing tables. Even if you cannot afford these it may be worth your while to check them out and you may then be able to improvise with what you already have available.

⁛ ⁛ ⁛

The questions and suggestions in this chapter have focused on you— because you are central to this book and to what, why and how you learn. Reading and following guidelines which tell you how to make your formal learning more effective is useful only if you adapt these guidelines to your own personality, lifestyle and surroundings.

> This above all; to thine own self be true.
> *Shakespeare*

Further reading

Faraday, Ann. 1973. *Dream Power*. Pan Books, London.

Faraday, Ann. 1976. *The Dream Game*. Harper and Row, New York.

Goodacre, Phillip, & Follers, Jennifer. 1987. 'Communicating Across Cultures' in Lovat, Terry (ed.). *People, Culture and Change*. Social Science Press, Wentworth Falls.

Iyengar, B.K.S. 1966. *Light on Yoga*. Allen & Unwin, London.

Luce, Gay Gaer. 1973. *Body Time: The Natural Rhythms of the Body*. Paladin, Granada Publishing, St Albans, England.

Stanton, Rosemary. 1990. *Health and Energy Cookbook*. Murdoch Books, Sydney.

2

Planning When and How You Study

This chapter looks at planning when to study and at how to go about studying and concentrating. It begins with examining your life to determine the place that study has in it.

All work and no play ...

> It is impossible to enjoy idling thoroughly unless one has plenty of work to do.
>
> *Jerome K. Jerome*

As a student you are likely to be involved in campus or community activities, socialising, sport, hobbies, personal relationships, domestic chores, childcare or a paid job. These involvements may enhance your learning, for example if you are a keen athlete taking physical education courses, or if you are a parent studying child psychology. Possibly they may conflict with your study—your family may expect you to put their needs first, or your drinking mates may scorn your study.

Learning can be one of the most creative and satisfying pleasures you experience. However, there are inevitably times in your formal learning when you have to make yourself work—when you are not interested in a topic, when you have difficulty with an assignment, or when you have other things on your mind. At these times planning can be useful.

Planning how to spend your time can give you the opportunity to explore the pleasures of using your mind and can help you cope with times when it is difficult to study. If it suits you to study according to a timetable, don't make it too ambitious, and don't let it rule your life so that you rarely do anything spontaneously. Any schedule needs to be flexible.

Whether or not you like to plan your time, examining your objectives and workload for a year is important.

Planning a year's study

The road to hell is paved with good intentions.
Western proverb

Your objectives

Planning a year's study involves formulating your objectives for the courses you will take, and drawing up a schedule of work to be done. For each course think about:

- where it fits into the overall objectives of your formal education
- how it is connected with your other courses
- your knowledge of the course content
- your interests or questions concerning the subject
- skills you want to acquire, and
- grades you hope to achieve.

Your workload

Plan your workload for the year, taking into account the time you spend in class, listening to tapes or reading course materials, preparing and producing assignments and reports, and reviewing material after a class or when preparing for exams.

One value of planning is that it minimises the stress that usually accompanies last-minute assignment writing or studying for exams. It is all too easy to delude yourself that there is ample time to complete an assignment or to study. Look realistically at your other study commitments for the same period and think about the activities necessary before each assignment is complete. Ideally, also allow 'just in case' time—just in case you have the 'flu in the week you plan to study, just in case your computer crashes, just in case you have an unexpected visit from an old friend when a major essay is due. Give yourself time for the pleasure of exploring areas arising from your study but not directly related to your current goals, needs or pressures.

A method to use

Try the following method of planning your year's study.

* At the beginning of a year, find out as precisely as possible what work you want to do or are required to do in that period. Do you have exams, major and minor assignments, weekly preparation for tests or classes? Draw up a calendar or buy and use a year calendar planner to show at a glance your study schedule and other commitments.
* For each assignment allow time for:
    * choosing and defining a topic
    * searching for and selecting material (including any field work)
    * researching, collecting and organising material
    * reading and notetaking
    * writing (or taping or filming)
    * typing or word processing, and
    * editing your work.

  Each of these is an activity in its own right and can require a deceptively large amount of time. Writing a report, for example, is not only a final chore to be hastily completed after your practical and field work is complete. If possible, allow more time than you think necessary for each activity.
* Estimate how much time you have to devote to an individual piece of work. This largely determines your approach to the topic, as well as the quality of the end result.
* Allow time prior to each exam or test to revise your work.

Within the framework of your long-term plan, you can also plan how to spend your week.

Planning your week

'There's lots to do; we have a very busy schedule—
'At 8 o'clock we get up, and then we spend
'From 8 to 9 daydreaming.
'From 9.00 to 9.30 we take our early midmorning nap.
'From 9.30 to 10.30 we dawdle and delay.
'From 10.30 to 11.30 we take our late early morning nap.
'From 11.30 to 12.00 we bide our time and then eat lunch.
'From 1.00 to 2.00 we linger and loiter.
'From 2.00 to 2.30 we take our early afternoon nap.
'From 2.30 to 3.30 we put off for tomorrow what we could have done today.

'From 3.30 to 4.00 we take our early late afternoon nap,
'From 4.00 to 5.00 we loaf and lounge until dinner.
'From 6.00 to 7.00 we dilly-dally.
'From 7.00 to 8.00 we take our early evening nap, and then for an hour before we go to bed at 9.00 we waste time.
'As you can see, that leaves almost no time for brooding, lagging, plodding, or procrastinating, and if we stopped to think or laugh, we'd never get nothing done.'

Norton Juster

To draw up a weekly study plan requires some knowledge of your lifestyle and of yourself as a learner, such as whether you often write with ease, or when during the day you are likely to be most alert mentally. Do you work best in bursts of intense activity for several days or weeks, with brief periods of relaxation in between; or do you prefer a regular daily or weekly work session?

If you prefer not to plan your time or you find it difficult to keep to a plan, try setting aside and using a regular time each day or week for concentrated study, or making and using a list of 'things to do'. These strategies can ease the worry of apparently having a lot of work and no time in which to do it. Use some of the suggestions in this chapter when your workload overwhelms you.

If you haven't thought much about how you spend your time, **the following exercise** will make you more aware of this. As it concerns a short period, the exercise is only an indicator of your current activities. But it can help you realise what priority study has in your life, how other activities can help or hinder your study, and where your time 'vanishes' to.

Time is like money. If you have lots of it to spare, you have more choice about how you spend it. If it is in short supply, knowing where it has gone can help you budget for the future.

Anon.

1 Examine how you spend your time

For several days or a week, preferably near the beginning of semester or term, keep a detailed timetable of how you spend your time. Record how much time is occupied by:

- formal classes
- private study
- employment
- relaxing alone and/or socialising
- exercise and active recreation
- domestic chores and family activities
- travelling, and
- sleeping and eating.

Note particularly any activities which take up a lot of time. Look for hidden time-consumers, such as watching TV. Indicate the times during your private study when you concentrated at your best. Make sure your record is accurate—recording three hours' work on statistics is misleading if you spent part of that three hours on the telephone chatting to a friend, daydreaming, or watering the garden.

At the end of the week, estimate the number of hours you spent in each of the areas listed above, and ask yourself the following questions about your data.

Were there times when I studied more effectively, such as early in the morning or when I had the entire day to study? Why?
Did I work more effectively in some places than others, for example, in the library or at home? Why?
How did the amount of time I spent in classes compare with the time I spent on study out of class?
Did I have a particularly heavy workload this week?
Did I usually work more effectively in short periods and then lose my concentration, or did it take me a while to settle into study so that I needed longer periods for serious work?
Is my study connected with any of my other activities?
Did I prepare myself for long periods of serious study? How? Was this effective? Did I relax afterwards?

2 Give study the priority you want it to have in your life

Now that you have some data on how you spent a few days or a week, are you happy with how you spent your time? Would you like to make any changes? If so ...

- List four activities which take a lot of time and energy in your life at present. List four activities which you think *should* take the most time and energy, and four on which you *would like* to spend the most time and energy.
- Ask yourself if you spend enough time studying effectively. Do your non-academic activities and interests leave you sufficient time and energy for formal learning, and do they increase or decrease your satisfaction with that learning?
- If other involvements prevent you from learning as well as you would like, consider limiting these involvements, reducing the number of courses you are taking, or reducing the time and effort you put into a course.
- If there is a significant difference between your current involvements and those you feel you should or would like to have, consider changing your priorities. Think about why you are at university or college, and how important your formal learning is to you.

3 Map out next week's work

Take into account your findings and do the following

- look at your long-term calendar and see what work is due soon
- chart in your short-term formal study commitments, such as giving a seminar paper
- mark in any informal commitments connected with your study, such as an appointment with your tutor
- indicate your other commitments
- write out a list of what you want to accomplish during the week, and when.

Then:

- plan to study when you are usually able to concentrate most effectively
- plan relaxation and social activities so that they and your studies complement each other, and
- set aside time at the end of each day's study to review your work.

At the end of the second week, think back on how your week has resembled your plan. Don't worry if you didn't keep absolutely to your schedule—instead, examine why you did not. If you are from a background in which the needs of your extended family network or your domestic responsibilities take precedence and you frequently find it difficult to meet the deadlines placed on you by the institution, discuss this with your teachers and with an adviser.

> Efficiency concerns the best ways of doing an assigned job. Effectiveness, on the other hand, concerns the best use of time—which may or may not include doing the particular job in question.
>
> *Edwin C. Bliss*

એ એ એ

Both your long-term and weekly study plans need to combine flexibility and a commitment to realistic goals. You can best use your plans by reviewing them several times during a course. Adjust them according to your current study needs and purposes, and to take account of other changes in your life. At the beginning of a course you need to explore and familiarise yourself with the topics and areas to be covered and the language used, so you probably spend a high proportion of study time in research and in classes. Half-way through a course you are likely to be relating new materials to what you have already learned, and to be planning and producing written work as well as attending classes and doing research. Near the end of a course you spend your time reviewing what you have learnt, and are probably involved in completing major assignments and preparing for exams.

Planning *when* to study is a beginning. To make full use of the time you have set aside, also think about *how* to study.

Concentrating while you study

'How can you go on talking so quietly, head downwards?' Alice asked, as she dragged him out by the feet, and laid him in a heap on the bank. The Knight looked surprised at the question. 'What does it matter where my body happens to be?' he said. 'My mind goes on working all the same.'

Lewis Carroll

Concentrating is not always something you have to work at—if you really want to know or do something you can concentrate easily, possibly for a long time. When concentrating fully you are so absorbed in what you are doing that you are unaware of time passing or of what is going on around you. Watch a small child building a sand castle, or two friends involved in an intense argument.

However, if you are required to learn about a topic which doesn't particularly interest you, or to study for a purpose which doesn't coincide with yours, or if you have to study at times or in ways which are difficult for you—then you have to make an effort to focus and sustain your concentration. Have you ever noticed that during a lecture many of the audience suddenly become restless, or that shortly before the end of a lecture many people change position, look at their watches and prepare to leave? The length of time for which you can concentrate fully depends on factors such as your enthusiasm for what you are doing, your skill at a particular task, your emotional and physical state, and your surroundings at the time.

You don't have to assume the position of a Zen Buddhist or a Rodin's Thinker or sit at a desk with pen in hand to concentrate. Why not let your ideas sort themselves out while you surf, watch the sunset, walk, or travel to college? When you do read and write, concentrating is not simply reading every word on a page or putting lots of words onto paper or a computer screen. Full concentration involves actively questioning your material and integrating it into what you already know. This questioning and integrating helps you understand what you read and organise what you write; it also helps you when you share your ideas and knowledge with others.

This section suggests a step by step process for concentrating more effectively in study sessions of at least an hour. These sessions might include reading, notetaking, writing, organising or editing material, or listening to tapes. Concentration during class or while working with other people involves similiar principles.

Experience as a mother has taught me a lot. Gone are the days of spending uninterrupted hours writing an essay or compiling a report. I'm lucky if I get half an hour now. But this maternal conditioning has its advantages. I'm now capable of making the maximum use of the time that is available and then switching off when family demands become pressing. Learning to use the available time to maximum advantage is one of the main secrets to success of the part-time student mother.

Vivienne

Have you consciously thought about your study habits—when, where and how you prefer to study? How do you settle down for a study session? For how long can you concentrate fully? What do you do when you find it difficult to concentrate? There will be times when you can only concentrate for short periods, or when you can't concentrate at all.

However, you can concentrate for longer periods and more effectively if you know how to cope with distractions which can arise at certain points in your study. While you are warming up or preparing for concentrated study you might be prone to procrastination, and your mind might be partly elsewhere. After you have been concentrating intensely for a short time, you may suddenly become impatient with your task, be unable to capture a particular thought or think through a specific problem clearly, and you may begin to feel stiff from sitting still. After sustained concentrated work, you feel less mentally alert because you are reaching the end of your concentration span for a particular subject. When you can no longer concentrate at all, outside thoughts or events intrude and you feel generally tired.

Warming up

Demanding physical exercise requires a warm-up session; so does strenuous study. You can begin this mental warm-up during your previous activity. When travelling to the library, you can plan what you will study; while doing household chores you can mull over ideas for an essay; while finishing a task, visualise yourself sitting down at your desk with a hot drink and beginning to study. When you actually sit down at your study place, deliberately preparing your mind for study can motivate you, help eliminate conflict or anxieties from your mind, focus your thoughts on the task at hand, and increase your ability to understand what you learn so that you remember it more easily.

If you have difficulty settling down to study, the following suggestions may help.

1 Consider **how you feel** emotionally and physically. If you feel good, direct this energy to learning. If you are not in the state of mind for studying, decide if you need to study at this particular time. If you don't, plan another time to work. If you do, use techniques that help

you set your problems aside (see 'Emotional energy', Chapter 1). Try a brief energetic walk, a run around the block, a cup of tea, or a short chat with a friend.

2 Seat yourself **comfortably**, with everything you need at hand (books, blank papers, a drink, lecture notes).

3 Decide on your **time limits** for this study session. Take into account your non-study commitments, then set a minimum study time to become involved in your subject. Set a maximum time, so you don't feel overwhelmed by apparently endless work and so you can focus your energy fully. Don't make these times so inflexible that you feel you must stop work precisely at the time planned. Plan to reward yourself after you have completed your study by doing something you particularly enjoy—go to the beach, visit a friend, watch a special TV programme or prepare your favourite snack.

4 Decide **what to study** while your mind is fresh. Will you start with the subject or activity you find easiest? Will you tackle an assignment that has been worrying you or which you have been intending to do for a long time?

Think about the study activities you have to choose from. You might, for example:

- read for a tutorial paper or an essay
- edit the final draft of an assignment
- write the first draft of an assignment, a short story, a lab report, or a journal entry
- prepare an annotated bibliography or illustrations for an assignment
- make a tape recording
- listen to a radio programme or a lecture tape, or
- learn data by heart.

Set yourself a goal to accomplish. If you have a large task, tackle it one section at a time.

5 Begin your study with a **brief warm-up task** which helps you concentrate. Use this task only if it is necessary—not if it is a form of procrastination.

- Do some routine tasks which are part of the subject, such as filing lecture notes or compiling a list of important vocabulary.
- Revise previous work in the area, for example, summarise notes, write comments on a discussion. This revision brings ideas to the front of your mind, and can give you a sense of achievement if you are overwhelmed by the study before you.
- Foreshadow a topic by asking yourself 'Why am I studying this topic?' 'To whom do I want to communicate my ideas?' For

example, are you studying to clarify ideas for your own benefit, or to prepare for a tutorial? Brainstorm your topic by jotting down as many ideas on it as possible—don't worry about the order of these ideas or how far-fetched they seem. Fill your mind with the subject.

• Preview a book you will use (see 'Previewing', Chapter 8), or read a section of the book and try to identify the central idea (see 'Central ideas', Chapter 8).

If you still have trouble concentrating, ask yourself why and what you can do about it. What must you change to help you concentrate better? (Try Chapter 1 for suggestions on coping with problems such as tension or a noisy study place.)

Sustaining your concentration

'Fan her head!' the Red Queen anxiously interrupted. 'She'll be feverish after so much thinking.'

Lewis Carroll

Some people study mostly in short, intense bursts with frequent breaks in between; others need to study for long periods to become fully immersed in their task. Your concentration span also varies for different activities and how involved you are in what you are doing.

• When studying intensely, you occasionally become aware you are distracted by something and feel impatient with your work. Set yourself another five minutes in which to work. If your impatience still persists, give in to it. After the five minutes, take a short break while you **physically loosen up**—stand up and stretch, walk around, consciously relax. Leave your study spot for five minutes or so—get a drink, glance through a newspaper, organise your desk. Don't take a break for too long or you may require another warm-up.

• When you have been studying for a long time so that your concentration is diminishing and can't be rejuvenated by a short break, you need to **recharge mentally**. Remotivate yourself by reviewing the material you have just covered and try to get an overall picture of it. This often gives you a feeling of achievement as well as reminding you why you are studying a particular topic. Look ahead at what you intend to do next. Preview the rest of the book or chapter. Jot down or tape record ideas for the next section of an assignment. Switch to another subject and work on that until it becomes stale, then return to your first subject or go on to a third.

Losing concentration

Try to recognise when you can't concentrate any further. There is no point in believing you are studying when you are simply staring at the words on a page, when you repeatedly can't find the words you want, or when your mind is far away.

- When you feel you are losing concentration, review what you have been studying. If your task is part of a large piece of work, think about where the part fits into the whole and which part you will tackle next.
- Decide when you will study again—in an hour's time, the next morning, a day later.
- Then stop studying and relax. Reward yourself—enjoy that special reward you promised yourself earlier.

> I do not happen to be a believer in the cliché that 'Virtue is its own reward.' As far as I am concerned, the reward for virtue should be at least a chocolate sundae, and preferably a cruise to the Bahamas.
>
> *Barbara Sher*

ऒ ऒ ऒ

It takes time and practice to plan when to study and to learn how to concentrate fully so that you enjoy your formal learning and accomplish what you set out to do. It takes time and practice to become aware of and create your own study patterns and to discover the concentration techniques that you find most helpful. The alternative to spending this time planning when and how to study is to study when others expect you to or to just bumble along as you always have. Being in control of when and how you study is crucial to learning independently.

Further reading

Bliss, E.C. 1977. *Getting Things Done—The ABCs of Time Management*. The Macmillan Co., Australia.

Lakein, A. 1973. *How to Get Control of Your Time and Your Life*. Signet, New York.

Mackenzie, A. & Waldo, K.C. 1981. *About Time: A Woman's Guide to Time Management*. McGraw-Hill, Sydney.

3

Becoming an Independent Student

Starting university or college can be bewildering as well as stimulating. In whatever discipline you are studying and whether your study is full-time or part-time, internal or external, the adjustments you have to make are considerable; and you will be faced with the challenge of becoming part of a new culture and of learning independently. You are likely to spend the first couple of weeks mostly in organising your timetable and in finding your way round campus and through administrative requirements. Hopefully you can do most of these things during an orientation period before classes start. You also begin to recognise faces among staff and students, and may discover some of the social activities that can be part of a tertiary student's life.

This chapter looks at adapting to independent study within formal institutions—thinking about why you are studying, deciding what to study, handling difficult situations, making contact with teachers and other students, and combining study with other work.

Tertiary institutions and you

The modern university has at least six distinct functions. It conserves knowledge, through library holdings and scholarship. It transmits knowledge by guiding the learning of students through community education programmes. It advances knowledge through basic research. It applies knowledge by applied research and consultancy. It refines knowledge through critical review and scholarship. It also fulfils the role of certifying standards of entry to a range of professions having different levels of commitment to intellectual endeavour.

Ian Lowe

Universities and colleges have a mystique which shapes expectations of them. *One* common image is that these institutions have little to do with the 'real' world, that they are full of professors who expound esoteric theories and young students who seem to spend more time playing than working. A *second* and somewhat contradictory image is that of superior training institutions where doctors, lawyers, architects, engineers, teachers and the like are prepared for their professions. A *third* image is of a community of scholars who dwell in the hallowed halls of higher learning, of professors who pursue ultimate truths and new scientific revelations and impart their insights to highly intelligent students. A *fourth* image which some staff and students come to hold is that:

> ... universities have become huge bureaucracies with an academic mind and no heart, careless and ignorant about students and their intellectual needs, organised by managers and managerial professors absorbed in their own pursuits, giving service to the existing social order and dispensing its conventional wisdom, bereft of a philosophy and the social imagination to create a new and compelling conception of their own future.
>
> *Harold Taylor*

If you enter university or college with high expectations, this fourth image may be disillusioning. On the other hand, it can help dispel the 'aweful' mystique embodied in the second and third images, and can help you realise that sometimes when you are having study problems the causes may not lie solely with you.

There is an ongoing debate about the role tertiary institutions should have in the modern world. For example, there are those who argue for an intellectual role, and there are arguments that higher education should respond to the market economy and to consumer demands. At various times there are attempts to 'streamline' and rationalise higher education and the level of funding varies accordingly. These changes will have a direct impact on your studies if, for example, severe budget cuts mean that your teachers are not so readily available to give you individual help, or that there are fewer tutorials and lectures and you are thus left more on your own to learn.

Tertiary institutions are usually divided into faculties, departments or schools, each representing a body or closely-related bodies of knowledge called 'disciplines'. Some of these disciplines provide professional training and some do not. Some institutions separate—and it seems at times even segregate—the disciplines into departments which teach what are considered to be 'subjects' in their own right. Each apparently discrete area of knowledge has an institutional hierarchy with a professor and senior and junior academics and senior (postgraduate) and junior (undergraduate) students. Each of these disciplines or body of knowledge is a culture in its own right with its own discourse, its own language and vocabulary and its own methodologies for choosing, analysing, interpreting and presenting this knowledge. In some institutions there are opportunities for interdisciplinary or multidisciplinary study, but this is the exception rather than the rule.

Thus, when you start tertiary study you enter not only the overall culture of the institution but the culture of the discipline in which you will study. As you progress through your studies you learn the current culture of your discipline through instruction in the content—through immersion in it. Only rarely do you get explicit instruction in the nature of the discourse—its language and methodology. And you may find that within some disciplines there is conflict about what constitutes 'knowledge' in that discipline—so there may be more than one appropriate methodology or language. At times it may be confusing if you find that the approach to knowledge in one discipline is different from the approach in another. Some students, for example, do very well when asked to write in one subject area but not so well when they use the same approach in another area.

But in your first year you are not expected to be highly knowledgeable in your chosen field or to be familiar with the languages or methods of the field; this is part of what you are at college or university to learn. The way you approached a discipline area in secondary school or elsewhere may no longer be applicable at tertiary level. Take nothing for granted and be prepared to ask.

You may enter the tertiary system after completing secondary school, from a workplace, or from an overseas educational institution. If you find your university or college strange and alien, remember that you are not alone in having to adjust to a new organisational culture and to many academic discipline-cultures. To become informed about how your university is organised and about your studies in general, attend orientation days, ask the staff in the areas in which you plan to study, consult a counsellor or study adviser, or read the relevant sections of this book.

You may find your cultural and social background at odds with the expectations of your discipline (see 'Your cultural and social self', Chapter 1). For example, if you are an overseas student taking a course which focuses on Australia, you may need to ask a teacher for a reading list to help you build the necessary background knowledge. And learning about the characteristics of 'good' study behaviours in your discipline is another aspect of becoming familiar with the field in which you have chosen to study: for example, whether or not there is a strong emphasis on critical thinking. Ask your teachers about these study behaviours, write these down and compare them with what other students think to confirm the acceptability of your approach.

> ... my time is exclusively occupied with study. It's a very bewildering matter to get educated in five branches at once.
> 'The test of true scholarship,' says Chemistry Professor, 'is painstaking passion for detail.'
> 'Be careful not to keep your eyes glued to detail,' says History Professor. 'Stand far enough away to get a perspective of the whole.'
> You can see with what nicety we have to trim our sails between chemistry and history.
>
> *Jean Webster*

Universities and colleges can be intellectually exciting places, but are also bureaucratic institutions like any other large work place. Academics are people with a variety of concerns which can include highly specialised research, a lively curiosity about things of the mind and the world in general, and an involvement with teaching; but like other people, they have their share of human bias and ignorance. Students usually manifest interest in learning, but otherwise are impossible to categorise.

Learn something of the systems and people who shape an institution and your opportunities for learning, and try to take part in the decision-making process. You will have your own decisions to make as well.

Choices and decisions

> 'Would you tell me, please, which way I ought to go from here?'
> 'That depends a good deal on where you want to get to,' said the Cat.
> 'I don't much care where —' said Alice.
> 'Then it doesn't matter which way you go,' said the Cat.
> '—so long as I get somewhere,' Alice added as an explanation.
> 'Oh, you're sure to do that,' said the Cat, 'if you only walk long enough.'
>
> *Lewis Carroll*

Your main experience of formal education may have been in the structured environment of compulsory schooling where from your first day at school the Department of Education and the teachers were responsible for directing what, when, how and where you learnt, and where the emphasis was on remembering and reproducing information correctly. You may have attended private schools such as a single-sex denominational school, or a boarding school where your learning and life were very structured; or you may have gone to an alternative school where ostensibly you were free to learn what and when you liked. Your early learning may have been in a country where questioning a teacher's authority is not acceptable.

In tertiary education you make many decisions about why, what, when, how and where you learn. Unless you were lucky enough to have teachers and schools that allowed you to develop your abilities for learning independently, this may be your first experience of making such decisions about your formal education.

Why are you studying?

You make your first choice when you decide whether or not to go to university or college. After secondary school, it should be your reasons which determine whether part of your learning takes place within the formal education system. Often there are pressures which seem to give you little choice, but the choice is there if you are aware of it. Why have you chosen to further your education? Because your parents want you to, you can't find a job, you want to become an engineer, you like discovering new ideas, or you think campus life will be a lot of fun? If you are returning to study after some years away from it, why?

> Most people let themselves be pushed by chance or other people's expectations into environments of which they make the best, rather than into those which meet their inner needs.
>
> *Michael Deakin*

A research study of students' motivations for studying identified four broad clusters of reasons which are categorised as orientations to study: *vocational,* or concern about future employment; *academic,* or a desire for continuing education; *personal,* or developing as a person; and *social,* or enjoying the freedom of university life. Within these four categories some students had an 'intrinsic' interest in study, that is, in learning for its own sake, and some an 'extrinsic' interest, that is, in education as a means to an end.[1]

Why you are studying will directly influence how you study. Thinking about and identifying your reasons for studying overall and for taking individual courses can give you useful insights into how you approach your work. It can also help you cope with the pressures that you face from peers or family who think you are working too hard or not hard enough. You have your own reasons for studying and as an adult you can make your own choices, but at times you will have to justify these choices to others. Your reasons for studying one course may be different from your reasons for studying another—one may be a pre-requisite in an area you don't like and your aim may be just to pass at the required level, while another course may be so intrinsically interesting to you at a personal level that you give it a lot of time and do very well in it.

What will you study?

When you applied for tertiary study you indicated in which discipline areas you wished to study. And your choices would have been directed by your interests, your previous studies, and by ease of access to your chosen area. Many students enter tertiary study with a clear idea of what they want to study, many start out on one track and then change to another. Some institutions are flexible and allow for these changes and others do not. If you have not been admitted to your first choice of discipline, it is up to you to accept this or to find out what you need to do in order to study your first choice at a later time. It may not be possible for you to study in your preferred area either because of educational factors external to you such as quotas or the need to have a high grade point average, or because of personal factors beyond your control, such as the lack of child care. In such cases you need to decide how important it is to you to pursue that area and to plan accordingly.

You also decide in which discipline areas to enrol, which courses to study, and whether to study full-time or part-time, internally and/or externally. In some situations you will have little choice, such as in a highly structured discipline with many required courses, or when confronted with yet another set of rules and regulations. Even so, you should be the one to decide whether to take that particular area, or whether to comply with a particular rule or regulation.

Choosing courses

Deciding which courses to take depends on why you are studying. It also depends on workload and how the course content fits into your primary discipline, and on the people who organise and teach the courses. Your choice is likely to be influenced by administrative and academic requirements such as pre-requisite subjects or quotas on course intakes.

To help decide on your courses, consult as many sources as possible. Look through the official handbooks and read any student guides to courses and teachers. Remember that most handbooks and guides go to press six to nine months before a course starts, so any information they give may be out of date. For recent information on courses, talk with staff, such as department or programme heads, deans, academic advisers and counsellors.

If you can't find a course on a subject you would like to study, ask a staff member in a related subject area if there is some other way you can undertake this study (see 'Pursuing your questions', Chapter 4). For courses which interest you, find out who organises and teaches in them, and look for students who have taken them. Talk to these staff and students to find up-to-date and detailed information on the aims and content of courses, on the likely workload for preparation and assignments, on assessment methods, and on books or materials you are expected to buy. The students will also have opinions about the teachers in the course. Attend any pre-course orientation activities and do any recommended preliminary work. If you can, find out what is expected of you in the first couple of weeks of a course and start on this.

If it is more convenient or enjoyable for you and if you can afford it, study part-time or take some or all of your courses externally. You can benefit from being a part-time student taking only one or two courses at a time, especially if you have a lot of other demands on your time, or have been away from study for a while. If you are an external student, your choice of courses may be more restricted than for internal students. Seek information on courses as early as possible, so you can enrol in time for course material to be sent to you.

If you are taking several courses, try to calculate your total workload and plan a weekly class timetable. If you have a choice of times and teachers, decide which classes to attend. The combination of courses you planned may be impossible because of timetable clashes or difficult because of a high combined workload. These difficulties can occur even for popular or required combinations of courses. So if you still want to take all these courses, check with the organisers if alternative arrangements can be made.

Unless your choice of courses is very clear, if possible delay your final choices until the end of the first or second week of teaching. This gives you a chance to find first-hand information on the courses which attract you, and to meet some of the teaching staff and students. You can't know all there is to know about a course at this stage, but you can check preliminary information against your own experience in the course.

Choosing teachers

> Learning grows and develops by the dialogue of teacher and student, becoming sometimes greater than anything an individual, however brilliant, could produce.
>
> *F.R Leavis*

Where you have a choice of teachers, sit in on their classes, read any handouts they write, and contact them personally. Look for a course organiser who clearly sets out objectives, organisation, content, workload and assessment for a course and who is open to your comments and questions. Select teachers who know their subject, stimulate your enthusiasm and are willing to help you improve and extend your skills in studying. A good teacher whose subject areas are only broadly related to your interests can help you follow these interests better than a poor teacher whose interests coincide closely with yours. How well you learn with a particular teacher also depends on how your personalities interact. The lecturer you listen to for several weeks or the teacher with whom you work for a whole course is important to your learning. If possible be prepared to change courses or teachers if, after a fair trial, you find you are not learning as much as you would like.

How you spend your time

The work pattern was one of alternate bouts of intense labour and of idleness, wherever men [*sic*] were in control of their own working lives ... The pattern exists among some self employed—artists, writers, small farmers, and perhaps also with students—today and provokes the question whether it is not a 'natural' human work rhythm.

E. P. Thompson

You largely decide on your study timetable—and you may be surprised at how much work is involved in being a serious tertiary student. The time you are expected to spend in formal classes or studying outside class time varies. For example, fine arts or architecture students usually spend much more time in classes than humanities or social science students, while courses without a large component of practical work usually require more time outside class for research, writing and preparation. Whether or not you attend a class, read a book or hand in an assignment early depends on your enthusiasm for a subject, your desire to pass a course at a particular standard and your response to teachers and programmes. Some teachers and programmes are more flexible about these matters than others.

Except for formal class time such as lectures, tutorials and laboratory sessions, you usually decide whether to study in the library during the day or at home in the evening, to sit in the cafeteria or the local student pub talking to friends, to work at a job or be with your family. Hopefully you will have time to explore both social and academic student life, even if you are studying part-time or externally. Universities or colleges are more than institutions with collections of courses, and being a part of campus life can be a lot of fun (see Chapter 2).

Adjusting to independent study

As well as changes you make as you begin to learn independently in formal education, becoming a student in a new culture entails practical and emotional adjustments in your life. (Some aspects of your self and your surroundings which influence study are presented in Chapter 1.) If the people you are close to support you as a student, the changes are easier and you can relax and explore what your new life has to offer. Without support, be prepared to spend time and energy in establishing a new lifestyle as a student as well as on study itself; but you need to be certain that you do want to be a tertiary student.

Coping with change

> I don't feel it is necessary to know exactly what I am. The main interest in life and work is to become someone else that you were not in the beginning. If you knew when you began a book what you would say at the end, do you think that you would have the courage to write it? What is true of writing and for a love relationship is true also for life. The game is worthwhile insofar as we don't know what will be the end.
>
> *Michel Foucault*

For some students the changes wrought by higher education are secondary to the other events in their lives. For others the educational process stimulates questions which force them to question their life, which in turn can lead to the desire (frequently accompanied by many difficulties and fears) to change their life to one that is more in keeping with these changing values. Many mature age students enter university at a time when they already perceive the need for changes. For a woman living in a traditional relationship with husband and children who expect her to fulfil the role of 'housewife' and 'mum', a course in Women's Studies can create exciting and confusing questions about her role. A student from Southeast Asia faces educational challenges as well as the possibilities inherent in adjusting to living in a new culture away from many supports and expectations at home. For some students changes occur that are independent of their studies, such as moving house, starting a new relationship, or a sudden bereavement in the family. If you are a school leaver starting tertiary study at 17 or 18 you are probably facing a time of intense personal growth; this can be a time of leaving home and finding your own social niche. These changes impinge on studies and there is a two-way exchange between learning and your life.

It may help to ask the following questions:

Is your education stimulating you to think about issues that make you want to change the way you live?

When the changes in your life are creating stress, how do you cope with your studies?

Where do you go for help when you are stressed by the changes occurring in your life?

How do you usually deal with change in your life?
Do you have a friend or acquaintance who will help you explore new possibilities
and listen to your problems?
Do you think you need to seek professional help to deal with these changes in
the most positive way?
How are these changes affecting the people close to you?

Foucault aptly points to the uncertainty of where life can lead and reminds us that changes are to be seen as opening new possibilities rather than as something to be afraid of. But if you are seeking certainty in your life and do not want to change your values or your ideas, then many of the courses offered in higher education may not be the best place for you.

> He believed to the end exactly the same things he started with. It seems to me that a man who can think straight along for forty-seven years without changing a single idea ought to be kept in a cabinet as a curiosity.
>
> *Jean Webster*

One of the fundamental approaches to coping with change concerns focusing in depth on why you want to study. When you are confronted with confusing changes and the decisions which go with them, it helps to be clear about the essence or core of why you are studying and what you hope to achieve; then to stay open to ideas on how to achieve this.

Imagine, for example, that you are studying because you want to work with people, so you have enrolled for a psychology degree. However, you find that the way that psychology is taught at your institution does not seem to coincide with your vision of how you would work with people. You then need to define as clearly as possible what are the essential characteristics of your vision. Do you want to work with people with severe problems or people who are having temporary difficulties? Do you want to work on your own, in a small team or in an institutional setting? Is your orientation towards a particular school of psychological thought because of its views of human nature? With these essential characteristics in mind you can then brainstorm to see firstly, what your current psychology degree programme offers you, and secondly, what other avenues might be open to help you achieve your vision. Of course your vision itself may well change with time and with changes in you. The important thing is to keep refining the essence of what you want, and not to mistake the means of achieving this for the vision itself.

One way of clarifying the essence of what you want and of dealing with changes is to talk with other people. While other people can't live the changes for you, you don't have to deal with the situation completely on your own.

Even if you feel alone now, talk with:

- other people who are going through similiar changes or have done so in the past
- possible new friends who care about you achieving your goals, or
- counsellors or sympathetic teachers who have seen other students going through similiar experiences and can pass on some handy hints and provide a listening ear to help you sort out how you want to handle the changes.

You may find that you look to one person to discuss your changing views of society, to another person to help deal with the repercussions at home of your changed lifestyle and to a third person for moral support when you have to write your first tertiary-level essay. Think creatively and stay open to all sorts of possibilities for help—words of wisdom and warm support can often come from unexpected sources.

Dealing with difficult situations

As a student you will inevitably find yourself in situations that are difficult. One technique which many students have found useful and which can be used to cope with difficult situations such as exams, is the **imagine the worst** approach.

Imagine you find yourself in an exam room, and are faced with a question which requires an essay answer. You have the sinking feeling that all you know on the topic could be put down in half-a-dozen sentences. What do you do? Panic instantly? Start scribbling furiously in the hope of inspiration? Leave the exam room? Most students worry about not being able to answer exam questions and imagine themselves in this situation. But their imagination stops there. You can help yourself cope with this problem ahead of time by also imagining what you will do about it.

Now continue imagining that you put down your pen, sit back, stretch a bit, and take several deep breaths. You read the question again, slowly and carefully. You pick up your pen and start to jot down anything which comes to your mind on the topic. You don't try to order this knowledge, but concentrate instead on recalling as much of it as you can. If you start feeling rushed, you deliberately pause for a few moments, and then continue. When you feel you have all your knowledge before you, you check that each item is relevant to the question. You then organise your information into one or two main points. When this is done, you start writing, concentrating on saying what you want to, as clearly as you can. You avoid the temptation to pad your answer with irrelevant facts or long-winded language. If at any stage you find yourself feeling rushed, you stop for a minute and concentrate on relaxing. You may just sit and look out of the window as a way of relaxing. When you have finished saying what you want to, you sit back and feel pleased at knowing more about the topic than you thought you did. Then you check your essay over carefully to make sure it answers the question and is clearly expressed. Finish.

Imagining the worst *and* imagining how you will handle it cannot guarantee you will answer the question successfully. Nothing can. However, it does make that outcome a lot more likely. (See 'Exams' in Chapter 5 'Learning and Remembering' for some help, and Chapter 12 'Writing Assignments' for ideas on essay-type answers.)

Part of the 'imagine the worst' approach is to think beforehand about why you are worried about an exam. Is it because you might fail a course, of which the exam is part? Imagine yourself failing the course, and then go on to imagine other possibilities once you have failed. Can you sit for a supplementary exam, or repeat the subject? Think about why you want to pass the course. Can you realise these aims in other ways? It can be invaluable to realise that there are often alternatives to some of the difficulties you face. If you know that you always panic in exam situations, despite knowing your subject well, it may be possible to arrange with your teacher for alternative forms of assessment. You may be able to select a course where exams don't count for all or most of your final assessment.

'Imagining the worst' can be used to help you cope with other difficult situations apart from exams. Are you anxious that you will make a fool of yourself in a discussion group? Imagine this happening—then go on to imagine yourself handling the situation. Think about why you are anxious, and what you can do about the causes of your anxieties. Do you need to prepare more thoroughly for the group so that you feel more confident about contributing to the discussion? Getting to know a couple of other group members outside the discussion time might make you feel that you have sympathetic listeners for anything you say during a discussion. Getting to know other students also enables you to share your feelings and experiences in discussion groups and other learning situations. Such sharing will probably lead you to discover that you are not alone in your anxieties. Other students may have helpful advice on how to cope with a situation which is worrying you. If you are all worried, try 'imagining the worst' together and see what alternatives you come up with.

Now stop, and think of a situation which is worrying you at present.

Imagine the worst that could happen—then imagine yourself coping with it. What are your alternatives after the worst has happened? Which ones seem most viable? Think about why you are worried, and what you can do to deal with the causes of your worry. Share your anxieties with others and see what they have to suggest. And perhaps most important of all—don't accept that you have to be worried. Is it really a matter of life or death?

Contacting people

> It is anything but easy to enter a classroom full of people whom you feel must be more intelligent than you, and quite demoralising when your worst fears are realised, you think. Still you must persevere.
>
> *Brian's Wife Jenny's Mum*

Adjusting to tertiary study takes time and practice and often courage. Many of the adjustments involve approaching other people—asking questions of a remote professor, seeking help from a teacher you see only once a week, putting forward your own thoughts in a seminar, or making contact with a stranger sitting next to you in a class. To deal with these anxieties, you often need to take the initiative in contacting people.

As a **part-time or external student**, you may have particular difficulty contacting teachers and other students. Perhaps you enjoy the pleasures of being a solitary scholar and your opportunities to learn independently, and your isolation can partly free you from the pressures of competing with other students. But you may miss sharing the pleasures and problems of study with other students, and if no one in your community sees tertiary study as valuable, you may feel particularly isolated.

Maximising your access to other people's ideas and to learning facilities is one aspect of part-time and external study which takes a lot of time and energy. Personal contacts with a teacher and students can make a big difference to the depth and enjoyment of your formal learning, particularly if you start your studies with high expectations or are worried about your academic abilities.

Approaching teachers

Only an unrealistic teacher would expect you to be an authority on a subject you have just begun studying or expect you to write a perfect first essay. You are expected to ask for the help and information you need. Teachers usually appreciate students whose questions and comments show genuine thought and enthusiasm for learning, and like most people, teachers take pleasure in discussing their special interest and explaining what they know to others. Often the students that a teacher comes to know best are those who ask questions, seek advice or are keen to discuss ideas—and it is more satisfying to teach people you know than to impart information to a collection of names and half-remembered faces.

What is the worst that can happen when you approach a teacher for help? Perhaps you persistently have trouble finding them. If so, try to arrange an appointment or leave a message. Perhaps you won't receive a helpful answer to your question. If the teacher is busy at the time, remember that tertiary teachers have responsibilities for research and administration as well as for students, so make an appointment for another time. If he or she isn't skilled at clear explanations, look to another teacher, a student, or a book for your information. Perhaps the teacher you approach is cursory or condescending. If so, maybe he or she is having a trying day, so ask if you can come back another time. Maybe the teacher is inadequate as a teacher. Nevertheless teachers are paid to help you learn, so if you want to, persist with your request. If you don't want to persist, look elsewhere for help. There are always one or two friendly, helpful teachers or advisers on campus who can help with your contacts with other teachers, with your study, and in some cases with your personal problems.

If you study at a distance, teachers like to receive communication from you other than the assignments you are required to submit. Send a letter telling your teacher a little about yourself. Make a 'phone call to ask about comments on an assignment or to thank your teacher for help. Send an informal tape to talk about ideas not covered in lectures or to discuss your concerns about your work or about course requirements. If you can arrange to visit your teachers on campus, you will be able to visualise the place and person to whom you are sending your work, rather than simply delivering it up to the postal service and to a red marking pen with a person at the other end.

These contacts help your teachers come to know you as an individual, and enable them to make comments on your work which are directed to your individual strengths and difficulties. Your teachers may also be encouraged to make more detailed comments and to return your assignments more promptly—important factors for all students, but particularly so when you have to wait anxiously for an evaluation of your work to arrive in your letter box or mail bag.

Getting to know other students

Having at least one or two fellow students with whom you can toss around ideas and share study problems is an invaluable part of a student's life. Sitting by yourself in the cafeteria, not knowing anyone in the first weeks of class, not being part of student social life or being an isolated student, can make you feel very alone. If you find university or college strange, if you have difficulties with your work, or if you feel shy with other students, you can be certain that other students feel this way too. Help someone else as well as yourself by talking to the person you sit next to in class, or by contacting another student and not always expecting them to contact you first. Take part in some of the social or academic activities on campus and take advantage of the multi-cultural community (see 'Your relationships with others', Chapter 1). If you have trouble with work or with a teacher, mention it to a couple of students in your class. They may have ideas on what you can do, and if they share your problem you can tackle it together. One of the most valuable learning experiences can be to find another student or a group of students studying the same subjects with whom you can share ideas and read and comment on each other's written work (see 'Share your writing', Chapter 12).

What is the worst that could happen when you try to make contact with other students? They don't seem interested? Perhaps they are shy, or preoccupied with other things—try another time or approach someone else. Perhaps they don't seem interested in your particular study problems—find other people you can ask for help. If you continue to have difficulty getting to know a few other students, talk this over with a friend or counsellor. However, most students are willing to talk about courses or teachers, the test next week or the essay you are supposed to finish in two days' time. You won't become close friends with everyone you meet, but you will find some people with whom you enjoy spending time.

If you are a distance education or open learning student, check with the distance education unit to see if there are other students in your area. Try to make contact with someone who has taken or is taking the same course as you, but even talking to somebody studying different courses can provide you both with invaluable moral support. If you can sit in on the occasional class on campus you will have a chance to meet other students and share your learning with them. If you are nervous at the thought of attending special on-campus sessions, you will usually find that some other students feel the same way. Once you actually meet each other, you are likely to have plenty to say.

Contacting the people around you and on campus helps you come to know them as individuals, to learn about the real people behind your images and expectations of what teachers and students are like. It is one of the most important parts of your learning.

Combining study with other work

Your job may be directly related to the subjects you are studying. For example, you maybe a veterinary student working part-time in an animal clinic or a parent studying children's literature. Even if your employment isn't directly connected with the subjects you study, it may require you to use your mind imaginatively to solve problems and to grapple with new ideas. In this case, your brain won't feel rusty when you tackle formal study. Useful connections between your employment and your study can be particularly important if you are an external or part-time student with little opportunity to discuss your learning with teachers or other students. However, close connections between your work and study can sometimes create problems if, for example, you read a book which criticises teaching methods you use, or if courses you take for further job qualifications seem irrelevant.

The amount of energy you put into your job affects your energy for studying. The high level of energy and creativity which you devote to a satisfying job can carry over to your studies. If your studies are less stimulating than your work, you may rapidly lose interest in them. A job which isn't satisfying but is financially necessary may demand a lot of your energy. If you do heavy outdoors physical work or spend your day looking after children, sometimes you will be too tired to study but at other times you will welcome the change to mental exercise.

If you work in a high speed job, you can find yourself impatient with the leisurely pace of some courses, especially if you have only limited time off work for classes. If a course doesn't regularly require work to be handed in, the apparent aimlessness of your study may be frustrating. However, study can provide you with a relaxing change from a high pressure job—and the workloads in most courses become demanding soon enough.

The overall time that your work requires, the particular hours that you work and the travelling time from home to work to class all influence your study. They affect your choice of courses, how much time you can spend on private study, and sometimes make external study the only possibility.

Financial decisions may affect your study. If, for example, you have to find a part-time job to finance your education, you will have less time for study itself. If you have been without an independent income as a secondary school student or housewife, you may have to justify your desire to study to the person whose income will now support you. You may feel under pressure to 'succeed' or to choose vocational courses, particularly if your study calls for extra money to pay for books or travel or child care.

ﻼ ﻼ ﻼ

Allow yourself time to discover what university or college is like for you. Expect to feel both confused and excited in the first six to twelve months while you settle in, while you begin to understand what is expected of you and to define some of your own objectives. During this time, as well as trying to pass courses, put some energy into learning how to learn and into making contact with staff and students. Remember that outside school you have learned many things on your own, and that you do know how to learn when you want to.

Think about what you want from tertiary study, and how you can reach your objectives. After a while it may make sense for you to defer your study for a short period or to leave university or college because of other interests, because your studies aren't sufficiently stimulating, or for pragmatic reasons. (If you are thinking of withdrawing from study, find out what you need to do in case you later want to return.) If you continue to study, your objectives in your formal learning will probably change. Any serious attempt to come to grips with new ideas, especially those which raise questions about yourself, your world and your beliefs about learning always engenders confusion and suggests new directions to consider. Learning what is important to you changes you, often in unexpected ways. Universities or colleges can offer you real learning if you explore what is offered and if you are able to make your own independent decisions about learning.

Have a broad picture of the place of tertiary study in your education rather than automatically thinking of it as the be-all and end-all. 'Lifelong learning' has become something of a catchcry and is a term with a multiplicity of meanings covering formal and informal learning. But just as some decades ago relatively few people went on to tertiary study and secondary school to the age of fourteen was seen as the end of formal education, now there is an increasing likelihood that you will need and be expected to continue your formal education and training beyond a degree or diploma. You may, for example, be required to update or broaden your professional knowledge or to acquire knowledge to enable you to move into a new field or to specialise in a particular area.

As well as any further formal education you undertake, your informal learning will continue for the rest of your life. Hopefully your formal study will enhance your ability to learn and to discover future directions you want to pursue both informally and in further education. Whatever directions your learning takes, remember to ask yourself 'What is my purpose in wanting to learn this?' just as you did during your initial education at university or college.

Further reading

Ballard, Brigid, & Clanchy, John. 1988. *Studying in Australia*. Longman Cheshire, Melbourne.

Buxton, Laurie. 1981. *Do You Panic About Maths? Coping with Maths Anxiety*. Heinemann Educational Books, Melbourne.

Edwards, Hazel (ed.). 1975. *Women Returning to Study*. Primary Education, Richmond.

Gilbert, John (ed.). 1980. *Staying the Course: How to Survive Higher Education*. Kogan Page, London.

McEvedy, M. Rosanna, & Jordan, Mike. 1986. *Succeeding at University and College*. Nelson, Melbourne.

Percy, Diana. 1989. *Adult Study Tactics: A Springboard to Learning*. Macmillan, South Melbourne.

Notes

[1] From Taylor, Elizabeth, *et al*. 1980. 'The Orientations of Students Studying the Social Science Foundation Course'. *Study Methods Group Report no. 7*. Institute of Educational Technology, The Open University, Walton Hall, Milton Keynes.

4

Asking Your Own Questions

> Knowledge is a process in the minds of living people. It is what we do as
> we try to find out who and where we are, and what is going on about us.
> *John Holt*

You ask questions all the time, both consciously and unconsciously. When you walk, as you take each step your foot is seeking out information to relay to your brain. When you pause at an intersection and glance both ways, you are checking the traffic. You learn when you have a question in your mind—whether as a small child continually asking 'Why?', or later as you learned about dinosaurs, gardening, jet aeroplanes, philosophy or toxicology. You learn when you are curious, when you want or need to know.

In formal education usually teachers ask the questions and you provide the answers. Much of your primary and secondary education would have asked questions that began with 'What ...?' and you would then have been expected to give correct answers which showed an ability to remember and reproduce information. While in tertiary education 'What ... ?' is a valid question, you are expected to ask questions that lead you to be more analytical or critical. These questions begin with 'Why ...?', 'How ...?', 'How important ...?' or 'How valid ...?'. Asking 'What if ...?' or 'What might happen if ... ?' are higher level questions intended to lead you to reconsider your assumptions and beliefs.

In tertiary education, it is usually the teacher who formulates the questions that you discuss in tutorials or write about in your essays, reports and examinations. Throughout your education many of your teachers try to lead you to an understanding that there are no correct and definitive answers, and some help you to formulate your own questions when you lead a tutorial, write on a topic of your own choice or undertake some form of independent study.

Some questions you ask constrain you and stop the learning process. Other questions enable you to ask other further questions, perhaps by generating initial answers that lead you to these. As a student in college or university you need to ask questions that explore your relationship to learning, questions that help you understand, criticise and evaluate what you learn, and questions that help you to integrate what you learn with your previous knowledge and ideas.

This chapter looks briefly at a few types of questions and suggests some fundamental questions you can ask when thinking about or researching a subject which interests you. It is designed to stimulate you to ask your own questions and to pursue them in your formal education.

What questions might you ask?

Just before she died she asked 'What is the answer?' No answer came. She laughed aloud and said: 'In that case what is the question?' Then she died.
Last words of Gertrude Stein, quoted by Donald Sutherland

What questions do you have on your mind right now? Questions about your work? Your personal relationships? Your ideas? Your social life? Who you are?

A **simple question** such as 'Should I cook lamb chops or a stew for dinner?', 'Did I leave my glasses behind?' can be answered without much imagination, perhaps with a 'Yes' or a 'No'. Questions such as these close off other possibilities and leave you with the option of only a limited answer. This may be all you need when checking if you know a fact, such as 'How many grams in an ounce?', 'Where is my clavicle?'

If you are looking for information on a subject such as basic human needs, to ask 'Do humans need food to survive?' is asking a closed question, while the **complex question** 'What types of food do humans need to survive?' opens many possibilities. Complex questions demand time and careful thought when you attempt to answer them. Some complex questions you can never answer. 'Did I make the right choice?' 'What would have happened if I hadn't gone to university?' Perhaps you check your horoscope or consult the *I Ching* in an attempt to find answers to such questions. It is tempting to believe that there are absolute or 'yes/no' answers to questions which can't be answered so simply and for which there is no one correct answer. Often an answer which is right today may be wrong tomorrow, or an answer which makes sense in one culture may be a mistake in another. Are there any answers which are always right? Much of what you are told is true later turns out to be not quite the whole truth; and many so called 'objective facts' are actually the results of a consensus of the subjective opinions of the people concerned.

> What men [*sic*] really want is not knowledge but certainty.
>
> *Bertrand Russell*

The way in which you ask questions shapes your answers. If you ask 'Is intelligence determined by genes or environment?' you have precluded the possibility that both of these or other factors might be important, as well as making assumptions about what intelligence is. Such 'either ... or ...' questions are examples of how language limits your exploration of a topic and encloses what you can learn.

> Every language conceals within its structure a vast array of unconscious assumptions about life and the universe, all that you take for granted and everything that seems to make common sense ...
>
> *N. J. Berill*

When you are curious about a subject, there are some basic questions you can usefully ask. As you read the questions suggested here, apply them to a topic which interests you and make notes on the answers and further questions that arise. (See 'Defining your Topic', Chapter 6.)

Why do I want to know?

> Tiger got to hunt,
> Bird got to fly;
> Man got to sit and wonder, "Why, why, why?"
> Tiger got to sleep,
> Bird got to land;
> Man got to tell himself he understand.
>
> *Kurt Vonnegut Jr.*

Asking why you want to know about a topic can clarify what you want to find out and how to go about your search. How did you become curious about the topic in the first place? What is your purpose for seeking the information? Perhaps you want to share it with others, use it to pass an exam, complete an assignment or progress through a sequence of practical skills. If you need to remember information for a short while, such as for a seminar paper next week, how you go about learning it will differ from your approach if you need the information for long-term use. (See Chapter 5, 'Learning and Remembering'.)

What do I want to know?

What do I want to know? What interests me about this topic? What seem to be the most important aspects? These are some of the *first questions* to ask yourself when you want to find information on a topic. For example, if you are interested in convicts in eighteenth-century Australia, ask yourself 'What do I want to know about this subject?' You might have questions about who the convicts were, why they were transported, how many were women, their living conditions, the number of convicts who were political prisoners, how they were organised and used in the colonies, and their role in the economy of the new colonies.

How do I know that ... ?

> Artists can colour the sky red because they know it's blue. Those of us who aren't artists must colour things the way they really are or people might think we're stupid.
>
> *Jules Feiffer*

Perhaps you 'know' that the sun will rise tomorrow because in your experience it always has. Perhaps you 'know' that the grass is green because your eyes tell you so. Perhaps you 'know' that Marie Curie discovered radium because you read that she did.

What are the *sources of your knowledge*? The first-hand evidence of your senses is one source which can be deceptive—for example, if you believe that the world is flat or that the grass is a particular shade of green because your eyes tell you so (see 'Research tools', Chapter 6). Much of what you know is not from first-hand experience. Much of your knowledge comes from cultural and personal biases of which you may be unaware, such as the belief that technological progress is always desirable or that a woman's primary role is to be a wife and mother. Much that is believed to be 'common sense' in your culture is not thought about or questioned (see 'Your cultural and social self', Chapter 1). It is thus crucial to question the nature and reliability of your sources of knowledge. Can you prove that Marie Curie discovered radium or that the sun will rise tomorrow? If you can't prove it, it may still be true, but you need to be careful before you assert its truth.

On the topic of convicts in eighteenth-century Australia, ask yourself 'What do I already know about this topic, and where does my knowledge come from?' If you 'know' that most convicts were petty thieves or that women convicts were prostitutes, asking yourself how you know these 'facts' should lead you to examine whether or not they really are facts.

Why?

> ... and books that told me everything about wasps except why.
> *Dylan Thomas*

'Why?' is one of the most important questions you can ask, especially if it enables you to *identify assumptions* which may be hidden. As an example of this, debates about education frequently ask 'How can we do this particular thing better?' while the question 'Why are we doing it in the first place?' is not dealt with. It might be more useful to start by asking 'Why are teachers trained?' instead of 'How can teachers be trained better?', or to ask 'Why am I going to write this report?' before you ask 'How can I best go about writing it?'

If you have a problem to solve, you might ask only how to solve it, for example, which methods you should use to remember material for exams. If you also ask why the methods are effective, you can decide if they suit you and will find it easier to remember how to repeat them and to use them in different exam situations. On the topic of convicts in Australia, asking why convicts were transported will uncover further questions about the social, political and economic conditions in England in the eighteenth century.

When? Where? How? Who? Why? What?

Asking these questions one after another is a *brainstorming* exercise to let your mind generate ideas without having to justify their immediate relevance. It is a useful way to stimulate your initial thinking about a subject and to provide new directions if you are stuck while researching. For example, if given the adage 'Know thyself', you could ask:

* who said this?
* when?
* where was it first used?
* what was its original context?
* what is the relationship between ...?
* how has it been interpreted?
* why has it been important?

What happens if ... ?

'What happens if ... ?', or 'What might happen if ... ?', are the *cause-and-effect* questions that experiments ask, whether the experimenter is a three-year-old child pulling a cat's tail or a professional researcher testing a hypothesis. Experimenting involves manipulating your environment to see what happens, sometimes predicting what is likely to happen, and then describing what happened. Here are some examples.

- What happens if you drop a piece of paper and a heavy lead weight from the top of a high tower?
- What happens if you write an assignment as a dialogue instead of in prose?
- What might happen if you always told the truth?

What if ... ?

Imagine living in the sixteenth century and asking yourself, 'What if the sun rather than the earth is the centre of our universe?' What answers might you arrive at if you ask 'What if our traditional energy sources are no longer available by the end of this century?', 'What if Robert Ardrey's theory that humans are predatory killers is true?,' 'What if most of the convicts transported to Australia were political prisoners?' or 'What might have happened if men were the sex that had babies?' These *speculative questions* require that you transcend your customary frameworks for viewing the world. Using your imagination and suspending disbelief enables you to look at the world through new eyes.

> Why, sometimes I've believed as many as six impossible things before breakfast.
>
> *Lewis Carroll*

❧ ❧ ❧

You don't need to ask the above questions in a particular sequence, but are likely to move backwards and forwards among them. What you want to know and the questions you ask will be influenced by how much you already know about a subject. For example, when confronted with a new subject you can immerse yourself in it by asking *basic questions* that uncover fundamental information about your topic, such as 'What is evolution?', 'What is Freud's concept of the unconscious?', 'What is carbon bonding?', 'What is Wall Street?', 'What are marsupials?'

In contrast, when familiar with a subject you can ask *analytical questions* which lead you to evaluate this information. For instance, 'How has Freud's theory of the unconscious been applied in late twentieth century psychoanalysis?' Because you already know something about marsupial reproduction you might ask if the reproductive process in kangaroos is an adaptation to the Australian environment. (Chapter 6, 'Defining and Researching a Topic', suggests a systematic way of asking questions about a topic.)

Pursuing your questions in formal education

> The teacher's work, therefore, begins when that other person asks a question ... If you ask me a question all I can do in my reply is try to put into words a part of my experience. But you get only the words, not the experience. To *make meaning* out of my words, you must use your own experience.
>
> *John Holt*

Without curiosity, learning is dull and mechanical if it occurs at all. Wanting to know, enjoying stretching your mind, feeling wonder or delight at a new experience or idea—all these need a mind which is receptive and questioning.

Unfortunately, the crucial part your curiosity and questions play in learning is often forgotten or disregarded. Formal learning is frequently based on a model which assumes that there is a body of knowledge to master, and a particular way to master it; and the proof of your mastery lies in correctly answering set questions. This model of learning is most evident in the exam process but can also underlie work such as essays, tutorial papers and laboratory reports. If you are given a topic for a tutorial paper, do you approach it by asking your own questions, or by doing what you think your teachers expect? If you read a lot for an assignment, but feel uncertain about what to write on the topic, perhaps you are trying to guess what you are expected to write, rather than reading and writing about what seems most relevant and interesting to you. In a discussion group, are you hesitant to take an active part because you fear you might say the 'wrong' thing, or give the 'wrong' answer?

> We kill, not only their curiosity, but their feeling that it is a good and admirable thing to be curious, so that by the age of ten most of them will not ask questions, and will show a good deal of scorn for the few who do ...
>
> *John Holt*

No teacher can tell you what you want to learn, but he or she can help you discover this. Teachers with an active curiosity who are interested in you as a learner can stimulate your curiosity in new ways; they can help you articulate your questions and help you ask more sophisticated questions. Such teachers also help you rediscover the confidence and skills needed to pursue your own questions in formal education. Obviously some teachers and assignments allow you more scope than others for asking the questions which interest you. If your learning is to be satisfying and mean something to you, you need to ask your own questions, even with teachers who prefer you to answer theirs.

Independent study

The basic questions of why, what, how and when you learn apply to any independent learning, and can be applied to an individual assignment or to your formal tertiary education as a whole (see Chapter 5). Studying independently requires thinking about and formulating your objectives. It involves studying a subject of your own choosing, on your own initiative, and making your own decisions about how and when you study it and with whom. Independent study differs from 'individualised' learning and self-paced methods, in which you study alone but are supervised and have limited choice as to what and how you study.

Studying independently entails asking yourself the following questions.

- What do I want to study, and in what depth and breadth?
- Why do I want to study this particular topic? You might explore an interest more fully, acquire specific skills, or examine previous work in a new context.
- How will I study the topic? Perhaps you want to conduct library research, interviews, or laboratory experiments, or to undertake field work, or to read extensively (see Chapters 5, 6 and 7).
- How do I want my work to be evaluated? You need to decide what work to produce specifically for recorded assessment, and who will evaluate your work and by what criteria (see Chapter 15).
- How much time will I spend on this study?
- With whom will I discuss my work?

If you usually rely on your textbooks and lecture notes for the 'right' answers without questioning their information or assumptions, you may find it frightening to consider asking your own questions. Perhaps you have become so accustomed to teachers asking you questions that you have largely forgotten how to ask your own, or have lost the confidence to ask them. Even if a teacher encourages you to approach a topic in your own way, you might be so unaccustomed to this that you prefer to retreat into the safety of looking to the 'experts' for the answers. In this case you are probably assuming that your task at university or college is to meet the requirements of courses and teachers, rather than seeing them as resources enabling you to move towards your objectives and to think about your questions. So perhaps the first question you should ask yourself is 'Why am I at university or college?', 'What are my objectives?' and 'What are my questions?'

A few universities and colleges allow you to complete part or all of your study programme independently. Sometimes you can obtain credit for exploring in depth a topic not available as a formal course. If independent study appeals to you, explore the possibilities for this method of learning within your institution or through cross-crediting from another institution. If you develop a serious academic interest which you want to explore further, you may decide to go on to study as an honours or postgraduate student.

Within a course, the extent to which you are allowed to work on your interests varies. In some courses you can spend most of the time exploring your interests without close supervision. Other courses allow you little scope for independent study; the work you do is assigned by teachers and you are told what to read, what experiments to conduct, and how to present your written work. When you do have the opportunity for independent study within a course, this often takes the form of an individual or group project for which you choose the topic and the methods of research.

  

Often your learning becomes largely a matter of asking more exact or more intricate questions, rather than finding answers. Despite a formal education system which talks of having 'done maths' or 'done history', it is impossible to learn all there is to know about any subject. When pursuing your own questions, you may realise that the more you know, the more there is to learn, which leads you on to further questions.

What questions would you like to pursue in your formal learning?

Further reading

Boud, David (ed.). 1981. *Developing Student Autonomy in Learning.* Kogan Page, London.

Dressel, P.L., & Thompson, M.M. 1973. *Independent Study.* Jossey Bass, San Francisco.

Lindsey, Crawford W. 1988. *Teaching Students to Teach Themselves.* Kogan Page, London.

Percy, Keith, & Ramsden, Paul. 1980. *Independent Study: Two Examples from English Higher Education.* The Society for Research into Higher Education, University of Surrey, Guildford, England.

5

Learning and Remembering

Oft in the stilly night,
When the mind is fumbling fuzzily,
I brood about how little I know.
And know that little so muzzily.
Ogden Nash

Why do you remember the things you do?
Why do you forget?

If you want to know how to ride a bicycle, you practise with great concentration, and persist with your riding despite the occasional spill. Once you can ride with skill, even if you sell your bicycle you always remember how to ride one.

A small child who wants to learn how to build a tower of blocks concentrates intensely while trying various ways to make the blocks stay put one on top of the other. After repeated attempts, she comes to understand the most effective way to build a tower of blocks. This skill is later remembered to build other towers—of books, of dolls, of cushions.

If you concentrate on learning what you want to know, you are more likely to understand and be able to use it. Remembering what you learn well enough to use it depends on why and how you learn. If you learn to ride a bicycle because you want to, and if you learn at your own pace, you easily recall the skill. You are less likely to remember it if you learn because someone else decides you should and teaches you in the way they think best. Whether or not you want to learn depends on you—what you already know, how you learn, your current interests and how you feel at the time.

This chapter begins by looking at how you filter what you learn and remember, and at why you might want to remember. It discusses how you learn in order to remember—by learning what suits you, when and how you wish, and by using methods which help you learn material thoughtfully. Deliberately learning in these ways makes it more likely that you will be able to use what you learn later and recall it in situations such as exams.

Filters on what you learn and remember

'I could tell you my adventures—beginning from this morning,' said Alice a little timidly; 'but it's no use going back to yesterday, because I was a different person then.'

Lewis Carroll

Your mind and body unconsciously select and interpret what you learn and remember from your daily life, and what you remember changes with time. Five people who witness the same car accident have five different versions even if asked soon afterwards to describe what happened, and a year later each person will have yet another version of the episode. They may even 'recall' things which didn't actually happen, such as events which could have been expected to occur but didn't or details of a 'long argument' between the drivers which was in fact only a couple of remarks. What each of the five recollects is their personal experience of the accident, modified by their experiences in the meantime.

What do you remember about today?
What immediately comes to mind?
Try recalling in order everything that has happened since you woke up.

What do you remember from yesterday?
What do you remember from last week? Why?
What memories do you have of your last birthday?

Do you remember your first day at school?
What is your earliest memory?

Spend about half an hour answering these questions. If you finish in less time, go back and see how much more detail you can recall. Can you work out why you recalled what you did?

Share the questions with someone else. How do your memories differ from theirs? How are they the same? Why?

> The past which we remember is partial and distorted; it has been edited by the censors to exclude events which are disturbingly painful or disturbingly pleasurable ... The history we recall tends to be propaganda which preserves the status quo of personal identity.
>
> *Sam Keen*

Now stop for a moment, and let yourself become aware of everything your senses are telling you. Smells? Sights? Sounds? Tastes? Touch? Of what are you most aware? After your first sense impressions, what else do you begin to notice? What thoughts are running through your mind?

Trying to be fully aware of even one fleeting moment makes you realise how much you forget—perhaps for a short time, or perhaps for all of your life. Some things you need to 'forget', in the sense of taking them for granted. Imagine if you wanted to be fully aware and decided to consciously breathe every breath. You would soon give up because you wouldn't have time for anything else. Other things you 'forget' by pushing them below the surface of your mind—items that have little interest for you, that have unpleasant associations, or that don't fit with your view of the world.

Sometimes you forget things you would like to remember. Have you ever read a childhood autobiography and marvelled at the amount of detail the writer recollects? Few people remember such detail without making a conscious effort to do so. Keeping a diary or taking photographs can make you more aware of your surroundings and help you remember them. Photos or diaries also help you realise how much you forget. Have you ever read back over a diary entry from several weeks or years ago and been amazed at how your memory of that time has changed and how much you have forgotten?

Try it now. See if you can find a letter, a poem, or a diary you wrote, or a photograph you took. Look at it and conjure up your memories of that time.

Remembering isn't just something you set your mind to do—**your senses** are involved too. Do you have a good memory for faces? For 'phone numbers? Or for jokes? Some people remember mostly what they see, and can see a word once and remember how to spell it; others remember what they hear, and can repeat verbatim snatches of dialogue from a movie.

Your experiences lead you to knowledge and beliefs about yourself and your world which influence what you are aware of at any moment. If you have been a keen surfer or sailor for several years, you are more likely to know and remember how the wind and waves have changed from one season to another than will someone who plays cards for their recreation. If you have worked as a carpenter, you can pick up and remember new information about the craft because of your previous knowledge.

Your active interest in a subject increases what you remember about it. A football fan can tell you in detail about the previous wins of her club, but if she is not interested in horse racing she may have no idea who won the Melbourne Cup. If you are concerned about the role of women in Australian society, you will remember facts from a history of Australia which others without your concern wouldn't notice. Such an interest can be kindled by another person's enthusiasm. Skilled teachers who care about their subjects can hold your attention so that you remember far more than you expected to. You may remember a conversation with someone you met at a party because you were entertained by them.

How you feel emotionally and physically also influences what you learn and how vividly you remember it. If you are alert, perhaps because you are feeling exuberant or slightly uncomfortable, your chances of remembering that particular time more fully increase. Your surroundings influence how you feel and are part of what you remember. Have you ever picked up a book you have read and been reminded of when and where you read it? And items you can recall in one situation you can't remember at all in another.

Your senses, experiences, interests and your current state of being act as filters on your life, both past and present. They affect what you are most aware of and what you find easy to concentrate on and to learn, and so influence what you remember from the information you are offered.

Why remember?

Remembering enables you to learn more about yourself and your world. Newborn human babies seem to operate mostly by reflexes rather than by consciously knowing and remembering. But toddlers in their second year are able to call on what they have learned, and can form a concept such as 'dog-ness' by remembering the characteristics of dogs which aren't present and comparing them with a dog which is. As an adult, the more you can remember, the less you have to relearn. The more you can remember concepts, the more you can solve problems and cope with new situations and ideas. If you can recall the fundamentals of Darwin's theory of evolution, you can move on to further related knowledge instead of relearning the theory repeatedly.

When you find **pleasure** in what you learn, you probably want to remember it. Perhaps you do this unconsciously because your senses and curiosity are more active, or perhaps you deliberately heighten your sense of awareness. You may relive the experiences in your mind, in a diary or through photographs. You may learn by heart the words of a song which please you. Maybe you want to remember an intriguing idea, so you can contemplate it further.

If you need **to use what you learn,** you are more likely to remember it. To cross the road and live, you learn and use an array of skills which become habits, or unconsciously recollected knowledge. If you need to prune fruit trees, you have a reason for using and remembering what you learn about pruning. If you want to use an idea in a discussion paper, you try to understand the idea and its links to your topic so that you remember it fully enough to explain it to others.

Some things you are required to remember for **reasons not directly your own**. You might enjoy learning the manual skills of flying an aeroplane but not want to study the navigation theory required for a pilot's licence. In your formal education you are expected to remember material so that your progress towards course objectives can be evaluated and recorded according to tangible criteria. For example, you may be required:

- in an exam, to show that you remember and understand the rudiments of a particular subject
- in an essay, to recall information well enough to argue a point of view
- in a report, to remember and describe a sequence of steps in an experiment
- in a tutorial, to review and present a summary of your reading on a topic
- to remember material in the short-term, such as dates or data for a seminar paper, and
- to remember material for long periods so you can take a final exam, a subsequent course or a future job.

These requirements are based on the assumptions that in formal education there is certain knowledge worth having, certain learning skills and abilities worth acquiring, and a specific sequence and time limit in which this learning should be acquired. These assumptions shape why and what and how you learn and remember. Those assumptions with which you disagree can still influence your learning and remembering if you decide to accept them as a means to your own ends. For example, even if some course material doesn't interest you, you may study it for an exam, because you accept the exam as necessary to acquire a qualification you want.

'But what did the Dormouse say?' one of the jury asked.
'That I can't remember,' said the Hatter.
'You must remember,' remarked the King, 'or I'll have you executed.'
Lewis Carroll

How you learn to remember

There are times when your assumptions and objectives about learning and remembering differ from those of your teachers. At such times, what you learn will be difficult to recall. However, you are likely to remember what you learn if your curiosity about a subject remains alive. To sustain your curiosity, there are certain prerequisites for learning.

1 What is important to you

You need to learn according to who you are—your interests, your experiences, your questions (see 'Beliefs and values', Chapter 1).

2 When you are ready

You need to learn at a place and time and in a way that makes sense to you, at 'the moment of readiness'. You are not always ready to learn in a school classroom between the hours of 9 am and 3.30 pm or during specified hours each week in a lecture theatre. If you are not ready, it is more difficult to concentrate on and to understand what you are supposed to learn, and you are more likely to forget what you do learn unless you use memory techniques such as those mentioned later in this chapter.

3 A way that suits you

If you have some insight into how you learn informally, your formal learning can be enhanced. Some people have strong visual memories, some learn by doing, others learn by discussion, others by reading and making notes. Which ways suit you best? If you are learning to drive a car, do you prefer to get in the car and start driving, to read a book on how a combustion engine works, or to talk to a friend who has just learned to drive? If you want to find out about kangaroos, do you go to look at them in the zoo or try to study them in their natural habitats? Do you ask other people about them? Do you read books on the subject? Do you take a course in marsupial physiology? Learning in a way that suits you enhances your ability to remember.

4 Building on what you already know

You need to learn by building on your skills and experience, on the patterns and beliefs which shape your world and your language. Even if you know only a little about a new area, having a context in which to understand your new learning helps you remember it more clearly. Have you ever attempted to read a book you don't understand and then some time later read it more easily and remembered it? By the second reading you have acquired new knowledge to which you can relate the book's contents.

There may however be times when you are required to suspend your previous understanding, and to think about and reassemble information in an entirely different way. For example, if you are concerned about drug addiction, you may have first learned about it in a psychology course which centred on changing the individual addict. If you then take a course in sociology which examines the social construction of individuality and looks to change individuals through changes in society, you will then need to try re-ordering your information and ideas within this new framework. Making these shifts can be extremely disorienting and it can be difficult to remember the information. Although it is tempting and comforting to hold on to your entrenched patterns of ideas, making an effort to understand and remember new ones is very challenging and can be rewarding.

If you are required to reproduce ideas or information that you can't relate to something familiar, you may have to resort to rote learning and mnemonics, acrostics and rhymes such as '30 days hath September'. One of the most powerful tools to help you remember unfamiliar material is linking it to familiar information and concepts. Here are some examples.

- Learn the principles which underlie a good book review before reviewing a book on a new topic, and your recall of the book will be more thorough.
- To help you remember the intricacies of Darwin's theory of evolution, test it against species differences with which you are familiar.
- Use analogies, similes and metaphors based on comparisons with familiar ideas and information when learning and remembering new material. (For example, the metaphor 'the body politic' helps you think about a political system in new ways by comparing it to your own body, and what you learn from such a metaphor is likely to stay in your mind).

> I can give you nothing that has not already its being within yourself. I can throw open to you no picture-gallery but your own soul ... I help you to make your own world visible. That is all.
>
> *Hermann Hesse*

When you come to learn about a new topic in a class, study session or assignment, spend some time recalling what you already know about it. Think about what you want to learn and, if you have a choice, how you want to learn. This preparation provides reference points or a framework for your learning and enhances your ability to remember.

Selecting what to learn

Even if you are able to learn what, when and how you want to, you can't possibly remember everything. Every minute you 'learn' a great deal of information, but most of it you remember only if prompted. To retain some things, you need to 'forget' others, focusing your conscious awareness to select what you take in and learn. To remember what a teacher is saying, focus on just that and ignore other thoughts which impinge on your awareness, such as what the teacher is wearing.

It is essential that you consciously select what you want to remember. If as a student you are confronted with large amounts of information, you quickly discover there is little point in trying to remember it all and some time needs to be spent selecting what you need to remember and in deciding how to record and retrieve it (see 'Filing information', Chapter 6). In your written work and tutorials, for example, your time should be spent selecting important points that you need to remember; and you might choose to remember and discuss a particularly striking example to illustrate a point when several other examples would have been just as valid.

How much material you need to concentrate on and remember for tests and examinations varies according to the course objectives and the preferences of individual teachers. Be aware of course objectives and find out from your course coordinators and teachers how much detail you need to learn and remember. Generally, you will need to remember the concepts, theories and ideas developed in your course, and be able to recall sufficient detail to explain them. In a biology course, for example, if the greenhouse effect has featured in discussion, in essay topics and readings you would be well advised to learn and remember the basic principles underlying the effect. Similarly, in a social science course if the concept of 'power' has featured prominently it is wise to study and remember the different meanings of this concept and to concentrate on the way the concept is used in the course. In an exam you may need to write an essay showing you understand the concept or you may need to apply it to a situation.

Learning thoroughly

Our memories have been impaired by print; we know we need not 'burden our memories' with matter which we can find merely by taking a book from the shelf. When a large proportion of the population is illiterate and books are scarce, memories are often tenacious to a degree outside modern western experience.

J. Chaytor

Once you have selected what you want or have to learn, you need to learn that material thoroughly. Even material you thought would be dull or difficult can be unexpectedly interesting if you set out to learn it thoroughly, if you make a game or challenge of learning it well.

A variety of ways for the same material

Take in the same information in as many ways as possible. If a friend explains to you the difference between a ketch and a schooner, you are more likely to remember these if you also see a diagram of each and then sail on them. If you read about a topic as well as discuss it and listen to a lecture on it, your recall of what you have learned will be greater. This approach is particularly important if you are trying to remember complex material like the elements of existentialist philosophy or the intricacies and implications of Einstein's theory of relativity. Such material can only be understood and remembered after different and repeated encounters.

Before, during and after classes and study

'—but there's one great advantage in it, that one's memory works both ways.'
'I'm sure mine only works one way', Alice remarked. 'I can't remember things before they happen.'
'It's a poor sort of memory that only works backwards', the Queen remarked.'

Lewis Carroll

Thorough learning from a class or study session partly depends on what you do before, during and afterwards. Many of the chapters in this book use this principle as their framework, and you will remember more of what you learn if you use the approaches they describe. 'Concentrating while you study' in Chapter 2, for example, describes warming up, concentrating fully, and concluding a study session. The chapter on lectures discusses how to make the most of a lecture by preparing, questioning as you listen, and reviewing and using the material soon afterwards.

Study session techniques

There are techniques which you can use in a study session to enhance your ability to remember what you learn.

• Vary the length of your study sessions according to the material. Your mind can only take in so many statistics at once and you won't remember effectively if you try to learn masses of figures all at once. In contrast, you need time to understand a philosophical argument well enough to remember it.

• When learning details from two similiar subjects, study a contrasting subject in between so you don't confuse information. This applies, for example, if you are trying to remember dates from two similiar history courses, or studying verb tenses in Spanish and Italian. Avoiding interference between subjects is especially important in the early stages of learning and for long-term recall.

• When trying to remember concepts, studying related subjects provides a framework, because the differences and similarities between them enhance your understanding of each. For example, this approach can help when studying concepts of human nature in Rousseau's philosophy and in humanistic psychology.

Memory keys

One way of consciously remembering is to précis the essential parts of what you have selected to learn, and then to find memory keys for each of these parts. These keys can then be used to open your memory of each part and its associated details. You unconsciously use such keys when an unexpected memory is evoked because you hear a particular piece of music, walk past a certain street, or drink a once-favourite drink. In your formal learning you can use memory keys consciously, for example to recall the discussion in a seminar. Summarise the structure and main points of the discussion, represent these by key words or phrases, and use these keys to review and recall the discussion.

What would you choose as memory aids to help you remember each paragraph in this section 'Learning thoroughly'?

Patterns and principles

If you learn by comprehending the patterns and principles, structures and relationships which link individual ideas and information, it is easier to remember these items than trying to do so one by one. Learning in patterns also makes it easier to recall information you thought you wouldn't need, since you can search for it by reconstructing the patterns in which you learned it. Use patterned notes, flow diagrams or charts to summarise information from a lecture, a chapter of a book, a section of a course or a topic. Depending on the way you remember information, these pictoral summaries can make it easier to recall information because they show at a glance central concepts and the links between idea. They can clearly separate main ideas from details (see 'Notetaking and/or underlining', Chapter 9).

Using what you learn

If you think back over an event from your day, what you remember depends on what has happened to you in the meantime, even if that time has been very brief. When you use your knowledge of an event in a new context, you don't reproduce it exactly unless it has absolutely no meaning for you. You extend your memory of the event to take in the context in which you remember it—if you describe the event in a journal, your surroundings, as you write, influence and become part of your memory.

Unless you continue your learning by recalling it, you forget even things you wanted to learn. Going over your day helps fix it in your memory, and recording the day in a journal makes it available for you to relive, to 'use' again. Discussing the ideas from a lecture with other people who have shared it has a similiar effect, with the added dimension of the others' perceptions now becoming part of yours.

Use what you learn as *soon*, as *often* and as *widely* as possible if you want to remember it. You recall the alphabet easily because you have used it over and over again in different situations. When you first learn to ride a bike, if you practise every day and in many different conditions you are likely to remember the skill more quickly than if you practise once a week and have to spend some of that weekly time in re-learning. Unless you have an exceptional memory for figures, you are unlikely to remember statistics, such as the population of Singapore, unless you use them frequently. If you want to remember an important idea, write it down and try it out on various people. You will come to a new understanding of it each time and remember the original idea more fully. To remember material for long-term use (for instance, for exams), use it by revising it periodically and relating it to new knowledge you have acquired.

> ...Funes not only remembered every leaf on every tree of every wood, but even every one of the times he had perceived or imagined it. He determined to reduce all of his past experience to some seventy thousand recollections, which he would later define numerically. Two considerations dissuaded him: the thought that the task was interminable and the thought that it was useless.
>
> *Jorge Luis Borges*

Exams

You are likely to need to remember material in exams and tests. Your memory in exams depends as much on being prepared for the exam situation as it does on learning material well. Even if you know material, you may be unable to recall it effectively if you become very anxious in an exam room. ('Coping with difficult situations' in Chapter 3 suggests how to handle the exam situation. Table 5.1 looks at techniques to help

Table 5.1 Exam techniques

1 If you are uptight before an exam, try to relax (see 'Tension and relaxation', Chapter 1).

2 When you are given the exam paper, and before you start writing, take the following steps.

- Carefully read the instructions which should tell you how you are expected to answer the paper, how many questions you should answer and the value of each.
- Read through all of the questions.
- If you have a choice, decide which questions you will answer or at least which questions you will do first.
- Decide how much time you will need to spend on each question because of its value and according to how thoroughly you can answer it.
- Decide on the order in which you will answer the questions. Answer first the questions you know most about and which are easiest. If you run out of time, you do so on a subject which will earn you fewer marks.

3 When you are allowed to start writing, jot down any thoughts or ideas you have about each of the questions you will answer. These jottings can be useful memory triggers when you actually come to answer the question.

4 For essay-type questions, analyse the wording of the question (see 'Analysing a topic', Chapter 6) and plan your essay (see 'Writing to a plan', Chapter 12). Include your plan in your exam booklet.

5 Write as quickly and as clearly as you can.

6 For multiple-choice questions, don't waste time over questions you can't answer. Be careful about guessing answers if points are deducted for incorrect responses.

7 When answering mathematical problems, include all of your calculations. Even if your answer is incorrect, the examiner can see where you went wrong and you may gain some points for your method.

8 If you have a memory lapse in the middle of a question, leave a few pages, go to another question, and later return to the first question.

9 In an essay-type exam, answer the required number of questions. Answer fully the questions you know well and write as much as you can on the others.

10 If you run out of time, jot down the main points you were going to make.

11 Try to leave time at the end of the exam to read back over your answers. Correcting poor expression or spelling or checking your calculations can make an important difference.

you remember what you have learned when you read the questions in
a limited-time, no-books exam.)

> I never told you about examinations. I passed everything with the utmost
> ease—I know the secret now, and am never going to fail again. I shan't
> be able to graduate with honours though, because of that beastly Latin
> prose and geometry ... But I don't care. Wot's the hodds so long as
> you're 'appy? (That's a quotation. I've been reading the English classics.)
>
> *Jean Webster*

ૐ ૐ ૐ

*Look back at the section on 'Why Remember?'. What do you remember from
this section?*
Why do you recall this material?
How could you remember this section more effectively?

Without remembering, each day, each event, each moment would be
a totally new experience. How fully you remember depends largely on
how thoroughly you learned in the first place, and the material you recall
is as unique to you as is why, what and how you learn. As you learn in
your formal education, think about how you can learn in order to
remember more effectively.

Further reading

Bolles, E. B. 1988. *Remembering and Forgetting: An Inquiry into the Nature
of Memory*. Walker and Co., New York.
Buzan, Tony. 1974. *Use Your Head*. BBC Publications, London.
Highbee, K.L. 1988. *Your Memory. How it Works and How to Improve
it*. 2nd edn Prentice Hall, Eaglewood Cliffs, New Jersey.
Orr, F. 1984. *How to Pass Exams*. George Allen and Unwin, Sydney.

6

Analysing and Researching a Topic

As a student in a tertiary institution, most of the work you are expected to do is in the form of assignments in which you communicate your ideas and knowledge to others. These assignments are usually written (essays, discussion papers, reviews, projects and reports), or oral, and occasionally audiovisual. In addition to assignments, you are expected to gather information for lectures, tutorials, practical sessions, field trips and for exams.

Before you choose and research a topic you should define your purposes and clarify what is expected of you in the assignment. If you have been given a topic, you need to analyse it; if you are free to devise your own topic, you need to state clearly your proposed title. These initial steps will largely determine the material you select for research and how you finally present it. However, as you proceed with your research the information you gather reshapes your original definition or conception of the topic and may even lead you to change to another topic. Analysing and researching your topic are interdependent processes, rather than two separate activities.

This chapter looks at defining your purpose for an assignment, at your teachers' purposes and the expectations of academic writing, and at choosing, analysing, defining and researching a topic. This approach is applied to essay-type assignments, but many of the suggestions also apply to researching a report, a seminar paper, a key lecture or tutorial. The chapter is intended for students who need to choose and analyse a topic and to find their way through reference lists, rather than for those undertaking advanced research. It is the first of several chapters directly relevant to students working on written assignments.

Your purposes for assignments

'Why, if a fish came to me and told me he was going on a journey, I should say 'With what porpoise'?'
'Don't you mean 'purpose'?' said Alice.

Lewis Carroll

Your purposes for a particular assignment in a course should reflect your reasons for enrolling in the course, and on a broader level, your reasons for being at university. You may enrol in a course to complete a prerequisite or to follow up an interest or to work with a particular teacher. When you are given a particular assignment, you may decide that the work you do for the assignment would enable you to obtain background information for your main area of study, to complete a required section of course work, to increase your knowledge in a new area, to read more in an area of interest, or so you can practise communicating your ideas and receive feedback on them. It is useful to write down these purposes and refer to them as you do your research. If you have trouble articulating your purposes ask yourself the following questions:

What do you hope to accomplish by writing this piece of work?
What skills do you want to improve?
What new skills do you hope to learn?
What aspect of your learning and writing do you most need to improve?

There are times when your purposes for an assignment conflict with what is expected of you by the course or teacher. You may be expected to give a seminar paper on a topic which doesn't interest you, or to present a written report when you feel that a taped essay would be more effective. When such conflicts arise, ask your teacher if you can choose an alternative. Many teachers welcome such initiative and allow you to pursue your own topic and form of presentation. If an alternative is not possible, your discussions with the teacher should at least give you a clear idea of the purposes of the assignment. It is then up to you to decide whether you agree with these purposes. If you can't use the assignment to pursue your own purposes and questions, you may need to find an alternative (see 'Independent study', Chapter 4).

Your teachers' purposes

> When we mean to build
> We first survey the plot, then draw the model.
> *Shakespeare*

Teachers who design and teach courses usually do so with particular purposes in mind and each assignment should have a place within a grand plan to instruct you in the subject area and discipline. These purposes may or may not be explicitly stated—at times your teachers may not have clearly articulated their purposes and underlying assumptions. Some of the purposes may be to acquaint you with an issue central to a subject area, to stimulate you to question your attitudes, to give you practice in the methodologies of the discipline, to diagnose your ability to write clearly and logically, or to give your teacher some tangible work by which to evaluate your progress. Most assignments are designed with several purposes in mind.

Your academic assignments are normally written for only one person and for the purpose of assessment. What does your individual lecturer or tutor expect of you? How do you find this out? You should be told the aims of an assignment and how you are expected to present it. Beyond these requirements you cannot be expected to second guess your teacher's mind and if you try to do so your assignments are likely to be cautious and dull. It is of course difficult to imagine exactly what this person wants from you and impossible to understand what this person knows. You are not an expert in your field and as yet you are not expected to be, but it is your purposes and interests which give your assignments originality, so spend your time researching and presenting these interests as effectively as possible. Most teachers prefer a well-researched and well-argued original approach rather than a rehash of familiar textbooks or their own lectures. One major purpose which your teachers have for your tertiary education is to help you learn how to analyse and criticise information, how to argue a case and provide supporting evidence, and how to do this in writing (and verbally) according to the methods of the discipline and courses that you study. To understand this fully, you need to give some thought to the expectations underlying all your university assignments.

Expectations of academic assignments

> Expectations is the place you must always go to before you get to where you're going. Of course, some people never go beyond expectations ...
> *Norton Juster*

Before you begin the major writing stages of an assignment it is important to be clear about what is expected of you in your work. What is expected of you operates at different levels. Firstly, there are the overall expectations of tertiary study, then there are the expectations or conventions of the discipline in which you are studying and then the genre or form (such as essays, reports, reviews) in which you are expected to write. There are also the expectations of individual courses located within this discipline and any expectations that your particular teacher may have.

In tertiary studies, with the exception of a few interdisciplinary courses, most of the courses that you study will be in broad subject areas which are defined as disciplines. In some instances there will be opportunities for an interdisciplinary perspective or there may be interdisciplinary courses that you can take. Each discipline is a developing and changing body of knowledge with its own languages and conventions for presenting knowledge. The term 'discourse' describes the broad way in which language and thus meaning is given to knowledge in different disciplines or contexts.

> ... discourse ... means that knowledge in any domain, in any social domain, is organised from the point of view of a particular institution ... like law for instance. The knowledge of law is organised by the institution of law so that when particular forms of social practice come into the domain of the law, it talks about them in certain kinds of ways and not other kinds of ways. For example, if my neighbour and I have an argument over the back fence which has deteriorated in a particular way then this is talked about by my wife and I in a certain kind of way, but when we go to see the lawyer it gets talked about in a different kind of way. And this is what I mean by discourse. Now discourses are important in schools, particularly in secondary and tertiary education, because the organisation of knowledge becomes more and more specific to the disciplines which a ... student enters into. Thus you have particular ways of writing which correspond to the ways of organising knowledge within particular disciplines.
>
> *Gunter Kress*

If you are a humanities or social science student you will be required to write essays in your courses. The essays you write in one discipline in a tertiary institution will differ in significant ways from those in another discipline. Thus, the essays you write in history (or sociology or philosophy) will be different in some ways from what is expected in politics (or literature or media studies). Similarly, the expectations of a written report in psychology is different from what is expected in the physical sciences, and report writing in chemistry is different from report writing in biology.

Essays, reports and examination essays are the dominant writing genres in tertiary education. Many students coming from secondary school expect that essay writing is the same as essay writing in their English courses in school. However, university or college essays are different in important ways and require a different approach. For example, in tertiary studies usually only students in creative writing and other highly specialised courses have the opportunity to experiment with fiction or with purely descriptive forms of writing. So writing a narrative story or dialogue or a poem is not something many students do as part of their tertiary education.

You are expected to build on your abilities in organising and expressing ideas and information. However, unless your secondary education has encouraged you to be analytical and critical in your thinking rather than to simply reproduce and select from given information, some of the advice you were given at secondary school is not applicable once you reach tertiary study. Similarly, much that you are told in one discipline arises from the conventions and methodologies of that particular discipline and does not apply to another. It is important to remember this and to read carefully any course instructions on written work which should outline the aims of assignments and how to present them. If in doubt, ask your teacher before you choose your topic.

Choosing a topic

Some topics are *general*, such as 'The ecology of eucalypt forests', 'Romantic literature', 'Journalism', 'The French Revolution', or 'Scientific Method' and you are usually expected to provide your own specific topic and define in detail the particular slant you will cover within these general areas. Other topics are more *specific*, for example, 'Discuss the Hindu ideas of forgiveness and tolerance', 'Define Marx's concept of the proletariat', 'Examine the likely effects on the local flora and fauna of the freeway proposed for your capital city', or 'Should Piaget's theory of stages in children's development be applied in teaching mathematics in Australian primary schools?'

Deciding on a topic can seem deceptively simple—a matter of choosing from a list of suggested or set topics, or selecting a topic from within the subject matter of a course. However, your decision also involves analysing and defining possible topics. Start making your choice by thinking about the possibilities of each topic. Explore a couple of options and choose between them as you analyse them in some detail, or decide on one topic at the start and change your mind if your initial exploration suggests that it has limited possibilities. Often a topic which at first doesn't seem very interesting may become attractive as you explore it.

- Your choice of topic is affected by what you already know. If you are given a list of topics and are uncertain which to choose because some of them are unfamiliar, find out more about these options from someone who knows about them and from a reference such as a specialist encyclopaedia or a course text. If you have limited time to gather information, choose a familiar topic. If you have ample time, decide whether to explore a previous interest further or to learn about a slightly familiar topic.

- Your enthusiasm for a topic also affects your choice. For example, if you are interested in women's history you might choose a topic such as the suffragette movement. If you are an athlete, you might write on the physiology of marathon runners.
- Your choice of topic is often influenced by the information sources available. Being aware of sources other than libraries, lectures and your teachers can increase your choice of topics (see Chapter 7).

Unless your choice of topic is quite clear from the start or unless you have little time in which to choose, keep several options in mind. Allow yourself time to analyse their possibilities further, and to find out if the resources you need are available.

When devising your own specific topic (perhaps from within a general topic), devise a clear and accurate title. Often it is useful to word your topic as a question which you want to explore. As you are still at the stage of analysing your topic, you are unlikely to be ready to choose a final title. As you proceed with your analysis, revise the wording as necessary.

The following section on analysing your topic applies both to specific topics which your teachers have set and to specific titles which you have devised yourself.

Analysing a topic

The questions listed below are designed to help you with the process of analysing a topic. They should lead you to a written statement which clearly defines or conceptualises possible main points, a theme (or thesis or argument) and a structure for your topic. Apply each of these questions to your topic before you begin your research and writing. It is not necessary to apply the questions in the order given here but it will help if you make notes as you go. You will be surprised how much you already know about the topic.

Questions to ask

1 What is the topic about?

- Think about the wording of the topic so that you understand more clearly what you are expected to write about and the possibilities that the topic offers.

- Does the topic contain words or ideas you don't understand? For example, the possible uses of the word 'concept' in the topic 'Define Marx's concept of the proletariat' may not be clear. Consult an appropriate concept dictionary such as *The Fontana Dictionary of Modern Thought*. Ask your teacher to explain words you don't understand or, if a topic isn't clearly worded, ask your teacher to explain it more fully.
- Ask yourself 'What assumptions seem to underlie the topic?' For example, the topic 'How should Piaget's theory of stages in children's development be applied to teaching mathematics in our primary schools?' assumes that Piaget's theory should be applied to maths teaching in our primary schools.

2 What do I already know about the topic?

- Ask yourself this question and jot down any ideas you have.
- Use any available lists of study questions to start your mind ticking over.
- Brainstorm your topic by asking, 'Why?', 'Who?', 'What?', 'When?', 'How?', 'Where?' about it, or ask, 'How do I know that ... ?' to check the validity of your existing knowledge. (See 'What questions might you ask?' in Chapter 4 for more questions to start you thinking about a topic.)

3 What are the possible main points of the topic?

In preparation for finding information, compile a list of the main points which seem to be central to the topic.

In a set specific topic, you may be given an indication of some main points. For example, briefly describing your understanding of central terms or concepts will form an early part of the assignment; so in the Piaget topic you would need (a) to describe Piaget's theory of child developmental stages before (b) discussing its possible applications to maths teaching in our primary schools. Otherwise possible main points are likely to come from your background knowledge, from course materials or lectures, from recommended reading or from tutorial discussions on the topic.

Make an initial list of alternative or related terms for each main point. A library catalogue or reference works can help you revise your list so that your information search is as effective as possible. For example, to find information on migrants in a card catalogue look at the cards before and after 'Migrants', and in particular look at associated reference cards which suggest alternative headings such as 'Emigrants', 'Immigration' or the nationality of a migrant group. To find references to the changing composition of the workforce, you may need to look up 'Unemployment',

'Trade Unions', 'Women, working', as well as the obvious heading 'Workforce'.

Use reference works such as subject dictionaries to look up your initial list of subject headings and to find any related terms which are associated with each heading. Consult a general thesaurus, or a specialised thesaurus such as the *APAIS Thesaurus*, as a way of coming up with alternative or related headings for your main points.

4 What might my theme, thesis or argument be?

University essays and seminar papers are expected to have a theme, thesis or argument. Just as the theme in a piece of music recurs again and again in a slightly different form, the theme of an assignment is a case or a point of view which you want to develop throughout your piece of writing in several different ways. The theme you choose depends partly on your purpose and interests, and partly on the stated aims of the assignment.

As a starting point for working out a possible theme, ask yourself the following questions.

- 'What interests me most about the topic?'
- 'What aspect of it do I most want to explore?'
- 'What seems most important about the topic?'

At this stage keep in mind that your theme will decide the relationship between the main points you choose and the way in which you order them.

5 How might I structure the topic?

Structure is the way in which your ideas and information are organised. It is the way in which your main points are presented to support your theme and the way in which your evidence, examples and explanations support these main points.

Some topics include process words such as 'define', 'discuss' or 'evaluate' which help shape the structure of your assignment (see Table 6.1).

- Decide which words are directive or process words. Analyse these words to work out how they will direct the structure of your essay.
- Find how many parts there are to the topic.
- Discover whether the topic involves description and/or analysis of this description.
- Decide whether to compare two different aspects of a topic, or instead to clearly define all of its components.
- Choose whether to argue a case for or against a particular controversy relating to the topic, or to review the range of opinions on it.

Table 6.1 Directive words

> 'When I use a word', Humpty Dumpty said, in a rather scornful tone, 'it means just what I choose it to mean—neither more nor less'.
>
> *Lewis Carroll*

Analyse	Show the essence of something, by breaking it down into its component parts and examining each part in detail
Argue	Present the case for and/or against a particular proposition
Compare	Look for similarities and differences between propositions
Criticise	Give your judgement about the merit of theories or opinions about the truth of facts, and back your judgement by a discussion of the evidence
Define	Set down the precise meaning of a word or phrase. Show that the distinctions implied in the definition are necessary.
Describe	Give a detailed or graphic account
Discuss	Investigate or examine by argument, sift and debate, giving reasons for and against
Enumerate	List or specify and describe
Evaluate	Make an appraisal of the worth of something, in the light of its apparent truth or utility; include your personal opinion
Examine	Present in depth and investigate the implications
Explain	Make plain, interpret, and account for in detail
Illustrate	Explain and make clear by the use of concrete examples, or by the use of a figure or diagram
Interpret	Bring out the meaning of, and make clear and explicit; usually also giving your own judgement
Justify	Show adequate grounds for decisions or conclusions
Outline	Give the main features or general principles of a subject, omitting minor details, and emphasising structure and relationship
Prove	Demonstrate truth or falsity by presenting evidence
Relate	Narrate/show how things are connected to each other, and to what extent they are alike or affect each other
Review	Make a survey of, examining the subject critically
State	Specify fully and clearly
Summarise	Give a concise account of the chief points or substance of a matter, omitting details and examples
Trace	Identify and describe the development or history of a topic from some point or origin.

— adapted from Harry Maddox, 1967, *How to Study*, 2nd edn, Pan Books, London, pp. 119-120.

6 How will I acknowledge and examine my subjectivity?

> The trouble is that essays always have to sound like God talking for eternity, and that isn't the way it ever is. People should see that it's never anything other than just one person talking from one place in time and space and circumstance.
>
> *Robert M. Pirsig*

To what extent will you include your personal opinions? How will you acknowledge your biases?

Your approach to a topic is always subjective to some degree. Even a set specific topic can be tackled in a variety of ways, and your particular approach is reflected in what you include and omit from the possible material. Even if you are presenting a report in which you try to eliminate as much subjectivity as possible, the words you use carry with them personal associations for you and your audience. So the question to ask is not 'Shall I take an objective or subjective approach?' but rather 'What is the most effective way of dealing with my subjectivity?' Examine your biases and preconceptions so that they distort your research as little as possible. State explicitly your approach or your preliminary hypothesis, and be prepared in your writing to let your audience know your beliefs and biases on the subject. (See the Appendix 'Discrimination' for examples of bias.)

In an assignment such as a laboratory report you are required to report only what you see as 'facts' and to make personal input only in your critical interpretation of raw data. In other assignments such as a philosophy essay you may be required to include your own ideas with supporting arguments. Many assignments are open to a combination of these approaches—and remember in reporting facts, no two people will choose to do so in the same way or in exactly the same language. Your scope for presenting personal opinions or theories often depends on the conventions of a particular discipline and the personal preferences of your tutor. If you feel unsure about including your opinions, even when asked to, remember that practice in communicating your ideas and arguing them is a vital part of learning—and given practice and some encouraging response, it does become easier. Usually it also makes your assignments more interesting to read. But remember that even a more subjective approach requires logic, evidence and argument—an outpouring of unexamined assertions and prejudices is not acceptable.

> ...my purpose is to employ facts as tentative probes, as a means of insight, of pattern recognition, rather than to use them in the traditional and sterile sense of classified data, categories, containers.
>
> *Marshall McLuhan*

7 How much breadth or depth can this assignment have?

Given any requirements of the assignment (such as length or format) ask yourself the following questions.

* Should I concentrate on presenting a broad overview of the topic, or on exploring one or two facets of it in depth?
* How many main ideas can I convey?
* How many questions can I answer?
* How much key information can I present?

For example, in the topic 'Scientific Method' you may focus on the question 'Is there a scientific method?', contrasting the opinion of Paul Feyerabend (who argues that there is no single scientific method) with the views of John Kemeny (who posits that there is one basic method common to all scientific activity). You make this decision because the length and time set for the assignment don't permit you to look at many writers in detail, and because you want to contrast two theories on the question.

Group Assignments Defining a group topic involves agreeing on a central theme or question which the whole group will explore; deciding which specific aspects of the topic each person will research; and clarifying how each person's work contributes to the main theme or question. (If you are working on a group assignment, see Chapter 10 for suggestions on discussing ideas and information with others.)

Your initial definition

Before you begin full-scale research for an assignment, write down a brief statement of your purposes for the assignment, and review the aims stated by your teacher. Then write down your responses to your analysis of the topic under the headings (i) *Theme* (or Thesis or Argument), (ii) *Possible main points* and (iii) *Proposed structure*. Also, under the heading (iv) *Approach* put down some notes on how much personal opinion you are able to include, and try to clarify any of your assumptions or beliefs which may affect how you choose to approach the topic. This definition may be reasonably clear at this stage if the assignment is short and straightforward. But it is more likely that you will have a couple of possible structures and a number of likely points from which you can choose as you acquire detailed information about the topic. At this stage, you may not be clear on the theme or argument. If you have trouble defining a topic, write down any ideas you have and discuss them with other people. Trying to express your thoughts accurately in writing or verbally to others often helps you clarify them.

Deciding which material to use in research

Once you are clear about what is expected of you in your assignment and you have analysed your topic as far as possible, think about where and how you will find material on it (see Chapter 7). You will be given information in lectures and tutorials, supplied with reference lists for courses, tutorials, lectures and assignments, and perhaps directed to sources such as the media and individual people. At times you may have to search out and know how to use less obvious sources so that you don't overlook significant material.

This plethora of material can be overwhelming, particularly as the information on any one subject is increasing rapidly all the time. You may feel bewildered because you want to or are apparently expected to absorb so much. When researching a topic it is easy to become sidetracked by fascinating but irrelevant information, held up by little or no information, or bewitched by mystifying technical language. You can avoid these pitfalls by keeping your purpose and initial definition of the topic in mind. Obviously you can't use or absorb everything, so as well as being aware of potential material, you need to decide which material is most useful to you.

This section gives some hints on selecting and evaluating material for your purpose, and for its relevance and complexity. It also looks at the practical aspects of selecting material—buying, copying and borrowing.

Selecting relevant material

If you are not given a list of references from which to choose, check the available information sources and make up a list of material relevant to your topic. Consult your teacher and any course guides, handouts or reference lists for suggestions. Ask for guidance on which material is essential and which material to read first. Look for both primary and secondary sources on your topic (see 'Identifying primary and secondary sources', Chapter 7). The length of your list should depend on the time available for your research.

When analysing your topic you should have drawn up a list of the main points and possible subject headings. Keep these firmly in mind and use them in your research. Browsing through material which is vaguely connected with your topic can be highly enjoyable and can lead to serendipitous insights, but it is time-consuming and shouldn't be confused with seriously selecting material for full-scale research. When browsing, however, you may come across material which isn't precisely on your topic but deals with the general principles underlying it. An article on scientific methods, for example, can spark off ideas about an individual question on physics. Other material may provide valuable background. For example, a conversation with a person who lived through the Depression years in Australia may help you understand a specific aspect of this era more fully. Occasionally an idea can be illuminated by juxtaposing it with material from an unexpected source; for instance, astronomy with Alice in Wonderland, semiotics with Sufi philosophy, poetry with popular music.

Look for material on your topic which is not obvious or recommended. One of your own books, for example, may contain suggestions for further reading, or an organisation you contact for information may refer you to another source.

> Like any kind of exploratory activity, library research benefits from good planning and proficient technique (e.g. subject searches, catalogues, indexes) ... but it also profits from unplanned encounters with the unknown. Contrast the tunnel vision effect produced by a data base that only reports what you ask it. Try wandering down the stacks; let yourself get distracted by what's in the vicinity of the item you're hunting. Who knows what exciting or inspiring adventures in knowledge lurk there?
>
> *Zoe Sofoulis*

Evaluating your selection

Once you have selected relevant material, choose from your selection by evaluating the material on the basis of the purpose for which you need it and its complexity for you.

According to your purpose

Why do you want to use the material you are evaluating? Is it preliminary reading for a lecture or for a discussion paper, follow-up reading to a field trip or study material for an exam? (Chapter 8 looks at the purposes you might have for reading a book, and Table 8.1 on previewing suggests questions which help clarify how useful a book is for your purpose.)

Some material, such as a course text, you use for more than one purpose. Sometimes different materials you use may complement each other, such as two books each with information on a different aspect of your topic, or a lecture and a course text which present the same information from different angles. Sometimes you have to choose between materials because they are repetitious, such as two radio programmes which cover essentially the same ground.

Complexity of material

You can only understand a textbook when you are at the point where you almost don't need to read it, where it helps you comprehend (if it is any good) some higher-order connections among things which you separately have already worked your way through or around.

David Hawkins

Previewing material can help you discover the complexity of the text or material for you and hence the background knowledge you require to use it.

* The subject may or may not be interesting or familiar to you and may or may not accord with your beliefs and biases. If an area is new to you, you won't understand all the material in it, but its very newness can be exciting. Don't automatically reject apparently difficult material —even as a beginning it may provide you with one or two important ideas, and later you may find it easier to understand and very stimulating.
* The organisation, format and writing style of material can make it easy or difficult for you to follow.
* Perhaps you are more comfortable using some media than others. For example, perhaps you usually take in more from journal articles than from lectures because you can re-read difficult sections in an article. Any medium becomes familiar if you use it often enough, but if there is no time for this before selecting material, opt for media which usually yield you the most information (and learn how to use the others later).

If material you are required to use seems too advanced or too simple for you, discuss this with your teacher and with other students. There may be other material you can use or you might need to choose another topic.

Buy, copy or borrow material?

Your choice of material depends on its availability. Sometimes you will encounter problems with material you want to use because you can't buy it or borrow it from a library. Often you can avoid these problems by doing your research well in advance, arranging to borrow material from friends, and asking your teacher if an alternative reference is possible. Otherwise you may need to reconsider your choice of a topic in the light of available resources.

Some material you are likely to want to refer to again, such as a course text or a reference book you need for a final exam or for a seminar paper. If you do need to consult material more than once, you may want to obtain your own copy—to buy a book, to tape a lecture or an interview, or to photocopy an article (subject to copyright laws). If you can't have your own copy, try to borrow the material, or if your information comes from a person or a place, arrange to visit them again. If you need to use borrowed material heavily, take full notes on the content and note source details such as page numbers.

When deciding which books to buy, be wary of relying on course booklists given in handbooks. Such lists are usually drawn up six months or more before a course starts and may change substantially, or a different edition or translation of a book may be recommended. Before you buy books or start your reading, check with up-to-date course lists or with a teacher from the course to find out if there have been changes.

Whether you buy, copy or borrow material depends on:

- the amount of money you have
- if the materials are easily available from the library, from another student, or from a teacher
- how heavily you will use the material in a course
- whether you have easy access to a library
- how heavily you rely on course materials and references for stimulation, for instance, if you have little opportunity to discuss your work with other students
- whether you prefer to underline books or articles you read, and
- whether or not the material will be useful in other courses or in a future job.

Using research material

Preparing to use material

Consider the practical steps for selecting information from the material you will use. For example, you gain more from a book if you are aware of what is involved in the process of reading and how you might improve your abilities as a reader. You learn more from a lecture or radio programme if you have thought about how these media convey information and what you need to do to listen more effectively. (See 'Examining a source' in Chapter 7, and the introductions to Chapter 8 on reading and Chapter 9 on lectures.)

Previewing material, that is, surveying material as a whole before you work with it, acquaints you with its general organisation, content and presentation. This previewing enables you to consider how you could best use the material for your purpose, for example, how detailed your reading of a book should be, or whether to take notes on a television programme (see 'Previewing', Chapter 8).

You have to record, store and retrieve useful information, so give some thought to how you will do this (see 'Selecting, recording and filing information'). A **filing system** evolves as you use it, but have a basis for your filing before you start researching. If you have thought about your purpose and topic, these can form the basis of your system. Will you record your information using computer software?

In the preliminary stages of your research, give some thought to **communicating ideas and information**. A written essay or report isn't automatically the most appropriate means for expressing ideas. If, for example, you are researching children's poetry, a taped essay which includes poetry readings may be most effective. If your topic is animal behaviour, you may decide to include photographs or a videotape to convey your findings. Asking yourself, 'To whom do I want to communicate the information I find?' can help you decide how to convey your information.

> 'Don't grunt,' said Alice, 'that's not at all a proper way of expressing yourself.'
>
> *Lewis Carroll*

As you work with material

Questioning and evaluating

> Where there is much desire to learn, there of necessity will be much arguing, much writing, many opinions; for opinion in good men [*sic*] is but knowledge in the making.
>
> *John Milton*

You should have already previewed your material for its overall relevance to your purpose and topic. As you work with a book, listen to a lecture or watch a film, question and evaluate the information offered. This involves examining the purpose, theme, content, structure and presentation of the material for its general quality and for its specific relevance to your topic and purpose. (See Chapters 8 and 9 for details on how to criticise information from reading and lectures.) Be prepared to discover that some of the material you have selected may not be as useful as you hoped, and don't expect that set or suggested references will automatically suit your definition of a topic. If you feel material is of limited use to you, abandon it as a source or try to incorporate a criticism of it into your assignment.

As part of evaluating information in your research, hopefully you will learn to *interpret primary sources confidently*. In some assignments you are expected to use both your interpretation of primary source material and opinion from secondary sources (see 'Identifying primary and secondary sources', Chapter 7). For example, when you conduct an experiment, you may be expected to interpret the data yourself and to refer to other people's interpretation of data from the same experiment. In an essay you may be expected to criticise a well-known author's works and use other critics' evaluations of these. If you feel uncertain about presenting mostly your own ideas, and think that you should play it safe and rely mostly on secondary sources, practise the following:

- get to know your primary source material thoroughly, and see what ideas and interests this sparks off in you
- refer to secondary sources to help clarify points you don't understand in the primary source material
- read selectively among secondary sources and critically examine other people's interpretations of the primary ideas or data you are studying, and
- use secondary sources for occasional new insights and for any unexpected connections they may make.

Above all, trust your own intelligence and common sense in questioning and evaluating ideas.

> In a private debate the scholar Salih Awami said to Sufi Rahimi:
> 'What you have just said lacks references and proofs through quotations from ancient authority'.
> 'Not at all,' said Rahimi, 'for I have them all here, chapter and verse.'
> The scholar went away, saying, 'That was what I wanted to know.'
> The next day he made his famous speech on Rahimi which began:
> 'The lecture which you are about to hear from Sheikh Rahimi lacks conviction. Why, he is so unsure of himself that he actually adducted written proofs and authorities to what he says.'
>
> *Idries Shah*

Selecting, recording and filing information

As you evaluate material, select information and record it in an easily accessible form. For example, underline an article, tape parts of an interview, or take photographs. You will probably record most of your information in note form even if preparing an oral or audiovisual assignment. (See Chapters 8 and 9 for more on selecting information and taking notes from reading and lectures.)

Some information you don't need to record and keep because it is relatively accessible or because it is unlikely that you will need it in future. However, some information which you may want again is available to you only once (such as material in an interview or radio programme) or is difficult to find again (such as information from a person who is awkward to contact or a book which isn't readily available). In these instances, as you select the information you want think how you can best record and store it.

The basic reasons for systematically filing information are so that you can easily find it again, add to or subtract from it, and re-arrange it when useful. Use stationery such as looseleaf paper and a ring binder, a box of file cards, a concertina file or several filing trays to make it easier to arrange and re-arrange material as necessary. Some computer software is designed to enable you to create a database or a filing system.

Methods for filing information depend on the specific purposes for which you need it. Often it is convenient to organise and file material according to its content or its source, as in the following examples.

- To follow the development of themes within a course, keep your lecture notes in sequence in a looseleaf folder. You can then interleave notes from tutorials, fieldwork and reading wherever their content is related to a theme.
- When preparing to write an essay in which you are expected to base your ideas on a careful examination of primary source material, keep your notes taken from the reading of primary sources separate from those from secondary sources.

Alternatively you might choose to organise and file your material in chronological order (such as dates on lecture notes) or alphabetical order (such as authors of books read) and/or numerical order (with each item or each page of notes numbered). Record the source of your information in detail, including page numbers, in case you want to find it again or cite the reference.

Read material and edit notes before you file them, ask yourself if you are likely to use the material again. Keeping all 'to-be-read-or-edited-material' together without attempting to file it before reading it indicates whether you are being realistic about the amount of information you think that you can take in and use. An efficient system is of little use if all it yields is an impressive collection of file card boxes whose contents you have mostly forgotten, or a stack of folders full of photocopied articles you intend to read one day, or a fancy computer programme which has been of more interest to you than its contents.

> Knowledge is of two kinds. We know a subject ourselves, or we know where we can find information upon it.
>
> *Samuel Johnson*

Organising and integrating ideas and information

As you research and think about your topic you need to organise and integrate your ideas and the information you find in a way that supports your theme/thesis/argument. The following method is one way of doing this.

- Write out a tentative statement of your theme. Ask yourself: 'What statement can I make which captures the essence of my argument?', 'How can I convey my central thesis to my audience?' Keep this in front of you as you work.

- Write each of the possible main points as a heading on separate sheets of paper or cards. If you have a computer and the appropriate software you might choose to use the outlining facility to help order these points.
- Enter relevant information and ideas (and references to any graphic or audiovisual material) under the appropriate heading.
- Add a new heading if you decide on another major point, or delete a point which comes to appear less significant. If you have much more information for one heading than for others, consider if you should base your whole assignment on the idea in that heading. If necessary, reorganise and delete material.
- Check the number of major points you want to make against the possible assignment length and the time available. It is usually better to err on the side of making a few points clearly, with plenty of evidence and examples and explanation, rather than trying to cover all possible major points superficially.
- Check that each of the main points is supported by evidence. reasons or examples and that each of the main points relates to your argument.

Organising your information and ideas in this way helps you see the main points more clearly. You begin to understand how they could effectively be related to your argument and to one another, and the order in which to develop them. Your researching, thinking and organising should extend and clarify your original analysis of the topic. As you continue your research, you revise your original definition of the topic and begin to structure the content.

Expressing your ideas

Talking to others about your ideas and the information you find helps you begin to sort out your thoughts and become accustomed to putting them into words. As you carry out your research, it is often valuable to write individual paragraphs or sentences (or to make part of a tape) so that you capture an idea you may use later. Put these ideas down when you think of them in case they vanish, and if you have a half-formed idea in your head, try expressing it without editing and see how it takes shape. (If you can use a computer for this, it is easy to refine later what you want to say.) Trying to express your current thoughts accurately can lead you to other useful ideas (see 'Free writing', Chapter 11).

Towards the end of your research

When your research is almost complete and you are ready to begin your assignment, allow yourself time to **sort out your ideas,** for your thoughts to sift and settle. Do this rather than read another book or conduct another interview, especially if you are finding it difficult to work out what you want to say. Look at your notes as a whole to refresh your mind about your ideas on the topic and to review the information you have selected from your material.

Talk again about your ideas and information with others, perhaps in a discussion or writing group, so that you begin to express your thoughts. New ideas and relationships will emerge, and any difficulties you might have in deciding and articulating what you want to say often resolve themselves. To provide yourself with a thesis for the assignment, look at the connections between your main points, and ask yourself again what strikes you as most important and interesting about the topic.

Your revised definition

Before you began your research you wrote down some thoughts on the purpose for your assignment, a probable theme and main points for your assignment, and outlined a likely structure.

After your research, review your written statement about the assignment's purposes; and produce a revised definition or conception of your topic. Look again at the topic and using the questions in the 'Analysing your topic' section of this chapter, make notes again outlining your theme/thesis/argument, the main points you have chosen, and the way in which you will structure them. Indicate the approach you will use in acknowledging your personal opinions. Compare the initial and revised definitions. Have you omitted anything important? Does your revised definition still reflect your purposes for the assignment?

Make sure, especially in the case of specific topics, that you are answering the question asked or sticking to the topic set. With topics of your own choice, re-read the assignment guidelines to ensure that you have incorporated all of the requirements when defining your topic. Remember that focusing your written work around a *theme, thesis or argument* is crucial and is a fundamental expectation of almost all tertiary assignments. Now that your research is more or less completed, the *main points* which you will cover should be definite. If you find that you have omitted any important content you may need to do some further research. The way in which you *structure* your assignment—how you will show the relationship between the main points and organise them so that they argue your case—may be quite clear now or may still be tentative. In either case, leave some flexibility so that if necessary you can revise your definition further when expressing your thoughts and information in writing your assignment (see Chapter 12).

❧ ❧ ❧

An assignment is designed for a specific, limited purpose, rather than to find out all you are ever likely to know on a topic. Analysing and researching a topic should enable you to select from your current knowledge of that topic, even if your knowledge continues to grow and expand in areas far beyond the focus of your assignment.

Further reading

Lane, Nancy D. 1989. *Techniques for Student Research: A Practical Guide*. Longman Cheshire, Melbourne.

Rottenberg, Annette J. 1986. *Elements of Argument: a Text and Reader*. St Martin's Press, New York.

Smith, David. 1988. *Becoming Your Own Researcher* in Lovat, Terry (ed). *People, Culture and Change*. Social Science Press, Wentworth Falls.

7

Using Libraries and Other Information Sources

We live in the midst of <u>information networks</u>. You are a point in many networks, <u>sometimes giving information</u> and <u>sometimes seeking it</u>. No one can learn all there is to know about a subject, so you can be both a learner and a teacher in subjects which interest you. Even as an interested beginner, you probably know enough about an area to teach someone else a little about it. If you can't answer someone's queries on a subject, you can probably direct them to another part of a network where they are likely to find what they want to know. Which network you plug into when seeking information depends on what you want to know, why you want to know it, and whether you know how to use available information sources.

This chapter centres on the processes involved in making effective use of libraries and other information sources, while emphasising the need to be aware of a wide range of possible sources. The chapter looks at choosing sources relevant to your topic and at examining the sources you decide to use. We begin by looking at libraries, since tertiary institutions rely heavily on them as an information source.

Libraries

Choosing libraries

If you have access to more than one library, explore each one to find out what it offers you. Look at each as a place to work. Consider the facilities, material in your areas of interest, and staff expertise and helpfulness. A large library may have most of the material you need, but you may prefer a small library where the staff are familiar with your interests and where you feel more at home. Or the small library nearby may be frustrating because it never seems to have the books you want, and you may prefer a large library with a more sophisticated range of collections.

Libraries have many different functions, and include:

- large state libraries, with special sections such as archives
- university libraries, often with individual subject libraries attached
- government departmental libraries
- specialist collections, such as a historical society library, a photographic collection, a substantial private collection
- public libraries serving a local community, and
- school and college libraries.

Don't forget your personal library, and those of your friends. Remember that through inter-library loans and computer-based information services you have access to material in libraries other than the one or two which you can visit most easily, or from which you usually receive books.

To use libraries fully, you need to know what materials they offer, learn how to gain practical access to the materials they contain, and learn how to find items in them.

Making full use of libraries

A Harvard Librarian of last century was notorious for his unsmiling countenance. One day a professor saw the librarian coming across the quad, beaming. 'You seem particularly jovial today' he said.

'Yes', replied the bookman, 'all the books are in except two, and I'm going to get them now.'

A Librarian

1 Knowing what materials libraries contain

Explore the libraries to which you have access to find out what materials they contain. The following list may include materials you hadn't considered or which are unfamiliar to you.

a Books and other printed material These are a familiar source of information to most of us. (Chapter 8 suggests ways of reading printed material effectively.) Apart from books, some libraries contain:

- periodicals, journals, newspapers, bulletins and other serials, with current issues usually on display and back issues shelved or available on microfilm
- government publications, such as reports, yearbooks, and manuals, and
- pamphlets on a wide range of subjects.

One important group of books in any library is the **reference collection**. You probably are aware of standard references such as *The Encyclopaedia Britannica* and *The Oxford Dictionary*, but reference collections can also contain works such as:

- specialist encyclopaedias or dictionaries, such as *The Encyclopaedia of Philosophy, Dictionary of Film Makers*
- atlases, gazetteers, guidebooks, such as the *Archaeological Atlas of the World, Bartholomew Gazetteer of Britain*
- yearbooks and almanacs which give relatively up-to-date statistical information and which are often government publications, such as *The West Australian Yearbook*
- handbooks which contain useful and detailed information for people in specific fields, such as teaching, writing, surveying, skin diving, and
- resource directories which are catalogues of useful material, people and places, such as a directory for a particular city or small interest group.

To find works on a subject, it can be extremely useful to consult some *bibliographies, indexes and abstracts* in the reference collection as well as using the subject catalogue. Many libraries now have CD ROM laser discs which hold bibliographical and statistical databases and other reference sources including some encyclopaedias. These discs hold the equivalent of 1500 floppy discs or over 200 000 pages of text, and CD ROM databases such as MLA and ERIC will give you references to five years of journal articles in literature and education respectively. CDATA 86 contains 1981 and 1986 census data from the Australian Bureau of Statistics. To access these databases you need subject keywords; and you can view the references on a workstation screen, print them out or capture them to disc.

Another form of technology which may be useful in the final year of a degree or in postgraduate work is on-line data retrieval. This connects you to a distant database via 'phone and is usually expensive to use.

- Bibliographies list books by a particular subject, author, printer or country, for example, *The Current Bibliographies on African Affairs*, *The International Bibliography of Economics*, *A Bibliography of Sex Rites and Customs*. The *Australian National Bibliography* lists recent Australian books and official reports, and *Books in Print* lists non-fiction books printed in the USA.

- Indexes are usually:
  - indexes to multi-volume reference works such as an encyclopaedia
  - indexes to government publications, for example *Australian Government Publications*
  - indexes issued by publishers of a periodical, for example the *Scientific American Cumulative Index*
  - indexes issued by an independent publisher for a number of general periodicals, for example *APAIS* (the Australian Public Affairs Information Service), a major indexing journal for the humanities and social sciences which is issued by the National Library, Canberra, and
  - indexes to periodicals in special fields, for example, *Index Medicus* in the medical field.
- Abstracts include a précis of books and articles in a field, as well as indexing them, for example *Psychological Abstracts*. The CD ROM database *Psychlit* contains the same material as *Psychological Abstracts* and the computer search software enables you to do in seconds what would take hours by hand in *Psychological Abstracts*.

To make efficient use of bibliographies, indexes and abstracts—especially in a computer-based catalogue—you need to develop a list of subject terms central to a topic (see 'Analysing a topic', Chapter 6).

b Non-print material This may include:

- graphic material, such as maps, prints, illustrations, paintings and models
- audiovisual material, such as slides and photographs, audio cassettes, videotapes, films, and overhead transparencies
- microfilm, for example, of back issues of newspapers
- microfiche, such as the Human Relations Area File, and
- collections of ephemeral material, such as newsletters, posters, advertisements and lapel buttons.

It takes time and practice to become familiar with the contents and organisation of a library, and to learn how to use library facilities. This familiarisation is a means to learning more about subjects which interest you, and the exercise at the end of this chapter can help you with this. To update and extend and diversify your knowledge of the information that any library has to offer, explore its resources when new subjects stimulate your curiosity.

Twenty-two acknowledged concubines, and a library of sixty-two thousand volumes, attested the variety of his inclination...

Edward Gibbon

2 Gaining access to information

To be able to use the materials a library offers means learning to use catalogues and equipment such as photocopiers, tape recorders, and video cassette players. Ask one of the library staff to show you how to use this equipment, as most students who are not initially confident with equipment rapidly become so once it is familiar.

Also ask for help if you are unfamiliar with particular information technologies such as CD ROM discs. Some convenient forms of storing information—such as microfilm and microfiche—can be demanding to use, so request help if you run into difficulties or if you want to make copies of the material in the least expensive way. If you find that using these information sources is tiring to your eyes, you may need to plan several short work sessions to obtain the information rather than one long one.

It is also helpful in gaining access to library material to find out when the library you use is busy and when it is quiet. Then if you possibly can, visit at the quiet times (such as Sunday morning) when staff are more available to help, when reserve collections are less in demand, and when access to catalogue terminals is easier so you can save time by searching for a batch of items all at once.

3 Learning how to find items

* Ask the *library staff*—they are usually helpful with anything from the most basic to the most esoteric of queries.
* Become familiar with the *layout* of a library—where the different types of materials are located, and where facilities such as photocopiers and audio visual equipment can be found. Most libraries have maps and publications describing their layout and operation, but it is easy to fall into the habit of only using one section of a library and being unaware of what other areas have to offer.
* Learn about the *operation* of a library, for example how the borrowing system operates or how to ask for an interlibrary loan. Since academic

libraries around the country have become connected through electronic catalogues it is possible to gain access to a much wider range of material (such as journal holdings) than before, although this service can be expensive. Conversely, in times of restricted funding the collections in libraries often do not increase in proportion to the increase in students, so more print material may be placed in limited-access reserve collections. This is done to try and make material available to a greater number of students, and you need to learn how to make the most of these collections.

- Find out what extra information *the information or reference desk* holds to enable you to locate material. There may be a printout of material currently on reserve, a list of journal issues, information about material in special subject libraries elsewhere on campus or information about branch library holdings. A large tertiary institution with more than one campus or with long-established departments may well have branch libraries in addition to the main one, and if so it is useful to have some idea of what each branch holds, both in the way of general collections and in specialist subject material which could be relevant to your interests.

- Find out which *system* the library uses for cataloguing, classifying, indexing and shelving the material it contains. For example:
  - some libraries use a classification system other than the familiar Dewey system
  - methods of shelving materials such as large books, pamphlets and audio visual material vary from one library to another
  - the alphabetical order of catalogue entries may vary, for example in how entries for authors with hyphenated names are filed,
  - some libraries have card catalogues for author/title and for subjects, while other libraries put all cards in one alphabetical file, and
  - many libraries have on-line computer catalogues while some use microfiche catalogues.

- Learn how to use *the catalogue system*. Taking time to do this (ask the library staff to help) can save you many hours later on and gives you access to a much greater depth of information. Some libraries (such as some local ones) still use catalogue cards, but most tertiary libraries now use on-line computer catalogues. To find items using on-line catalogues, you choose from a menu on the screen which is accompanied by instructions directing you how to search for an item by author, by subject or by title. In this initial search you will find information on:
  - the call number, which gives you the exact shelf location and also appears on the item itself

- a location symbol, which indicates the sequence of materials with which the item is shelved—with oversize books, for example, or with journals, pamphlets, or general books. (Your next step is to find where such material is shelved and how each of these categories of material is organised.)
- the classification number, which arranges material by subject
- the author's symbol, which is used to sub-arrange material on the same subject, and
- publication details for an item, which include the publisher, place, publication date and edition. (Note that the date of first publication may differ from the publication date of the particular edition or reprint which the library holds.)

To look up an item using the author's name or the title, you need the correct spelling of the name and the correct wording of the title. If you know the title of a book you are looking for, then search for that first. There may be several authors with the same name and each one may have written several books. Most titles are unique so that is the most direct way to find the book in the catalogue. If you can't find an item in the catalogue, check that you have been given an accurate reference.

Once you have located the item and the relevant information from your initial search using author, title or subject, you can carefully follow the instructions in on-line catalogues to find further information such as other books by the same author or the loan status of the item you're seeking. In most catalogues you will also come across reference entries which direct you to alternative headings for a topic (such as 'Motor cars ... see Automobiles'), or to related headings (such as 'Naturalists ... see also Ecologists'), or to more specific headings (such as 'Biology ... see also Marine Biology').

- *If the item isn't on the shelf in its exact location:*
  - check if it is on the shelf but slightly out of order
  - check the catalogue to make sure that you copied the call number accurately
  - if you did, find out if the item is on loan
  - if it is, you can ask for it to be recalled, and
  - if it is not on loan, check if it is being held elsewhere in the library such as in a reserve collection.

  If none of these steps help you find the item, it is probably in use in the library by another reader or waiting to be re-shelved. Try the shelves later on.
- *If you are not able to visit the campus library easily*, perhaps because you are a part-time or external student, be particularly well-informed about

the facilities you need to use most often, such as photocopying services and special loan arrangements. When you send in a request for help, or if you do manage to visit the library, be very clear about the sort of information you are seeking. Explore any other library facilities near you, work out which books you will use most heavily, and be prepared to buy them (see 'Buy, copy, or borrow material?', Chapter 6). The cost of mailing books or making special trips to a library can soon add up to the price of several books, and libraries don't regard provision of textbooks as one of their functions.

Choosing relevant sources

> Not even the largest 'multiversity' can offer all the resources needed by students today.
>
> *University Without Walls*

An initial step in choosing information sources for a topic is to become aware of a range of possible sources. As a student in an educational institution, you have some obvious sources such as:

- classes—including lectures, laboratory sessions and discussion groups
- people, including teachers and other students, and
- printed and audio visual material, such as course guides, laboratory manuals, handouts, recommended books and library materials.

You limit your potential sources if you look only to educational institutions and libraries for your information and ignore the groups and individual people in your community. So before automatically consulting your lecture notes or going to a library for information, ask yourself 'How would I find what I want to know if I wasn't a student with access to these sources?' You can learn much in your formal education from people who are not considered experts or teachers. If you are studying local history, for example, you can gain a wealth of information from people who have lived in your community for a long time. If you are studying insect behaviour, the person next door who has kept bees for many years can be extremely helpful. But it is easy to overlook sources of information outside libraries unless specifically directed to them. And as a learner in the late twentieth century, the mass media form a large part of your information networks and a large part of the reality in which you live.

Being able to use a range of information sources requires:

- defining your purpose and topic as clearly as you can
- locating a range of potential information sources
- choosing sources which suit your subject, and
- examining sources to find out how to use them most effectively.

Defining your purpose and analysing your topic are discussed in Chapter 6. This section and the next look at the other processes involved in using a range of information sources, and as examples of these processes refers to three broadly different sources of information—organisations, people and the mass media. We now look at identifying primary and secondary sources in relation to your topic, and at mastering the skills necessary for using a source, in this case for gathering primary information.

Identifying primary and secondary sources

The information sources available to you vary according to your subject. Sometimes you can go directly to your subject for first-hand information. For example, if your subject is the ideas of Mao Tse-Tung you may be able to obtain and read his writings, or if you are studying goldfish behaviour you might have facilities so you can conduct experiments on this. At other times, you will have to rely on other people's reports about your subject. For example, you may read a journal article about Mao Tse-Tung if you can't obtain his books, or you might ask an aquarium owner about the behaviour of goldfish. Often you will use both first-hand (or primary) and second-hand (or secondary) information.

If you are studying a local community group and you gather your information on them by attending several meetings, your source is also your subject and is described as a *primary source*. If you read a newspaper article on the group to obtain your information, the article is a *secondary source*: that is, the information doesn't come directly from your subject.

Similarly, if your subject is a scientific research organisation, a filmed interview with the head of the organisation is a primary source, whereas someone else's written report about the interview is a secondary source. If you are studying an historical event, the testimonies of participants and witnesses are primary sources, while a source of secondary information would be a book written by an historian using these testimonies.

You can limit your choice of material and your choice of topics by classifying an information source as either primary or secondary when it can be both. Teachers and libraries, for example, dispense secondary information about a range of subjects, but they themselves can also be subjects for a study and thus a primary source. You may study a commercial organisation such as a mining company and use it as a primary source, but overlook the secondary knowledge the company holds on subjects related to its operations

Communities offer a wide variety of organisations which can be used as primary and secondary sources, depending on your topic. The following are just a few of the possibilities:

* public agencies and institutions, such as museums, government departments, art galleries, courts, scientific research organisations
* commercial businesses, such as mining companies, factories, insurance companies, shopping centres, and
* community groups, such as church organisations, business associations, environmental groups, women's health care houses, ethnic broadcasting groups.

Some organisations offer library and public information facilities. You also have access to services and organisations designed to provide information, such as Legal Aid, Citizens' Advice Bureaux, and local government information offices. Often a person or group can refer you to further sources.

Do some preliminary research and decide on some questions you want to ask before contacting people and organisations for information (see 'Analysing a topic', Chapter 6). Make inquiries to find out who is most likely to be helpful for your purpose and don't hesitate to make an initial polite request for information. You may be surprised at the help people are willing to give, and this process of finding material is a valuable learning exercise in itself.

Research tools

Other chapters in this book look at tools for using sources such as books and lectures. Here we look briefly at the tools needed to gather primary information (see 'What questions might you ask?', Chapter 4).

When you are curious about a subject you can learn much by **observation**. Listen and look closely, and use your senses of taste, smell and touch if appropriate. If you can observe a subject more and more intently over a period of days or weeks, you will come to see it with new eyes. You can observe the natural physical environment—phenomena such as a sunset, a bird, trees, rain and mountains. You can observe your manufactured and technological environment, with its aeroplanes and advertisements, its transistors and telephones. You can observe the people in your world such as parents, friends, work colleagues or strangers.

Observing people and seeking information from them are activities you engage in for many of your waking hours, and you consciously or unconsciously learn much of what you need to know from your interactions with others. Deliberately seeking information from and about people requires carefully directed observation if you are to obtain useful information on a specific topic. You need practice in the skills of observation, even if you are 'only watching' people to describe them, or 'just talking' to a person to find out very specific information.

However, observation alone can't tell you all you want to know. No matter how acute your observations, don't mistake them for a sophisticated analysis. Skilled researchers are very cautious about drawing conclusions from their research.

> Natural science does not simply describe and explain nature; it is part of the interplay between nature and ourselves; it describes nature as exposed to our methods of questioning.
>
> *Werner Heisenberg*

As well as careful observation you also need considerable familiarity with the **appropriate research techniques** if your observation is to be extended and directed towards specific ends. Research techniques are more of a hindrance than a help if used without sensitivity to the complexity of people and of environments, or if used in the belief that they provide 'objective' answers. But if used cautiously they can be appropriate tools in your search for information. For example:

> Anyone interested in human beings and why we act as we do won't want to limit their inquiry to reading books or listening to lectures. The raw material of all our understanding of human behaviour is observations of people—ourselves and others. These observations include study of how people act in certain situations and what they report about how they feel and why they do things. From these observations we infer their motives, their values, their attitudes, and their opinions. Social science has developed a whole array of tools to assist in these analyses. These tools include questionnaires, interviews, field studies, participant observation, laboratory studies, and unobtrusive measures.
>
> Each of these techniques is an entire skill area in itself and consists of a whole series of sub-techniques. For example, an interview may be open-ended or closed, structured or unstructured, in-depth or limited. The proper construction of a reliable and valid questionnaire is a skill requiring months or years of training and experience. Unobtrusive measures for observing people can range from activities such as measuring carpet wear patterns in an art gallery to find out which paintings are most popular, to gathering statistics from pharmaceutical companies about sales of oral contraceptives to Catholic and non-Catholic communities.
>
> Each technique has its own characteristic strengths and weaknesses. The nature of the question being asked, the population being studied, the resources available, and the preferences of the questioner, all influence the choice of appropriate techniques. This area of 'research methodology' is one of the most complex and difficult in the social sciences and scholars spend entire lifetimes studying small aspects of it.
>
> The interpretation of the results of these information-gathering techniques is equally complex and requires a sophisticated level of skill if it is to be properly done. The path which leads from initial formulation of a question in the mind through gathering data from observations of

people to drawing valid conclusions from those observations, is a long and thorny path which is pitted with traps for the unwary. Expert guidance is essential.

John Raser (1980, written for this book)

Humans don't follow neat patterns of behaviour, don't act in totally predictable ways, and are distinctly prone to present a researcher with a mass of complex material to analyse. As you acquire information, your clear definition of what you wanted to know will hopefully remain the same in substance, but it will inevitably change in shape as you come to grips with the uniqueness of another human being. To acquire skill in using research techniques, practise them and learn from your successes and failures how each technique can best be applied.

Even when you have considerable skill with such tools you will continue to learn more about their use because of the unpredictable nature of your 'subjects'. This very unpredictability shows the limited use of even sophisticated research tools unless you seriously consider the nature of the relationship between yourself as a researcher and the people from whom you are seeking information. For example, if in a series of interviews you treat your interviewees only as information sources who should confine themselves to passively answering your questions, you are ignoring the input that these individual human beings can make to the substance and validity of your research.

Another aspect of the relationship concerns your respective social backgrounds, since these affect how you interpret the responses you receive from someone whose background differs from your own. Imagine, for example, how the responses of an older female factory worker might be interpreted differently by a young male student, by an older woman who works in a professional occupation, and by an older unemployed man whose mother worked in a factory. When you do not share the cultural background of the person you are interviewing, it is advisable to seek guidance from a cross-cultural specialist when planning and interpreting your research.

> ... the active voice of the subject should be heard in the account. Our interpretations should avoid transforming the acting and thinking human being solely into an object of study, while recognizing that some objectification is inherent in the process of interpretation or reconstruction. Moreover ... the theoretical reconstruction must be able to account for the investigator as well as for those who are investigated.
>
> *Joan Acker et al.*

Examining a source

As well as choosing relevant sources, examine each information source you use so that you can plan how to use its contents effectively and how to understand and evaluate it more fully. If, for example, you are going to interview a person, think about the process of interviewing and about the skills you will need to obtain information on your topic. Other chapters in the book look at the processes involved in using the sources of books and lectures. Here we look at the mass media as an example of analysing a source and at planning how to use that source systematically.

The discoveries to be made from observing and using the information in the mass media are plentiful—if you accept them as a significant information source in your formal education. How can you observe and analyse the nature of the mass media?

The medium used

The mass media are part of your daily life. When you read a daily paper or watch the TV news, you see your community, your society and your world as they are reflected, selected and shaped by the media. What you see, read and hear is happening now, and you expect the media to provide you with more up-to-date information than in books. But this simultaneity makes it difficult to stand back from the information the media convey. For example, it is difficult to evaluate and use a documentary shown on TV last night in the same way as you would a book. And because the media deal almost entirely with topical issues and events, they frequently select information which will make 'a good story' rather than presenting a balanced view of a subject. In cases where the ownership of large sections of the media is concentrated in the hands of a few people, the information with which you are presented is likely to be limited in its scope. Use the media but keep their limitations in mind.

1 Comparing mass media with traditional sources

One way to learn about the nature of mass media is to compare them with information sources traditionally used in formal education. Listening to a ten-minute current affairs commentary or a full-length play on the radio requires a different approach from listening to a fifty-minute lecture. To criticise the content of a radio programme as though it were a lecture delivered by a person in front of you is to ignore the way the medium itself shapes the content and your perceptions in each instance. The same is true if you evaluate feature articles in a daily newspaper as though they were written with exactly the same aims as a chapter in a book which took a year to write and which you can take a year to read.

> The newspaper format ... offers short, discrete articles that give important facts first and then taper off to incidental details, which may be, and often are, eliminated by the make-up man. The fact that reporters cannot control the length of their articles means that, in writing them, emphasis can't be placed on structure, at least in the traditional linear sense, with climax or conclusion at the end.
>
> *Edmund Carpenter*

Like books and traditional lectures, radio programmes and newspapers present you with information in a one-way process. Their messages come to you with little possibility of engaging in immediate dialogue with them. If you recognise this, you can see that you need to question and evaluate and use the information they convey if you are to understand and remember it. This entails discussing it, writing about it, or applying it to a problem you need to solve. In this way you think actively about the information, and make it your own. As with listening to a lecture, it is easy to delude yourself that you have learned something from listening to and looking at a TV programme, when in fact all you have done is passively receive words and images.

You may also realise that, unlike books and lectures, the media mix direct information with advertisements and trivia which convey information indirectly. When using the media as sources, look out for both types of information.

Indirect information includes:

- examples of attitudes to sex in our society, as seen in a family comedy series or in recent films
- political attitudes and issues, as presented in the 'letters to the editor' columns and the cartoons in daily newspapers, or
- a mystification of science and technology, revealed in the way advertisements use the word 'scientific' and in the lack of informative and accessible technical reporting.

Much directly informative material is broadcast on television, including:

- regular programmes in areas such as science, women's issues, current affairs, wildlife and music
- individual series or programmes on the ideas of people such as Jung and Einstein and on issues such as nuclear power and racial discrimination, and
- performances of Shakespeare's plays and dramatisations of novels by modern authors.

2 Practical experience

'Hands on' experience is another way to learn about the nature of the mass media—making films or videotapes, writing or taking photographs for a student newspaper, preparing a broadcast for community radio, working in public access television. Learning about the media by only observing them is somewhat akin to expecting to learn how to conduct experimental scientific research only by observing experiments conducted by others.

How to use a source systematically

Plan how to use the mass media systematically according to their particular demands. The media present you with masses of information, much of which you won't want to use in your formal learning. But be aware of the valuable information that is offered, and make the most of it when you do use it. If you see a TV programme only once, how can you best take in and select the information it offers? If you buy a newspaper every day, how can you decide which items to re-read and keep?

Prepare, evaluate and review material as suggested in Chapter 8 on reading and Chapter 9 on lectures. Think about the nature of the media and how they influence your information. For example, if you have been listening to a radio programme, ask yourself how the same material would have been presented in a lecture or on television.

Electronic media

TV, radio and film are essentially transient. You usually see a TV programme or a film only once, you listen once to a radio programme. There are several ways to take advantage of the information they offer.

- Use *guides* to films and to TV and radio programmes. Don't overlook the less obvious alternatives in these areas such as community radio or a cinema screening 16 mm films. Go through the guides and pick out programmes which you know or expect will be useful. Note the times for these in a 'Things to do' list, a diary, or a weekly study plan.
- Make arrangements for *recording* a radio programme (subject to copyright laws) if you can't listen when it is broadcast or if you think you may want to replay it. Keep a couple of blank tapes on hand, and buy or borrow a tape recorder with a time switch. Some libraries video-tape programmes for you if you don't have access to facilities for this.
- Think about *the topic* of a programme or film ahead of time, talk about it with others, and perhaps arrange to watch or listen to it together and discuss it afterwards.
- If you will hear or see a programme only once, concentrate fully so that you can absorb and select information quickly and competently. Take notes if these would be useful, for example to remember certain facts or figures, or to record impressions (see 'Understanding as you listen', Chapter 9).
- If you haven't made *notes* during a radio or TV programme or film but would find these useful, write notes immediately after while the material is still fresh in your mind.
- Review any notes you have made or listen to a tape recording or video-tape you have made as soon as possible after a programme (preferably the next day).

'She reads at such a pace,' she complained, 'and when I asked her *where* she had learnt to read so quickly, she replied, 'On the screens at Cinemas.'
Ronald Firbank

Print media

When you read newspapers, magazines and periodicals, you probably browse and skim, glancing through some items, reading a few others in detail, and passing over most. You can re-read newspapers and magazines, but except for a few items of special interest you are unlikely to do so. After all, there is the next day's paper and the next issue of a favourite magazine to be read, and today's news article loses much of its impact by tomorrow or next week or next month. What can you do to discover and select the information available in the print media?

• Regularly skim read a daily and weekly newspaper (perhaps in a library) to see if they often contain any information useful to your study interests.
• Survey several issues of the magazines, periodicals and newsletters in your areas of interest, and decide which ones you really find useful. Subscribe to them for yourself or on a shared basis, or find out if your library will subscribe to them. Look through their contents regularly for useful material.
• Practise the skills of surveying material, selecting what to read and deciding how closely to read it when looking through newspapers, magazines and periodicals (see 'Approaches to reading', Chapter 8). Clip out useful items and note on each the page number, date and title of the paper or periodical.
• File clippings so they can easily be found again (see 'Selecting, recording and filing information', Chapter 6).

People don't actually read newspapers—they get into them every morning like a hot bath.
Marshall McLuhan

≈ ≈ ≈

Using the media as learning sources requires that you think about the general nature of mass media and about their roles as information providers in both formal and informal learning. Theories about the nature of the mass media are many and complex, and offer insights into the nature of knowledge and its social contexts, and into the effect of a particular medium on the forms of language used and on the distribution of knowledge. If your teachers only occasionally direct you to the mass media as significant sources of information, being aware of what you can learn from the media is essentially something you choose to do for your own reasons. The choice is important if your education is to include an understanding of the nature of learning in the late twentieth century.

One way to use this chapter

The aim of the following exercise is for you to become more aware of a wider range of information available to you in a particular area. To do this, set aside a couple of days at the beginning of your academic year to do the exercise, or return to it at intervals over a longer period of time. Continue it for as long as you like or regard it as successfully 'completed' when your knowledge of your topic has been noticeably increased.

1 Choose a topic which strongly interests you but which you haven't systematically researched.
2 Define the topic as clearly as possible by asking yourself what you want to know and by listing subject headings (see Chapter 6).
3 Write down as many possible information sources from your community as you can think of. Don't bother at this stage to evaluate how helpful they might be—simply list any people or organisations that might be useful.
4 Use a library catalogue to list material on your subject, and use the library's reference collection to discover further references to your topics.
5 Choose four or five information sources from your community list which you think will be the most helpful for your purposes. Choose another four or five sources from your list of library references.
6 Follow up each of these information sources to find out more about your subject.

Further reading

Babbie, Earl R. 1973. *The Practice of Social Research*. Wadsworth Publishing Company, Belmont, California.
Burdess, Neil. 1991. *The Handbook of Student Skills for the Social Science and Humanities*. Prentice-Hall, Sydney.
Eichler, Margrit. 1988. *Nonsexist Research Methods*. Allen and Unwin, Boston.
Goodacre, Phillip, & Follers, Jennifer. 1987. *Communicating Across Cultures* in Lovat, Terry (ed). *People, Culture and Change*. Social Science Press, Wentworth Falls.
Guenther, Elsa. 1978. *How to Study Through Your Library*. 3rd edn, Australian Library Promotion Council, Melbourne.

Keats, Daphne M. 1988. *Skilled Interviewing*. Australian Council of Educational Research, Hawthorn, Victoria.

Lane, Nancy D. 1989. *Techniques for Student Research: A Practical Guide*. Longman Cheshire, Melbourne.

8
Reading

I would sooner read a time-table or a catalogue than nothing at all.
Somerset Maugham

As you silently read this paragraph, your eyes are moving from left to right in a series of quick jumps along the line of print. Each time your eyes stop and focus on individual words or a cluster of words, the number of words you take in depends on your eye span and your word recognition skills.

You instantly perceive and recognise familiar words by their shape without needing to think consciously about their spelling, pronunciation or origin. However, sometimes you need a context to give a familiar word meaning. For example, how do you read 'read' in 'I have read six books' or in 'I'm about to read the paper'? At other times you need knowledge or experience to identify the intended meaning of a word. For example, do you interpret 'The East is red' to mean that the sun is rising or that China is a communist country?

When you come to a word you have never seen before, such as 'transmogrify' or 'simulacrum', your eyes focus on it for longer. You might re-read the sentence or paragraph to understand the meaning of the word from its context, or you might refer to a dictionary. Perhaps you recognise parts of the word ('trans-' in 'transmogrify'), or you attempt to divide the word into syllables (trans-mog-ri-fy, sim-u-la-crum) and pronounce it to see if you have ever heard the word spoken. Sometimes the word reminds you of another familiar word ('simulacrum' may remind you of 'similiar', 'simulate', 'simultaneous' or 'fulcrum'). You might skip the word and move on.

There is much more to understanding what you read than the physical movement of your eyes and your ability to recognise words. When reading the paragraphs above, you gained an overall impression of what was written without needing to identify every word or literally reconstruct the printed message. You filtered the message through who you are as a reader and this has been influenced by your cultural background and your individual experiences. Your background in turn has influenced your knowledge of and interest in the subject, your reading purpose, your reading abilities, your feelings about reading and your understanding and interpretation of what you read.

> Recent theory ... argues that experience is not personal but cultural. That is, although you, as an individual, may have an experience—such as falling off a bike, loving someone or winning a prize—you can only think about those experiences in particular ways that are available to you. So, it is argued that texts are read and gaps filled by readers, not with ideas that they personally 'make up', but with meanings that are already available in their culture.
>
> The different ways readers can make meaning from texts—the range of reading positions they can take up—depends on their access to different ideas in their culture.
>
> *Bronwyn Mellor, Annette Patterson and Marnie O'Neill*

Stop for a few minutes to think about and answer the following questions about **you as a reader**.

Do you like to read? Why?
If you don't enjoy reading, why?
What genres do you like to read? Historical novels? Scientific journal articles? Biographies? Cookbooks? Newspapers?
When do you read? Before you go to sleep? Whenever you have a spare moment? While cleaning your teeth?
Where do you most enjoy reading? In the bath? On the bus or train?
Do you have several books on the go at the same time?
Do you talk to others about what you have read?

As a reader, you differ from other people in what you read, when and where you read, and how much you enjoy reading. You have your own reading 'personality' which was influenced by your cultural backgound and which began developing when you first made contact with words and books as a small child. This reading 'personality' influences the type of reading material or genres that you prefer, and your attitudes and approaches to reading as a student. If you like to read novels, you can sit absorbed in them for hours. If you prefer magazines, you may be accustomed to reading in short bursts. If you usually read the paper, you probably read some articles closely and glance through others.

When confronted with reading material for a tertiary level course, only some of your previous reading habits are appropriate. The way in which academic materials are presented can differ from discipline to discipline and the way in which you are expected to read it also varies. You shouldn't read medical texts as you would science fiction, and novels in a literature course require a different approach from magazines. However, if you enjoy reading and read a lot, you can build on this enjoyment and utilise the appropriate reading abilities when you come to tackle academic reading.

It is important to learn to read actively as opposed to passively. A passive reader looks at and recognises the words on a page but doesn't actively engage with the material. Have you ever read a passage or several pages and realised that you haven't taken any of it in? If when you read you sit looking at the printed text and your mind is elsewhere, if you cannot recall or explain or ask questions about what you have read, then you are reading passively.

Reading actively means attending to the meaning of the text, the ideas expressed and how they are organised. It means trying to discern the author's intended message (theme, thesis or argument[1]) and to evaluate how effectively this message is supported by the information given. Active reading involves analysing and criticising the material to uncover how the message has been affected by the author's purpose, biases, experience, and beliefs. And it also involves determining how what you are reading relates to other material in the field and to your own learning and purpose for reading. An active reader is aware of the author's writing style and method of presentation.

> ... she continued with the process of taking a fragment here and a sentence there, and built them into her mind, which was now the most extraordinary structure of disconnected bits of poetry, prose, fact and fantasy ... She had in fact not read ... any ... author, if reading means to take from an author what he [*sic*] intends to convey.
>
> *Doris Lessing*

This chapter is about reading actively. It focuses on you the reader, and on how you can become involved with what you read so that you come to know and understand it fully. The chapter is designed to help you formulate your purposes for reading, and suggests a range of techniques appropriate for different purposes and materials. You are likely to use the chapter most often in conjunction with material you are reading thoroughly, such as a course text, or when discussing material with others. But it is a long chapter, so first look through the headings and then either start at the beginning and work through it slowly, or dip into sections which are most immediately useful to you.

Use the previewing section to help you decide whether to read a book which is one of a dozen suggested references. If you want to improve your notetaking, read rapidly through the chapter to that section. The techniques described here apply to reading a whole book, a part of a book, a journal article, a research paper or a government report, and some of the chapter is useful for reading fiction.

Preparing to read

Your purpose

Your purpose for reading influences any preparation you do before you read, your reading rate, and whether you underline or take notes. Before you read, clearly articulate why you are reading. Ask yourself questions such as: 'How thoroughly do I want or need to understand this material?', 'Why?', Do I need to read for an in-depth understanding?', 'How much do I want to remember?'

Imagine that you are reading to prepare for a lecture on an unfamiliar topic. A day or so before the lecture you look through a couple of references and try to identify some of the main points or issues of the topic, using guides such as the introduction, index or chapter titles to help you. Or imagine that you have to write a detailed critique of an article. First, you read for an overview and then you read slowly, underlining or taking notes on the thesis, and the important points, and you re-read if necessary.

Sometimes you read the same material for several purposes. For example, you may be required to read the same text for background information for a course as well as to understand it to answer an assignment question. You approach the material differently to meet each of these requirements.

Examining your material

When browsing in a bookshop or library, why does one book appeal to you more than another? When leafing through an academic journal why do you pause over some articles and not others? Perhaps a book's appearance or title attracts you or the author is someone whose writing you usually enjoy. Perhaps an article seems relevant to one of your interests or useful for a particular purpose. The layout, writing style or author's approach to the subject may lead you to buy a book or borrow a journal. Each book or article is different and your response to each will depend on who you are as a reader.

Previewing

To get the feel of a book you might glance through it, read the dust jacket, look at the pictures or diagrams, think about the meaning of the title and perhaps check through the table of contents and read the introduction. *Systematically* previewing material helps you to read actively and is one of the first steps you take to become thoroughly familiar with material. Such preparation gives you some understanding of why the material was written, the author's theme, the information the author has selected, and how that information is organised and presented. Previewing can indicate which parts of the material could be most useful for your purpose and how thoroughly you want or need to read different sections.

This section looks at previewing a book, but most of the steps described also apply to parts of books or to articles. There are various systematic steps you can take when previewing a book, but the order of these depends on your preference. You might start by reading the first chapter to become immediately involved with the content and the author's style, or you may prefer to check through the information that surrounds the text, such as the publication details and the index. As you preview, write down any ideas, questions or statements which seem relevant to your purpose and that might help you understand and criticise (or produce a critique of) the book. This helps you read actively because you have a framework into which the information fits; and you consciously look for answers to your questions, and for information that supports or disagrees with your original ideas on the book.

Apply the questions in Table 8:1 for a fuller sense of what a book is about. For example, a quick thumb through the index can tell you the major areas covered by the book; and a glance at the publication details gives information about the book in its field, such as how recent it is, whether it has sold enough copies to be reprinted, and whether it has been published in more than one country.

Table 8.1 The anatomy of a book

Title/subtitle
What is the author trying to convey in the title (and any subtitle)?

Cover/dustjacket
What information does the cover of the book give about the contents, the author, and the book within its field?
How reliable is any information on the cover of the book?

Author/editor/translator
Is there any information inside the book about the author's (or editor's or translator's) background, other publications, or experience relevant to the subject?
Do you know anything else about the author or any other of his/her writings?

Publication details
When was the book written?
What is the publication date of your copy of the book?
Has the book been revised?
Which edition is the book? Has the book been reprinted?
If the book is a translation, what is the date of this?
Who is the publisher?
In which countries has the book been published?

Table of contents
Is the table of contents sufficiently detailed to be helpful?
Which sections appear to be interesting, familiar or difficult to you?
How do the contents relate to your purpose and to other material you are studying?

Preface/foreword/introduction
If the book includes a preface, foreword or introduction, have they been written by the author or editor, or by someone else?
What information do these sections give you about why the book was written, its place in its field, how to read it?

Text of the book
What do the introduction and conclusion tell you about the book? Are there guides to your reading of the book, such as summaries of chapters, sub-headings?
Does the author spell out the theme, thesis or argument of the book in the introduction or in chapter headings or elsewhere?

Graphics/layout
Is any graphic material—such as diagrams, photographs, graphs, tables, charts, maps—easy to follow?
How are headings and sub-headings used?
How is emphasis indicated within the text? For example, are italics used?

Glossary
If the book has a glossary, are many words unfamiliar to you?

Bibliography and references
How comprehensive are any footnotes, endnotes or a bibliography?
Does the author use recently published items in references and the
bibliography?
Is the bibliography divided into subject areas?
Is it a summary of all sources consulted or only the major ones?
Do the references include other than written materials?

Index
What does an examination of the index add to your understanding of the
contents of the book? Which subject areas are given prominence?
Docs the index list mostly ideas and concepts, or more factual entries
such as names of places and people?
Has the index sufficient detail to enable you to easily locate your areas of
interest?

Complexity of material

> ... one of the stupidest things [to] do is insist that children comprehend
> everything they read, and read only what they comprehend. People who
> read well do not learn to read this way. They learn by plunging into books
> that are 'too hard' for them, enjoying what they can understand, wondering
> and guessing about what they do not, and not worrying when they cannot
> find an answer. Few children in school are allowed to act or feel that
> way.
>
> *John Holt*

How complex material is for you depends on your knowledge of the
subject, your interest in it, and whether or not the material accords
with familiar theoretical perspectives or with beliefs that you hold. Even
if you are familiar with a topic, material can be complex because it is
poorly written, organised or presented, because it expresses new ideas
in unfamiliar language, or because of its style and format. ('Evaluating
your selection' in Chapter 5 looks at determining the complexity of
material when deciding whether to use it in research.) If material seems
too simple for your purpose, you may need to check that you really do
understand it thoroughly—even basic material sometimes has one or
two points to offer, and can provide useful revision. Here we suggest
how to read material which seems difficult, and the first step in doing
this is to try to articulate why this is so.

- If the material is difficult, because the subject doesn't interest you,
  read a little of it and use the techniques described later in this
  chapter to make your reading more effective. On closer acquaintance
  the material may become more interesting and you can try to relate
  the subject to one which interests you.
- If the material conflicts with your 'common sense' understandings or
  with your beliefs and biases, discuss these conflicts with a sympathetic

person who doesn't share your attitudes. It can help you see your beliefs and biases in a new light if you play devil's advocate to them.

- If the theoretical perspectives or key concepts on which the material is based are unfamiliar to you, you may need to read other material which deals with the same perspectives or concepts, and it may take you time to understand the material fully.
- If the material is in an area unfamiliar to you or if you have a mental block about the subject, preview the material first, then read the easiest sections before you attempt more advanced ones. If you can't get past the basics, ask for help.
- If the material appears complex, read it slowly and look for one or two important ideas—sometimes material which at first seems complex becomes clear after a careful reading. You may later find it both easier to understand and very stimulating.

The discipline area

She took the book to her refuge, the tree, and read it through; and wondered why it was that she could read the most obscure and complicated poetry with ease, while she could not read the simplest sort of book on what she called 'facts' without the greatest effort of concentration.

Doris Lessing

How you read is also influenced by the discipline area of the material. The methodologies and conventions for presenting information vary from discipline to discipline, and within disciplines writers have different styles and ways of presenting information. This influences the way you read. For example, in maths, understanding what you read can depend on mastering one step at a time. In geography, you frequently refer to maps and other visual material as you read. In literature, reading a literary work to savour the language differs from reading literary criticism to select the central points. How much you are expected to read varies from one subject to another, and this in turn also influences how you read. For example, in subjects such as the social sciences and law you are usually required to read more than in subjects such as engineering or the physical sciences.

As a newcomer to a discipline area you may find the specialised language of that discipline difficult to understand, and even familiar, everyday words may have distinct meanings. For example, the word 'programme' has different meanings in psychology, computing and education, and the meaning of 'character' is different in literature, mathematics and biology. Some words embody concepts that have changed over time; for example, the words 'culture', 'power' or 'class' can have specific meanings in different disciplines, and their meaning today differs from several years ago. You need a subject dictionary to understand the meanings of some words and to be clear how the words are used in the context of your reading.

Some terms will be new to you and you will in effect be learning a new language.

- Talk about difficulties with a teacher or in a discussion group, listen carefully to relevant lectures, ask for a glossary of terms, or consult a specialised dictionary on the subject.
- Compile your own list of terms and try reading some basic books on the subject.
- Make a real attempt to understand the new language, then if you still have difficulties or think too much is expected of you, let your teachers know. The language may be second nature to them, and they can easily forget that it may be incomprehensible jargon to you.

'Twas brillig, and the slithy toves
Did gyre and gimble in the wabe:
All mimsy were the borogroves,
And the momeraths outgrabe.
Lewis Carroll

Developing your vocabulary

Reading widely is an ideal way to improve your vocabulary, both the words you use in writing and speaking and your understanding of the words you read and hear. You can actively work at improving your vocabulary by consulting a general dictionary, technical glossary or subject dictionary and by developing a system for recording and using your new words. Try a notebook or card system in which you write the unfamiliar term, the context in which it appeared, its dictionary definition and your own sentence using it. Practise using these words in your writing and speaking. Try them out on other students and your friends. Try a word a day or several a week.

When you begin studying in a new discipline or embarking on a new course or subject, pay particular attention to the vocabulary. If you find there are many words that you don't understand, start with those that are central to the area or those that keep recurring. When you understand these terms start on the others.

Before you read, use your preview to look for frequently used or unfamiliar words and concepts and look these up before you read. Use the index or leaf through the text to find these words. This will help you read more quickly and you will not be slowed down by continually consulting a dictionary. However, if you are reading and you do come across words that you don't understand, don't skip over them. Take the time to stop and look them up.

As you read

How you read material depends largely on why and what you are reading. You probably read a detective story straight through to find out 'What happens next?'. With many academic books you identify with an idea, and affirm or reject what you read on the basis of your theoretical perspectives and your experience. Maybe you read with pencil in hand, jotting notes or underlining anything which strikes you as useful, puzzling or appealing. Perhaps you ask yourself questions about what you are reading. Are you conscious of varying your reading rate according to your material? Do you talk about what you are reading with your friends and urge them to read it too?

How you read is also influenced by whether or not you are **sharing your reading**. Reading with others gives you the opportunity to share immediate reactions to material. Some material, such as poetry, plays or novels, lends itself readily to being spoken and listened to with another person or a group. You may also like to share with your teachers and other students the problems and pleasures you have with material. Because peoples' perceptions of what they read differs, opinions vary, and so hearing different viewpoints can help you understand material more fully. (To set up a group to read each others' writing, see 'Sharing your writing' in Chapter 11.)

Approaches to reading

> Some books are to be tasted, others to be swallowed, and some few to be chewed and digested; that is, some books are to be read only in parts; others to be read but not curiously; and some few to be read wholly, and with diligence and attention.
>
> *Francis Bacon*

Different reading techniques are sometimes given names, such as 'skimming' or 'scanning', and actual reading rates of words per minute are suggested for each. Such terms can be confusing, and while generalised reading rate figures may apply, in practice how you read varies. It depends on your purpose, the material and your concentration when you read.

This section describes five different reading approaches which arise from your reading purpose and the material, but it doesn't assign reading rates to each approach. It looks first at the breadth and depth of the understanding you are seeking from your material and then at reading rates.

Reading in depth and breadth

Imagine you are planning a visit to a city that you have never visited before. Why are you going there? Five possible purposes are:

* to stroll around the central shopping area for pleasure
* to experience the city atmosphere
* to visit a famous art gallery or a zoo
* to familiarise yourself with the key features of the city, or
* to explore thoroughly as much of the city as possible.

Your purpose in visiting the city influences how you go about preparing for your visit, what you do when you arrive, and how long you stay.

Imagine that you are planning to read a book you have not read before. Are you going to read this book:

* for entertainment?
* to gain an overall impression of the book?
* to locate a specific idea or section?
* to familiarise yourself with the central concept or theme? or
* to understand the whole book in detail?

These five purposes and how they influence your approach to reading are explained below.

1 *Entertainment reading*   What do you read for relaxation? A favourite magazine? A detective story? A collection of poems? An abstract philosophical work?

Entertainment reading, that is, reading without any specific intention of criticising or remembering what you read, can be other than reading for relaxation on free evenings or holidays. When studying, it can be a pleasurable way of getting yourself into the right frame of mind for in-depth study on a topic, and can provide you with general background on the subject.

When you read for entertainment, you probably read fairly quickly or browse through the material. You might pause to ponder over a particular passage, image, or item of information, but you probably do not make a conscious effort to remember what you read. You might use entertainment reading as part of formal study when you intend:

* to read the quotes in a chapter of this book as stimulation for reading the chapter in detail
* to enjoy an historical novel before beginning an intensive study of the era in which the novel is set, or
* to read quickly through a biography of a scientist who has worked in your research area.

2 *Overview reading* Reading for an overview of material entails reading quite rapidly, reading the introductory and concluding paragraphs, noting the main themes or points and forming an overall impression of what you read. You are not concerned with specific details or a complete understanding of the material. Read for an overview when, for example, you want:

- to find out how this book might be useful to you
- to decide whether to read a book in detail, or
- to add to your store of information on a familiar subject area or topic.

3 *Reading for specific information* To locate (or re-locate) a specific item or section in material, read through most of the material quite rapidly, using such features as the table of contents, the index, chapter headings and sub-headings to guide you to the item or section you want. Then read the section thoroughly, possibly taking notes or underlining. Use this technique if, for example, your purpose is:

- to look for a specific section in this book
- to locate biographical details on a literary figure, or
- to find evidence for or against a case you will debate.

4 *Reading for central ideas* To familiarise yourself with central ideas in material, first take an overview of it. Then read so that the structure of the material and its central theme, thesis or argument becomes clear, clear enough for you to write it down or explain it to someone else.

Read for the central message or ideas when, for example, you want:

- to familiarise yourself with the main approaches to study presented in this book
- to read an article as background for a research paper, or
- to understand the central conclusions in an experimental report.

5 *Reading for an in-depth critical understanding* When reading to understand an entire book or article as thoroughly as possible, first preview or overview the material. Then read the material in detail, section by section, criticising or evaluating it. As you read ferret out the structure to understand its main thesis, the information supporting this, its theoretical perspective and the underlying assumptions.

Reading in this depth doesn't mean laboriously reading every page word by word. It does involve making sure that you read actively, understanding each section so that you can reproduce clearly what you have read with the material set aside and so that you can see how each section fits into the whole. Seeing clearly how material is organised or structured can help you to understand its content. (Refer to Table 12.2 'Transitional words and phrases' to alert yourself to the words and phrases that are signposts to the structure.) Take notes or underline important information to help reinforce your understanding.

Read for an in-depth critical understanding if, for example, your purpose is:

- to identify the assumptions underlying this book and to evaluate its usefulness to you as a student
- to follow a complex argument
- to understand each stage of an experiment in order to repeat it yourself, or
- to understand material thoroughly so you can build on it in further learning.

Reading rates

> Speed, which becomes a virtue when it is found in a horse, by itself has no advantages.
>
> *Idries Shah*

When feeling overwhelmed by long reading lists or by the time it takes to get through a book, you might wish you could increase your reading rate or speed. Although learning to read more rapidly can save you study time, fast reading rates are useful only if you can understand and recall what you read as fully as you need to. They do not in themselves ensure better comprehension.

Reading effectively involves varying your reading rate according to your purpose and to the difficulty of material for you (see Table 8.2).

You can **improve your reading rate** while still understanding what you read.

- Check how fast you can read while still understanding what you read. Time the number of words you read per minute for:
  - a light novel you are reading for background
  - a journal article you are reading to familiarise yourself with the central ideas, and
  - a chapter in a course text that you have to understand in detail.

  Read at least ten paragraphs of each one. In each case, when you finish reading, set aside the material and try to recall it in as much detail as you need. If you have trouble remembering the material, your reading rate probably needs to be slower and you may need to try the techniques in the following points.
- Preview all material before you read it. Although this may appear to take extra time in the beginning, if you have a framework in which to put what you read, as you read it you can vary your rate according to

Table 8.2 Varying your reading rate

The following example suggests how you might read a chapter in this book.

Chapter 9 'Lectures'

Your purpose	The material	Your rate
To warm up	Boxed quotes	Fast
To read for an overview of the chapter	Whole chapter, especially the introduction and conclusion	Quite fast
To identify main ideas so you can explain them to another student	Whole chapter	Slowly
To locate specific information to help you take more useful lecture notes	Section on 'Taking notes'	Fast until you locate the section you want, and then slowly within the section itself
To gain a detailed critical understanding of the nature and purposes of lectures	The introduction to the chapter	Slowly and thoroughly, underlining or taking notes

the importance of the information and ideas. This framework will also help you remember the material later.

- Push yourself to read as fast as you can for 10–15 minutes each day for a week, then check your rate and comprehension. Remember your reading rate regresses if you seldom read and if you don't practise reading faster.
- Make a habit of reading material which is as complex as your study material. Becoming accustomed to reading material which is more demanding than light fiction or the sports pages, makes it easier to read most of your study material.
- If you find that it slows you down to consult a dictionary or technical glossary as you read, make a list of unfamiliar words before you read and then look them up as you need them. (See a method for doing this in 'Improving your vocabulary'.)

The aim of improving your reading rates is to save you time, but you only save this time if you understand and remember what you read as thoroughly as you need. Without understanding, you have to go over the material repeatedly until you do understand it, and your initial time-saving is lost.

Questioning and criticising

You should already have evaluated the material before reading to find out if it is useful for your purpose, how complex it is for you and to check if its subject matter is relevant and interesting (see 'Evaluating your selection', Chapter 6). You can begin to criticise material as you read it but you also need to think about it critically when you have finished reading and you can see the text as a whole.

To produce a critique of material as you read, take the text section by section. A section may be a group of chapters, a chapter, a paragraph or even a sentence, depending on your purpose and on how complex or familiar the material is. Before you begin a large section, preview it. As you read, ask yourself the questions in Table 8.3. These questions should help you identify the author's theoretical perspective, purpose and assumptions; understand the message or argument and how the content and structure is used to convey this message; and evaluate the style and format of the material. At the end of the section, recapitulate what you have read. Check if you understand the contents of the section as thoroughly as you need to, and try to understand the relationship of the section to the whole.

> To communicate ... experience through print means that it must first be broken down into parts and then mediated, eye dropper fashion, one thing at a time, in an abstract, linear, fragmented, sequential way. This is the essential structure of print.
>
> *John M. Culkin*

If you have difficulty answering the questions in the table, try working on the material with other people. First try to reach agreement on the theme. Then discuss any differing opinions on aspects such as the central ideas in individual sections and in the material as a whole. Ask 'What did the *author* intend to be the central ideas?' When you finish reading each section, put the material aside and evaluate its usefulness for your purpose. Decide which information you want to underline or include in your notes.

> It is possible to question readings of stories which may seem 'natural' and normal by paying attention to the ways a story conforms to or differs from familiar patterns.
>
> *Bronwyn Mellor, Annette Patterson and Marnie O'Neill*

Table 8.3 Asking questions as you read

As you read a section of a book or article, look for information to help you answer the following questions.

The author's purpose
- Why has the author written the material? Are these purposes explicitly stated? Are there other implicit purposes?
- For whom is the material intended?
- What theoretical perspective has the author taken? How does this perspective relate to other material in the field?

Content
- What is the main theme (thesis or argument) in the material?
- What main points are used to justify or support this theme?
- How does the author develop the theme from one main point to another?
- What explanation or evidence is used to support the main points?
- Do the evidence and explanations seem well researched and accurate?
- Is the factual information correct as far as you know?
- Which aspects of the topic has the author chosen to concentrate on and which to omit?
- Is the material presented in breadth or depth? Is the material dealt with superficially or in too much detail?
- Has a contemporary issue or a particular philosophy influenced the author's purpose? Is the author defending a particular point of view?
- What are the author's underlying assumptions? Are these explicitly stated?
- Is there any evidence of deliberate bias, such as interpretation of material or choice of sources or factual information? (See Appendix A for examples of discrimination in language and attitudes.)
- Is any irrelevant material included?
- Does any graphic material illustrate or restate the written content?
- Which of your questions about the subject does the author answer? Which are not answered?
- How do the contents relate to what you know about the topic?
- Do any items puzzle or intrigue you?

Structure
- What framework is used to organise the material? Is the framework clearly explained?
- How is the theme/thesis/argument reflected in the structure?
- How is the content organised and developed within the framework?
- How does the author introduce the subject?
- Does the author recapitulate what has been said at appropriate points?
- How does the conclusion relate to the introduction and to the rest of the material?

Style and format
- In what style has the material been written? For example, is it formal or informal, simple or complex, didactic or persuasive, narrative, analytical?
- How does the style and format influence your reaction to the material?

Notetaking and/or underlining

Books that you may carry to the fire, and hold readily in your hand, are
the most useful after all.

Samuel Johnson

You might underline your own books because you want to make your
responses to what you read part of the book itself. You might take
notes because you don't want to mark your books, because referring
to the book later is difficult, or because a précis of the information
is more useful for your purpose (see 'Buy, copy or borrow material?',
Chapter 6).

On rare occasions you come across a piece of writing which encap-
sulates ideas that are especially significant for you, so that you want to
photocopy or buy the material. However, usually it is better to close the
book or article and try to express what you read in your own words, as
this helps you remember it. Avoid photocopying material which you will
never read, as when under pressure and short of time, you may tend to
photocopy everything rather than read any one item carefully (see
'Selecting, recording and filing information', Chapter 6).

Why take notes or underline?

You might do this:

- to help you see a structure in what you read
- because what you read strikes you as useful, puzzling or interesting
- to remember what you read
- to be able to refer to it later, for instance, for an assignment or for an
  exam in a few months time, and
- to help you concentrate on and understand what you read.

What to note or underline

This includes:

- key elements, such as the theme/thesis/argument, central ideas, major
  characters or crucial information
- the author's purposes and assumptions (explicit and implicit)
- single phrases or sentences which encapsulate key elements or the
  author's purposes and assumptions
- details or facts which appeal to you, such as a useful statistic or a vivid
  image, and
- items to follow up, such as a question, an idea that offers further
  possibilities, a puzzling comment, an unfamiliar word, an explanation
  you don't understand, or an opinion you question.

How much to underline or note

The amount of underlining you do or the quantity of notes you take depends on what you read, why you read and whether you have easy access to the material again.

If you have limited time and access to material, it is easy to opt for the apparent safety of taking notes of everything you read 'just in case' you need the information later. However, if you analyse your topic before reading, you need fewer notes and underline less. Having a clear idea of what you are looking for prevents you finishing up with masses of notes and no idea of how to organise or use them.

Check that you understand what you have underlined or written down (see 'Questioning and evaluating', Chapter 6). Underlining a lot or taking detailed notes can be necessary, but it may indicate your inability to discriminate what is important from what is not, and can give you a false sense of achievement because you have a large quantity of work to show, regardless of its quality.

If you record lengthy quotes or paraphrases to use in assignments because the material 'says it much better than I can', select quotes and paraphrases to use within the framework of your ideas and approach to a topic. Although your teachers usually expect you to discuss other people's ideas and work, relying mostly on authorities shows a lack of confidence in your opinions and a belief that there is a Right answer for a topic (see Chapter 4).

You probably don't need to underline or take many notes if you are reading mostly for entertainment, if you are familiar with the subject or if you have an excellent visual or conceptual memory. But if you need the material later, take down at least a bare outline of its contents and notes on where to find it again. Two weeks and six books later you will find it surprisingly difficult to recall what you have read unless you have some record of it.

> 'The horror of that moment,' the King went on, 'I shall never, never forget!'
> 'You will, though,' the Queen said, 'if you don't make a memorandum of it.'
>
> *Lewis Carroll*

How to take notes or underline

Develop your own method of note taking or underlining which differentiates between the central ideas or arguments and the details or evidence. Work out a way of indicating the author's assumptions or attitudes, the details which appeal to you, and items to follow up. If you use patterned notes creatively, for example, when planning an essay, the open ended nature of the pattern enables your brain to make new connections far more easily. Note that you can create a pattern as part of the assignment preparation process to help you to link the concepts in your assignment.

When beginning to take notes:

- write down full details of author, title and publication
- on each page of notes, write the title or author and list the page numbers of the book or article in the margin of your notes. This habit is essential for quoting exactly, referencing assignments, and checking the content of an idea you want to paraphrase
- use quotation marks to clearly indicate the beginning and end of material you have copied exactly
- clearly identify the beginning and end of material you have paraphrased (see 'Paraphrasing and plagiarism', Chapter 14).

(To integrate your own ideas with those from your reading try the system suggested in 'Organising and integrating' in Chapter 6. See Table 9.1 'Note making' in Chapter 9 for ideas on how to take notes.)

After you read

Some of the girls sell their textbooks when they're through with them, but I intend to keep mine. Then after I've graduated I shall have my whole education in a row in the bookcase, and when I need to use a detail, I can turn to it without the slightest hesitation. So much easier and more accurate than trying to keep it in your head.

Jean Webster

When you have finished reading, do you close your book or article with a sigh of satisfaction or relief and not think about it again unless you have to use it? To remember and use what you have read, review the material as a whole, and use it as soon, as often and as widely as possible.

- Look at the material in relation to your reading purpose. If you are researching an assignment, ask yourself the following questions. Does the material lead you to revise how you have analysed your topic? Is the book central or peripheral to your understanding of a topic? Does the material provide the necessary level of information for your research? What parts of the material particularly apply to your theme for a topic?
- Find out whether your initial impressions and any questions raised during your preview have been confirmed or answered. To help revise what you learnt from the text, look again at those parts of the material you examined during your preview. Check through the index, for instance, to help recall what you read and to give you a fuller understanding of the scope of a book.

- Look at the material as a whole and ask yourself the same questions about the purpose, content, structure, style and format as you asked about each section while reading.
- Review your notes or underlining to ensure that you remember what you have read and to see how the various sections fit together. Draw up patterned notes of the whole chapter or article or write a summary of it.

Table 8.4 Writing a book review

'... What is the use of a book,' thought Alice, 'without pictures or conversations?'

Lewis Carroll

The overall purpose of a book review is to interest and inform potential readers and to give them your considered opinion of a book. It should evaluate a book from your perspective rather than simply summarising or describing the book's content.

Depending on your specific purpose in writing it, your review should contain some or all of the following points:

- full details of title, author and publication
- a brief résumé of the book, or what the subject of the book is, its theme/thesis/argument and how the content is organised
- comments on the author's style, or how the book is written
- information about the author's purpose in writing the book, or why the book was written
- comments on the theoretical perspective taken
- comments on the book in relation to other material in the field including when the book was originally written (and revised), the author's qualifications and experience, whether the book introduces any new concepts or data, and whether the author is reviewing material
- comments on how the book relates to your knowledge, your experience, your beliefs
- comments, where possible, on what other reviewers said about the book (check indexes such as The Australian Book Review Index)
- information on the standard of the details such as an index, a bibliography or graphic material
- comments on the overall quality of the presentation, such as layout, quality of paper and binding, and
- an evaluation of the overall strengths and the weaknesses of the book.

Support any statements you make, including your opinions, with reasons and examples. A few well-chosen quotations can convey the flavour of the author's style as well as illustrating a point. (Give the page reference for a quote immediately afterwards.)

Your own honest and well thought-out opinion of a book is of more value to your learning and to your readers than your version of someone else's opinion. A book review can be technically excellent but dull to read unless you convey to your reader the impact the book has on you.

- List questions which the material has raised and which you want to follow up. Edit your notes, or summarise them further if necessary, and file them (see 'Selecting, recording and filing information', Chapter 6).
- Think about the material and how it relates to you—your knowledge, your experience, your beliefs.
- Think about how the material is written in relation to your own writing. Perhaps the material can provide an example on which you can model your own writing, especially in relation to how you might organise what you write or how to use the languages of a discipline. Try writing in the style used by the author. The material might also provide an example of what not to do.

Whether or not you think about what you have read when you finish reading depends largely on the impact it had on you and whether you are required to use it. You might remember ideas or information, or recall a particular character. You may read further works by the same author or on the same subject, and in time reread the original book. If a book pleased or irritated you, stimulated or satisfied your curiosity, you are likely to think about it and discuss it with other people. Articulating your ideas and responses to material helps clarify them, and you may also want to articulate your ideas about a book in a written review (see Table 8.4).

Reviewing the chapter

1 Look through this chapter, taking each heading in turn and recalling what you can about it. Which section can you recall in most detail? Why?
2 Choose one section which is useful to re-read. As you re-read it, think about how you are reading and why.
3 Could you explain the structure and contents of the whole chapter to someone else?
4 Summarise this chapter using patterned notes. See p. 134 for information on how to draw up these notes.

Further reading

Buzan, Tony. 1971. *Speed Reading*. Sphere Books, London.
Drewry, John E. 1974. *Writing Book Reviews*. Greenwood Press, Westport, Connecticut.
Kress, Gunther. 1985. *Linguistic Processes in Sociocultural Practice*. Deakin University Press, Deakin University, Victoria.
Mellor, Bronwyn, Patterson, Annette, & O'Neill, Marnie. 1991. *Reading Fictions*. Chalkface Press, Scarborough, WA.

Morris, A. & Stewart-Dove, N. 1984. *Learning to Learn from Text : Effective Reading in the Content Areas.* Addison Wesley, Sydney.

Packham, Gillian, McEvedy, M. Rosanna, & Smith, Patricia. 1985. *Studying in Australia: Reading Efficiently and Note-making Accurately.* Nelson, Melbourne.

Notes

[1] Throughout the remainder of this chapter 'theme', 'thesis' and 'argument' are used interchangeably. For a definition of these terms see chapter 6.

9

Listening to Lectures

Depending on who you are—your experience, your interests and how you are feeling—you react to and select from what you hear. Each person responds differently to the pitch and intensity of sounds. One person's music is someone else's noise. If you live in the country the noise of traffic can be deafening when you visit the city; for an enthusiastic motorbike rider the roar of a 750 cc engine is melodious to the ears; and the 'snap, crackle and pop' of a favourite breakfast cereal can be irritatingly loud to someone with a hangover.

Do you consider yourself a good listener?
Do you listen closely to your friends when they talk about their troubles?
Have you ever felt your eyes glaze over as you listened to a teacher's monologue?
Have you ever found your mind far away from the lecture theatre towards the end of a lecture?

There is a difference between hearing sounds passively, and actively listening. Concentrating on what you hear is one of the basic requirements for listening to lectures. But even when you are keenly interested in a subject, it can be difficult to concentrate for a long time while sitting passively without the opportunity to respond.

This chapter is about understanding lectures well enough for them to be genuinely useful for your purposes in learning, rather than attending classes largely because you think you should. The chapter looks at how you can actively prepare for a lecture and how you can concentrate on what is being said and on taking notes. It suggests that after a lecture you need to review and use the material which has been presented to you.

Lectures are essentially a one-way communication process. The lecturer lectures and you listen, whether the lecture is delivered to ten students in a high school classroom or to several hundred people in a large lecture hall, whether the lecture lasts for five minutes or for an hour and a half. A lecturer may follow the customary format of university and college lectures and talk for almost the entire time with little or no student participation, or he or she may set aside part of the lecture for students to respond to and discuss what is said.

Why lectures?

Lectures are the most common form of tertiary teaching, so it is worth thinking about their purposes. These can include:

- imparting information to large numbers of people
- providing a common ground for formal discussion in a subject
- serving as a starting point for private study
- drawing together the main ideas in a new research area
- providing a preliminary map of difficult reading material
- reviewing literature which is difficult to find, and
- adapting a subject for a particular audience in a way that a standard course text can't.

However, educators debate the effectiveness of lectures in achieving many teaching aims. For example, it is often stated that lectures don't encourage students to think for themselves and that students should discuss ideas thoroughly rather than simply listening to them in lectures. It is also argued that lectures are widely used not because they are effective, but because they are the cheapest way of teaching large numbers of students. You probably have your own opinions on how valuable lectures are in achieving your purposes for learning.

I cannot see that lectures can do so much good as reading the books from which the lectures are taken.

Samuel Johnson

Some lecturers think seriously about what lectures can teach and about what they want students to learn from a particular lecture. They adapt their lecturing methods to their purposes, and are willing to depart from the traditional lecture format.

- If the lecturer intends to take a class in stages through difficult subject matter which involves a sequence of reasoning or events, he could use a series of five-minute lectures, each of which is followed by a few minutes for students to discuss or work on a related question.
- If the lecturer wants to exchange questions and comments with students in a small class, she doesn't plan a set lecture or time for student participation beforehand. Instead she relies on knowing the subject well and on being able both to present it logically and to restructure it in response to discussion.
- If a lecturer's purpose is to encourage maximum participation from a large class, she might lecture for half the time and divide the remaining time equally between a preliminary class discussion, individual student work, small group discussion and a brief summary by the whole class.

'Should a lecturer cover the ground laid down in his [*sic*] syllabus, even when some students don't understand, or go at a slower pace and get behind?' ... If lecturers considered their courses in terms of the learning being achieved by students rather than as a succession of performances by lecturers, this question would seldom be asked.

Donald A. Bligh

A lecturer's effectiveness partly depends on their personality, particularly if—as is often the case—they are not trained in the skills of communicating to an audience. And because lecturing styles and abilities differ, you inevitably learn more from some lecturers than others. Skilled lecturers vary their method of presentation, pace of delivery, voice, and position in relation to the audience. They may be story tellers, actors or humorists or someone whose pleasure in the subject is catching. Some lecturers read their lectures, while others use brief notes or speak extemporaneously. A lecturer who is sensitive to an audience and responsive to their shifts in mood and attention is always more enjoyable. You may or may not share a lecturer's enthusiasm for a topic, but a talented lecturer is a pleasure to listen to and can hold your attention almost regardless of the subject.

However, all lectures require at least some effort on your part. If you consistently prepare for lectures, actively concentrate on what is said, and think back over it afterwards, you will get more out of lectures, even poor ones.

Preparing for a lecture

Usually you will hear a lecture only once, so preparing beforehand will help you understand it more fully.

- Think about how useful a lecture could be in achieving **your purposes** in learning. For instance, if you are attending a lecture as well as discussing a topic or reading a book on it, why? You might do so to find information which is difficult and time-consuming to locate elsewhere, or to listen to a gifted lecturer present a familiar topic in a new way. Your main incentive could be to absorb information for exams and assignments. You may go to lectures simply out of habit or because they are compulsory.
- Prepare for a lecture by thinking about where **the topic** fits within the broader framework of a course—review previous lectures and the course outline. Do some of the suggested reading on the topic and look for other relevant material. You may find material (such as a summary of main points of the topic, a map, a time line or a list of biographical dates) you can take to the lecture to help you follow it. List any questions or ideas that come to mind as you prepare. You can use these as reference points when listening to the lecture, so that you are less likely to be overwhelmed by a mass of unfamiliar information and should be able to listen and take notes more intelligently.
- Consider your alternatives for **recording the lecture**. You probably take notes on a lecture, so think about how you can best do this. You may want to arrange to compare your notes with someone else's after the lecture (see 'Taking notes'). Check if the lecture will be taped. If not, you may want to tape it yourself if, for example, the topic is unfamiliar or if you want to listen without taking notes. However, don't tape lectures indiscriminately—think first about your reasons for wanting a tape rather than notes (and always ask for the lecturer's permission before using a tape recorder).
- Immediately before a lecture, think about **how you feel**. If you are feeling physically or emotionally low, do what you can to make yourself feel better. (See 'Your emotions', Chapter 1 for suggestions on how to put your worries aside.) If you need to miss the lecture, have someone else tape it or take notes for you.

To help you follow a lecture, arrive before it starts to collect any handouts and so that you don't miss the introduction. In an introduction the lecturer often outlines the lecture, relates the topic to reference material or to the rest of the course, states a problem the lecture will address, or tells a joke or a story to lead into the topic.

Understanding as you listen

'I think I should understand that better,' Alice said very politely, 'if I had it written down: but I can't quite follow it as you say it.'
'That's nothing to what I could say if I chose,' the Duchess replied, in a pleased tone.

Lewis Carroll

Thoughts can move faster than speech, so your attention can easily wander during lectures unless you actively concentrate on what is being said (see 'Concentrating', Chapter 2). To sustain your concentration so that you understand more fully what you hear, try to question what is being said, anticipate what will be said and frequently review what has been said. Take notes, and try to deal with situations which make concentration difficult.

Questioning and evaluating

Ask yourself questions about the purpose, content, structure, style and format of the lecture. Most of the questions suggested in Table 8.3, 'Asking questions as you read', also apply to lectures. You may have other questions specifically related to lectures such as 'What is the lecturer conveying by his or her position, distance from the audience and voice tones?' The questions you ask as you listen can form the basis for any notes you take.

Taking notes

'Write that down,' the King said to the jury; and the jury wrote down all three dates on their slates, and then added them up, and reduced the answer to shillings and pence.

Lewis Carroll

It is impossible to reproduce most of the content of a lecture exactly and very rarely do you want as much detail as this. Instead your notes should be your consciously selected version of the material offered. The previous chapter on reading suggests why you might take notes and what your notes could include (see 'Notetaking and underlining', Chapter 8), and the same points apply to lectures. But how you take notes when listening to a once-only live lecture differs from taking notes from printed material you can re-read. (Table 9.1 makes some suggestions on note making that you can apply to both your reading and lectures.)

Find a balance for each lecture between taking useful notes and listening carefully—taking notes constantly or taking none at all are both of dubious value. In lectures which are meant to stimulate your imagination, spend most of your time sitting back and listening. In lectures which are densely packed with information and ideas you will take more notes, but select from and condense what is said so that you can listen closely enough to understand. For instance, if you are given a lot of data or examples, you can often summarise what they mean rather than frantically trying to copy them all. Sometimes lecturers use phrases such as 'the following three factors are ...' or 'It's important to note that ...' to help you identify the structure of the lecture and indicate which points to note (see Table 12.2 'Transitional words and phrases').

If you prepare for a lecture and go over your notes very soon afterwards, you can usually strike a happy balance between taking satisfactory notes and listening fully to what is said. Try the following **methods** to experiment with how detailed your notes need to be and how much time you need to spend listening.

- Take as many notes as you think you will need. Go over these immediately after the lecture, asking yourself if you understand all you have written, and try to reproduce the way in which the lecture developed. If you can't, you have possibly spent too much time writing during the lecture—or the lecture itself was very confusing.
- If you have access to a tape of a lecture or if you can make your own tape, don't take notes but sit and listen intently. Immediately after the lecture and before you listen to the tape, see if you can write down a satisfactory summary of what you have just heard. Then listen to the tape and compare your notes with what you hear.
- If you are listening to a taped lecture, listen to the whole tape once without taking notes. Write notes on the lecture before you listen for the second time. A taped lecture gives you the advantage of being able to stop and replay it at any point—something you can't do with a lecturer.

The above are suggestions, and you should develop your own method for distinguishing the structure of what is said—the main points, subpoints and supporting details. Lecture notes in which you can see the structure are easier to remember. Leave space for your own comments, questions or references to follow up, and items to think about further. Include on each page the lecture title and date, and the lecturer's name.

Table 9.1 Note making

You make notes from your lectures, from your reading and from discussions. The term 'note making' is used here to indicate that you need to take an active role in creating your notes and that your notes are more than a passive record of a reading or lecture. As a learner you should be making your own individual notes—processing and selecting information so that you make notes which are useful for your own purposes. These notes should show at a glance the relative importance of information—that is, you should use methods of note making that clearly separate the main points from the minor points.

Linear notes

Most people find the easiest way to make notes from reading and lectures is to start at the top left hand corner of a page and write from left to right until they reach the bottom right hand corner. If you prefer a linear note making method, try some or all of the following suggestions:

• use headings and subheadings which break up your text
• note key words
• use numbering
• use different coloured pens to differentiate the relative importance of information.

Another idea to try is to divide your page into two columns by folding your page lengthwise, then to use the left hand column for headings and main points and the right hand column for minor points or details. This method ensures that before you write anything you have to decide the relative importance of the information.

As you become adept at the method add a third column, a narrow left or right hand column, in which you record your responses to the information. These responses might include: references to check, points of particular interest, questions to ask about the material you don't understand, aspects you know about, or rude remarks.

Patterned notes

These notes are also called 'explosion charts'. (See the graphic on p. 134 for an example). The method involves starting in the centre of the page and branching to the edge. The theme or argument of the information is in the centre of the page and the main and sub-points radiate from it. The minor points or details radiate from the sub-points. You can also show 'cross-connections' between, for example, main points. The pattern can be drawn to represent the structure of the material as presented, or the structure that most closely suits your intended use of the material. Patterns of notes are a visual aid to learning the material that complements the usual oral/textual format in which we store information.

The advantages of this system over the linear form of note making are outlined by Buzan:

1 The centre or main idea is more clearly defined.
2 The relative importance of each idea is clearly indicated.
3 The links between the key concepts are immediately recognisable because of the proximity and connection.
4 As a result of the above, recall and review is both more effective and rapid.
5 The nature of the structure allows for the easy addition of new information without messy scratching out or squeezing in.
6 Each pattern looks and is different the each other patterns. This aids recall.

From: Lorraine Marshall, 1991, *Learning Skills Tutors' Guide*, Murdoch University, Western Australia

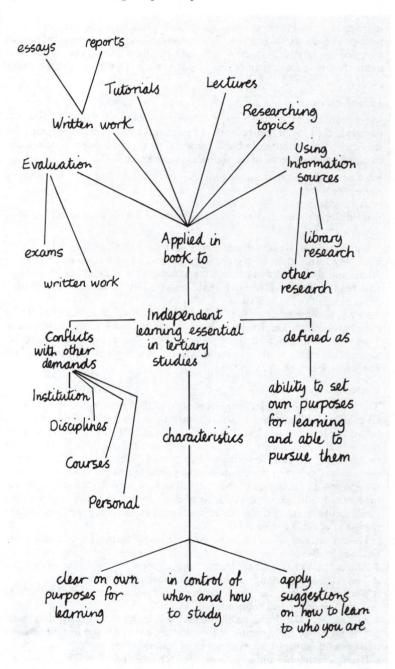

A student's patterned summary of the points they found relevant in **A Guide to Learning Independently**.

Overcoming concentration difficulties

Now I lay me back to sleep,
The speaker's dull, the subject's deep.
If he should stop before I wake,
Give me a nudge for goodness' sake.
Anon.

Try to overcome difficulties which prevent you concentrating on and understanding a lecture. Your concentration is usually better at the beginning of a lecture—if you are able to put aside the thoughts or distractions which were occupying you before the lecture began. You also concentrate better when you know that the lecture is nearly over—unless you are impatient to leave. During a lecture your concentration span is probably about twenty to twenty-five minutes. In a long lecture, revive your concentration by changing your sitting position, by quickly reviewing your notes, or by asking the lecturer a question.

- Try to minimise distractions in your physical surroundings—a hard chair, a wobbly desk, a cold room or loud hammering near-by are not conducive to full concentration.
- If you find it difficult to listen to a lecture tape because you can't see the lecturer's expressions or gestures, listen intently and replay parts of the tape if necessary. If you still have trouble, ask the lecturer for a written copy or an outline of the lecture.
- If a lecture seems to offer little that is new to you, ask yourself 'Am I really listening to what is being said?' If you are, try to anticipate what will follow, relate what is being said to what you already know about the topic, and review any notes you have made as you listen. Make a game of trying to find new information.
- If a lecture contains too much unfamiliar material, make a list of questions on points you don't understand, and ask the lecturer to clarify a couple of these points.
- If the content of the lecture seems irrelevant or uninteresting to you, jot down at least an outline in case the topic becomes relevant or interesting at a later date. Leave the lecture quietly and do some other work rather than sitting through it and complaining afterwards.
- A lecturer may make it difficult for you to follow a lecture because he or she doesn't organise material clearly, doesn't provide a written or oral lecture outline, or doesn't adequately prepare overhead transparencies and other aids. When you can't follow a lecture easily, leave plenty of space for your notes so that you have a chance to go back and add and edit as you write.
- If a lecturer's style is difficult or dull for you, think about why this is so. You can probably do little to change the idiosyncrasies of lecturers' styles, but let a lecturer know if you can't hear or follow what is said.

Don't dismiss lecturers you find difficult to follow as useless after only a couple of lectures. They may know their subject well, and as you become more familiar with their individual styles, it is often easier to concentrate on and understand what they are saying.

After a lecture

Before I came here I was confused about this subject. Having listened to your lecture I am still confused. But on a higher level.

Enrico Fermi

As you hear most lectures only once, **reviewing your notes** as soon as possible—preferably immediately after a lecture or the same day—helps you remember what you have heard.

- Do you understand everything you have written?
- Can you identify the structure of the lecture—the theme, thesis or argument, the main points, sub-points, and how the lecture developed from one point to another? It may help to underline or highlight the main points as you review your notes.
- Do you need to edit your notes so they reflect the lecture more accurately and read more easily?
- Do you need to expand your notes so you can still understand them in a month's time? Do you have a relevant article or other material to file with your notes?
- Would it be useful to express all or part of your notes in another form, for example as a flow chart, or diagram or in a pattern? (See Table 9.1 'Note making'.)

If you have **persistent problems** in identifying the structure of lectures and understanding your notes:

- listen to lecture tapes if you need to
- make sure that you are preparing thoroughly for lectures
- compare your notes with someone else's, and discuss the differences to help clarify ways to improve your notetaking
- read some more on the topic so the lecture isn't your only source of information, and
- ask a lecturer for help with the problem (see 'Contacting people', Chapter 3).

Your problems with lectures may be due to the lecturer. If you have difficulty understanding an important lecture, go and see the lecturer soon afterwards to talk about the topic. Sometimes a person who's awkward in front of an audience is helpful when discussing information on a one-to-one basis. (Think about how you feel when delivering a seminar paper and when discussing the same topic with one other person.) Lecturing is a talent which few people possess naturally, so constructive comments can help lecturers improve their skill. Such comments can be made tactfully by asking questions on points you don't understand and suggesting alternative lecture formats (see 'Why lectures?'). Part of being an active listener is to suggest to lecturers how their lectures could be more effective.

Since most lectures are a one-way communication, **using and discussing the lecture material** is essential if you are to understand it fully.

- Do you have items you want to follow up, for example an idea which interested you, a reference you noted, a point you didn't fully understand, a quote you want to check out?
- Did the lecturer suggest any follow-up to the lecture such as a reference to read, a problem to solve, an exercise to do, or a couple of questions to think about?
- File your notes for easy future reference (see 'Selecting, recording and filing information', Chapter 6).

Some lectures contain ideas or information that are especially significant for you. These lectures are easy to remember and use. Otherwise, you are most likely to use what you have heard and written down if you need the material for an assignment or an exam, or when talking to friends, in a tutorial or seminar, or with a teacher. In a discussion over coffee after a lecture, for example, you can compare notes, clarify points you didn't understand, exchange ideas which excited you, and decide on questions or suggestions with which to approach the lecturer if necessary.

&a. &a. &a.

If you find some lectures boring and pointless, is it because you are sitting back and expecting to be entertained? If you are, think about your purpose for attending a lecture and prepare to take an active part as a hard-working listener. Inevitably some lectures seem a waste of time, and very few people deliver an ideal lecture. To make the most of the range of knowledge and lecturing styles you are offered, take the time to learn how to get the most out of lectures and, if necessary, pluck up the courage to try to change them.

Further reading

Bligh, Donald A. 1972. *What's the Use of Lectures?* Penguin Education, Penguin Books, Middlesex, England.

Brown, George. 1978. *Lecturing and Explaining*. Methuen, London.

Buzan, Tony. 1974. *Use Your Head*. BBC Publications, London.

10
Participating in Tutorials and Seminars

Do you think of yourself as a 'talker' or a 'listener'?
Which people or situations encourage you to talk?
Who do you talk to, in your daily life, about the weather? about personal matters? about current issues?
Do you find that many of your conversations are about other people? yourself? ideas? events? sex? religion? politics?
To whom do you particularly enjoy listening?
Do you think that you learn more from talking with people, from reading, or from watching TV?

Your discussion with other people may be an intense debate, a rambling conversation, a casual chat, an exchange of brilliant repartee or a ritual of polite remarks about the weather. These discussions may be very brief, go on for several hours, or continue intermittently for weeks or even months. Perhaps you use the discussion to sort out ideas, share experiences, play with words, or learn something new.

As a tertiary student, you probably learn a great deal from discussions over endless cups of cappuccino in the cafeteria. However, formal small-group discussion in universities and colleges is mostly conducted in tutorials and seminars. Such groups meet specifically for discussion as part of a course, and usually consist of a teacher as leader and a particular group of students.

These formal group discussions vary widely in structure and content. For example, they may be:

* a mini-lecture where the teacher imparts information
* a group in which the leader remains relatively unobtrusive and the rest of the group decides what to discuss
* a seminar series where each member takes a turn as chairperson
* a discussion structured around a paper given by a group member or based on set reading
* a meeting which sets out to debate an issue formally, to solve a specific problem, or to work on a particular piece of research
* a group which uses role-playing exercises to learn more about the dynamics of human values and attitudes
* a session which emphasises the less subjective, rational aspects of learning, or
* a group which often shares experiences and feelings as well as discussing intellectual issues.

Such variety is the spice of discussion groups. Within a group, people of different ages, experiences, backgrounds and beliefs have much to offer each other when exchanging ideas, and a varied format and content for group meetings is stimulating.

> I dogmatise and am contradicted, and in this conflict of opinions and sentiments I find delight.
>
> *Samuel Johnson*

If you are in a group which lacks variety, this chapter suggests some alternatives. The chapter also outlines principles and techniques which can be used in informal discussions with other students as well as in tutorials and seminars. It deals with some aspects of how discussion groups work, and suggests how you can learn from and enjoy groups more by preparing for them, participating actively, and reviewing and using what is discussed.

Why formal discussion groups?

Formal discussion groups can offer an opportunity:

- to integrate what you learn from your reading, writing and lectures
- to clarify your ideas and feelings on a subject
- to sort out misunderstandings and problems in your work
- to practise communicating ideas to others
- to have relatively close contact with a staff member, and
- to learn about the uses and dynamics of formal discussion groups.

Sharing your learning in discussion groups can be a co-operative exploration of ideas which offsets the competitive pressures on you as a student. Discussion groups also provide an alternative to the solitary activities of private study and listening to presentations such as lectures. If an educational institution doesn't include formal discussion groups, you might ask that these be established as part of a course you are taking, or create informal ones with other students so you can actively use the information you receive from lectures and reading.

Preparing for a discussion

If *few* people prepare for a discussion group, these people can challenge the waffle that others are likely to contribute. It would be useful to discuss why most people didn't prepare, and agree to prepare fully next time. If *everyone* in a group prepares, the discussion at least has the basis for success. If *you* prepare, you will have a clearer idea of what you want to discuss and you will remember the discussion more clearly.

Be sure you know as precisely as possible **the topic** planned for discussion, what preparation is required, and why. Ask the group leader as soon as possible for suggestions or information if you find the preparation required is too much or too difficult, if you have trouble obtaining necessary materials, or if you have other demands at the time which make it difficult for you to prepare fully.

- Do any required preparation such as reading or exercises.
- Formulate in writing at least one brief item to contribute to the discussion—a thought, a question, a piece of information, or a comment on your reading or lectures on the topic (see 'Asking your own questions', Chapter 4).
- Revise your relevant lecture notes.
- Check reference books and audiovisual material on and around the topic and follow up with more specific reading if necessary.
- Read any notes you made during or after the last group meeting.

Prepare thoroughly if you are to give a **discussion paper**. Your efforts will be assessed according to the content, how you structure your material, and your presentation.

- Research, plan and prepare the content of your paper (see Chapter 6). In a short paper, limit yourself to one or two main points. You need a clear introduction, and a summing-up which could be a statement or question for the group to debate. This is especially important if you do not make copies your paper, as your listeners will have the material presented to them only once.
- Prepare visual materials or handouts to help your audience follow you. If you plan to use data, maps or other information which may be difficult to absorb quickly, prepare photocopies or a blackboard display so the group can read the information.
- Decide whether to speak from notes or read a paper. You may feel more confident if your paper is written out fully. Rehearse aloud, so that you know how long your presentation takes. Most listeners become restless after 15–20 minutes, so time your presentation with this in mind.
- Practise varying your presentation to hold the group's attention. You are more likely to engage your listeners if you invite questions or ask the group questions at appropriate points in your talk.

Immediately before the group meets, be aware of how you feel and try to put distractions behind you (see 'Your emotions', Chapter 1). You might read thoroughly a section from a relevant book to focus your mind on the discussion topic.

Taking your part during discussions

Most groups spend time talking about academic or practical matters such as the next topic for discussion, the set reading, or who will deliver a seminar paper, but they usually neglect to consider explicitly the personal interactions within a group—the '**hidden agenda**'. Even group interactions of which every member is aware, such as frequent silences or an over-talkative person, aren't usually discussed by the whole group. The following are a few examples of this agenda.

- The particular combination of people in a group plays a large part in shaping the discussions. For example, groups made up of school leavers who are full-time students approach a subject differently from groups made up of part-time students from a variety of backgrounds. People who are in a minority in a group, such as women in a predominantly male group, often feel less free to speak.

- If people always sit in the same place or two or three people always sit together, this can set up habits of who talks to whom and where discussions centre.
- A person who decides the direction of a discussion may not be a teacher or a person who talks a lot, but someone who asks pertinent questions or who brings an aimless discussion back on track.
- How people contribute to a group is influenced by whether each person's participation is assessed, and if so whether it is assessed by a teacher or by the whole group.
- When people contribute to a group discussion, they may be trying not to appear naive/over-clever/aggressive while at the same time seeming to be witty/intelligent/confident/sexually attractive.

If you have little experience of taking responsibility for formal discussions and are anxious not to appear foolish in front of the other students and a teacher, you are unlikely to initiate discussions on how a group is working. If a teacher is unskilled in dealing with group dynamics, he or she is unlikely to initiate discussion with students about what is happening in a group. But the personal interactions within a group can't be separated from its intellectual discussions, and a group needs to spend time talking about both if it is to realise its full potential. If you feel that a 'hidden agenda' item is being ignored at the cost of group effectiveness and your own learning, try to work up the courage—perhaps with someone else in the group—to bring the problem constructively into the open, using some of the suggestions which follow. A basis for discussing both academic work and the interactions within the group can usually be established in the first two or three meetings.

The first few meetings

Instead of plunging straight into talking about a course topic or assignments and assessment, people in a group can devote some time to *becoming acquainted*, perhaps over a cup of coffee or a glass of wine. Names and faces become more familiar if each person, including the teacher, introduces themselves briefly and talks about their interests and hopes for the course. If the group divides into pairs for a brief period to discuss a specific question about a topic or the course, people have another opportunity to get to know each other.

Discussions are influenced by the *physical setting* in which you meet, so consider how you can adapt a meeting place to the group's needs. A cold box-like room occupied by standard institutional chairs and tables and a blackboard is more conducive to monastic silence than heated discussions. What can you do with an inappropriate room? It is often possible to rearrange seating or desks so that everyone is more comfortable, and most importantly, can see everyone else. A leader need not be isolated in front of the group; a large open space in the middle of a group can be closed up; and if the room is carpeted people may be more relaxed sitting on the floor. Sometimes another place can be found for a group, or you can meet outdoors or in a private home. Meeting outside the formal setting—to have coffee or go to a movie, for example—has an impact on the group's formal discussions.

One of the first topics for discussion should be the *group's role in a course*. Group meetings could serve as a forum for discussing lecture topics or the special interests of members. Some people in the group may see its main role as enabling students to exchange ideas, while other people see the meetings as an occasion for the teacher to tell them more about a subject. Group members need to decide (or be told) if participation in the group will be assessed formally or informally, and if so, how.

Contributing to a discussion

'The time has come,' the Walrus said,
'To talk of many things:
Of shoes—and ships—and sealing wax —
Of cabbages—and kings—
Of why the sea is boiling hot—
And whether pigs have wings.'
Lewis Carroll

Each member of a group influences how that group operates, even if by remaining silent. The success of a discussion group depends largely on whether everyone takes responsibility for how the group operates and whether everyone feels free to contribute fully.

The size of a group

A group should be small enough to enable everyone to say something within the time available. Seven to ten people is often recognised as a useful number for a group, but this varies with the purpose of the discussion. Most people feel hesitant about speaking up in front of a large group, yet there should be sufficient people to provide a variety of ideas. If a group is too small, combine it with another group if possible. If the group is too large, it might break into smaller groups for a part of each session or permanently.

Attending regularly

If the same group of people come to the meetings regularly, they become more comfortable with each other and more confident about suggesting ideas, asking questions, admitting ignorance, and responding honestly to what is said by someone else. The give and take that develops lessens the pressure to say something on most topics and to impress others, and because continuing discussions are built up when everyone knows what is been talked about previously, people find it easier to make their own contributions.

Talking and listening skills

'... I find discussion as a whole ... difficult, because I've never had to discuss anything before and haven't put my feelings into words ... It takes me an awful long time to think about what I want to say and, sometimes, by the time I've thought about it, it's gone.'

A student

Participating fully in a group discussion requires practice in the skills of talking clearly and concisely, asking useful questions and listening carefully. These skills take time to acquire, particularly with a group of people who initially are strangers, and you need to find your own balance between talking and listening for each combination of people. In particular, studies have shown that men often dominate discussions in which both sexes are involved. Some people don't see asking questions as an essential part of conversations, so they may need to practise the skills of asking questions and genuinely listening.

Participating in a group is not the same as talking a great deal. Some of your *alternatives* are:

- listening closely for most of the time, occasionally contributing a well thought-out remark or question
- attempting to paraphrase what someone else said, to make sure you understood them
- asking questions which begin 'Do you mean that ... ?', 'What do you think about ... ?' or simply 'Why?'
- commenting in response to someone who has spoken, as long as you really are responding and not just waiting until they have finished so you can have your say, and
- expressing support for an idea that someone else has put forward.

If you have prepared for the discussion you will have your own thoughts and questions to contribute. If a discussion group is to help you sort out your ideas and become aware of your biases and beliefs, articulate these and bring them out from inside your head so other people can respond to them. Don't hold back because you feel you have to utter perfectly complete thoughts or always be serious.

You may come from a cultural background or an educational system in which you do not expect to speak up unless addressed directly by the teacher or in which your main contribution is to respond to factual questions asked of the class. In universities and colleges, you are expected to contribute ideas as well as information and to comment thoughtfully on what the other members of the group say. Practise this, and talk to the group leader or to other students about how you can more effectively contribute to the discussion.

If you lack confidence in a discussion group, remember that it takes time to gain experience in the skills of formal discussion and to settle into a new group of people. Even if you like the group members at first meeting, you may still be cautious about venturing opinions until you know them a little better. If you continue to feel uncertain of yourself in a group or if you are not confident about a topic, you can gain confidence by preparing for the discussion, getting to know some other members of the group outside the formal discussion time, and talking to the group leader or a helpful staff member about how you feel. Others who at first seem to know more than you often don't; and even if they do, you still have your contribution to make (see 'Your cultural and social self', Chapter 1).

If you talk too much and are aware of this, you will probably also be aware that other people stop listening or find it difficult to follow what you say. For several meetings try to ask other people questions whenever you feel tempted to talk—you will probably be surprised at how much they have to contribute.

How much time do you usually spend in talking and how much in asking questions and listening to what others say?
How much response do you usually give to other people's ideas?
Your answers to these questions will probably vary for each group to which you belong. Can you work out why you put more effort into some groups than into others?

Taking responsibility

Each person in a group influences the nature of the discussion, and the absence of even one person can change the atmosphere of a group. Everyone needs to prepare for and participate in discussions rather than seeing the group solely as the leader's responsibility. If only one or two people contribute, even a skilful leader can do little to make the group satisfactory.

• If you are giving a *discussion paper*, let the group know if you are happy to deal with questions or comments during your presentation, or if you would rather these were kept until you finish. If you are responsible for the discussion afterwards, try to encourage other members of the group to take part. As well as helping them and improving the discussion, directing this effort to others usually reduces your anxiety about being the centre of attention.

'Begin at the beginning,' the King said, very gravely, 'and go on till you come to the end: then stop.'

Lewis Carroll

- The amount of time each person in a group talks depends on their enthusiasm for a topic, amount of preparation, and well-being at the time. A common difficulty in a group is having one or two people who are persistent *talkers* or *non-talkers*.

Some people prefer to contribute to a discussion only occasionally, but the person who rarely says anything needs encouragement. Most people indicate by facial expressions or body movements when they're ready to speak, and if other people are sensitive to these signs they can give a shy person an opportunity to speak. Someone who is quiet may gain confidence if the group divides into smaller units for part of the discussion. You could suggest that each person prepares a specific contribution for each session or takes a turn to comment briefly on a topic which comes up, as this gives reticent members of the group practice in speaking while limiting more garrulous individuals.

However, the whole group needs to discourage a person who talks too much, and usually this can be done politely but firmly by remarks such as 'That's interesting—I'm curious to hear what other people have to say now'. If what the talker says is irrelevant, the whole group will be grateful to someone who restates the original topic. But if the offender fails to take the hint, someone in the group needs to deal with the problem after the meeting.

The teacher's authority in a group

The authority of those who teach is very often a hindrance to those who wish to learn.

Cicero

The official group leader may not always be a teacher—he or she may be a student who is giving a paper or is responsible for chairing the discussion. Most groups also have unofficial leaders, even if 'leaderless'. The authority of a teacher-leader usually overrides that of a student, even when the teacher tries to prevent this.

A teacher may have authority in a group because she or he is:

- a group leader appointed by the educational institution
- an assessor of the group members' work
- a specialist in a particular field of knowledge
- a skilled group leader

- a person older than most students in the group, or
- a dominant personality.

Leadership styles

Some teachers consciously try to step back from a position of authority in a group, to encourage students to articulate their own ideas and learn from each other. Such teachers face the challenge of trying to be *a resource person* in a subject rather than an expert or an appointed leader. They try to use their personal skills with people or groups to foster the development of individuals and the whole group, instead of attempting to direct this process. If you are accustomed to having your learning firmly directed, you may find this approach disconcerting.

There are teachers who consciously prefer to be *the definite leader* in a group. This choice is consistent with a model which defines formal education as students receiving information from experts. Teachers who base their teaching on this model are likely to expect to be the focus of the group's comments and questions and use group meetings to give mini-lectures. (For help with taking notes in such groups see 'Taking notes', Chapter 9.) This approach can work when both teacher and students feel under pressure to cover a prescribed amount of material, but it discourages discussion between students and ignores much of the potential of small-group work.

Some teachers remain as *automatic leaders* because they haven't given much thought to the bases of authority in a group—and even teachers who want to encourage student participation occasionally fall into accepting this authority. An inexperienced teacher may be glad of the security that the role of leader offers, and some older teachers expect younger students to defer to them. Some teachers, because of their personality and experience, are accustomed to leading most groups in which they find themselves.

He was leader by default—by de fault of de rest of de group.
Anon

Coping with a teacher's authority

If you are a student in a group where the teacher takes the authority you may find it helpful to cope with this authority if you can work out *why* the teacher is the group leader. For example:

- Some teachers don't recognise that their familiarity with the concepts and language of a subject gives them a position of authority in discussing it with students. It is often difficult for these teachers to understand how complex a subject can be for beginners (see 'Improving your vocabulary', Chapter 8).

- Other teachers have their own plan for a tutorial or seminar because they are anxious to cover a syllabus or eager to convey what they see as the important or exciting issues in a topic. Such teachers may ignore or belittle contributions which don't fit their plan, or ask questions for which they have a Right answer in mind. They may attempt to start a discussion at too advanced a level or at a pace too fast for most of the group, so that discussion is only possible if there are one or two students who are self-confident and familiar with the subject. Other students are left either to drift off or to try to guess the teacher's plan, rather than having a chance to think about and articulate their own ideas.

- Teachers who don't know how to encourage participation may leave a group floundering because they fail to realise the need for a clearly-defined starting point for discussion. Or they may hover over a group—rushing in to break up any silences instead of allowing people to collect their thoughts, asking questions to which the answer is obvious, or answering questions so conclusively that further discussion is pointless.

> All the tutors say, you know, do ask a question if you don't understand me, but if you really have no idea of what on earth they're going on about you can't very well say 'Well, would you start again at the beginning'. You can't ask a question because you just don't know what to ask it about.
>
> *A student*

How can a group cope with a teacher's authority? Start with the assumption that it is the responsibility of the whole group, not only the teacher, to make a group work and ask yourself if you have contributed as fully as possible. A teacher who takes a dominant role may appear to determine a group's character, but she or he can only dominate if the rest of the group allow this to happen—if, for example, you seldom address comments or questions directly to each other. As a group, work out clearly what you expect and want from the discussions. Keep in mind that if you aren't prepared to take action, you can't expect the situation to change.

- What aims would you each like the group to have?
- What do members have to offer each other in discussions, and what skills and knowledge does the teacher have which are valuable to the group?
- If you find the teacher difficult, can you work out why and together decide on ways to handle the problem?
- What activities could the group undertake which would help each person participate fully?
- If you think that assessment of contributions to the group is preventing full discussion, can you suggest alternatives?

- If you don't understand an aspect of the discussion, are you each willing to ask about it?
- If the discussion seems aimless, are you each willing to say so, explain why, and suggest a definite direction the discussion might take?
- Are you each prepared to renew the discussion after a silence?

You may want to talk about these and other questions during or outside group meetings. If at all possible, talk directly with the teacher concerned about any problems rather than suffering in silence or grumbling and doing nothing. Teachers who are concerned about their students and their teaching know that they can often learn from students and welcome thoughtful suggestions. Such a direct discussion may require considerable courage if a teacher is authoritarian, and more than a little tact if a teacher is well-meaning but unskilled (see 'Approaching teachers', Chapter 3). It is usually easier to talk with a teacher if you have met on a one-to-one basis early in the course, so that you see each other more as individuals with particular interests in a course rather than as a 'Teacher' and a 'Student'.

After a group

After a group meeting, **review the discussion** to think about how it relates to you, your learning and the course. To help you remember what was discussed, as soon as possible make a brief summary and follow up anything you haven't understood. If you gave a paper, think back over your presentation and the ensuing discussion. If required, see the group leader to evaluate your paper. Make sure that you know what the next topic for discussion will be and precisely what you are expected to prepare.

Another way to learn more from a formal discussion is to get together afterwards with one or two other students to **talk informally about the topic**. You can sort out points you didn't understand, make some of those comments which were lost in the larger group, and consolidate and build on what you did understand. The moral support that such discussions can give is invaluable, particularly for less confident students.

> ... all my confidence diminished as I was to hear someone talk of *The Plague* all the time referring to the Germans in France during the War. What in heaven's name was she talking about? I had also read *The Plague* and found it a most interesting story of a town infested by bubonic plague, but it never entered my head that these things were all symbols. From that moment I was frightened to open my mouth. At coffee break, however, I was to learn a couple of others felt the same reaction to this piece of news.
> *Brian's Wife Jenny's Mum*

You may have **persistent problems in a group** and feel dissatisfied or unhappy. If you have contributed as fully as you can, you may want to discuss your feelings privately with the group leader. You could sound out the other group members to see if they share your feelings and if so, arrange to devote some of the formal discussion time to dealing with the problem. You may be able to change to another group if these attempts to deal with the problem don't succeed. Such a change often only involves asking the teachers concerned and is preferable to wasting your time.

ॐ ॐ ॐ

Do you usually enjoy discussion groups? Most students feel confident and interested in some groups, and uncertain or bored in others. Perhaps the most important thing about groups is that even good groups have their off days. The success of a group as a whole depends on every member assuming responsibility for it; the success of a group for you as an individual member depends on your willingness to participate both by speaking and listening.

Further reading

McEvedy, M. Rosanna, Packham, Gillian & Smith, Patricia. 1986. *Studying in Australia: Speaking in Academic Settings: Oral Skills for Seminars, Discussion and Interacting with Supervisor*s. Nelson, Melbourne.

Young, Robert, & Lovat, Terry. 1988. *Communicating all Around* in Lovat, Terry (ed). *People, Culture and Change.* Social Science Press, Wentworth Falls.

11

Developing Your Writing

... becoming a writer is all a question of learning to trust yourself, to trust your own voice.

Katherine Anne Porter, quoted by Erica Jong

If writing is one way you often express yourself and communicate, you probably enjoy writing and feel at ease with the process; your formal academic writing will be enriched by your experience with the craft. In tertiary institutions, written expression is emphasised, and learning is assessed primarily through writing essays, reports and examinations. You may have opportunities to take an oral exam, to deliver a paper orally, to present an assignment in film, on tape, as a collection of photographs or drawings, or by writing a play, a short story or poem. Don't overlook these. However, the reality is that to pass courses in tertiary institutions you must be able to write prose. In particular you are expected to become familiar with the languages and methodologies of your discipline (see 'Expectations of academic assignments', Chapter 6) and you may find that you acquire some more quickly than others. Similarly, although you might find that while essay writing comes easily it may take you time to learn to write reports in the style expected.

This chapter is the first of three dealing with writing and suggests ways of developing your writing. The chapter discusses academic writing and offers suggestions on informal writing which is not for assessment. The next two chapters deal with two of the dominant genres used in tertiary study: essays and reports. Whether you currently find writing a pleasure or a chore, the suggestions offered in this chapter can help you explore, develop and have confidence in your writing. The chapter suggests that you try different methods of writing, that you make writing a regular activity in your life and that you write for different purposes and in different genres. It also suggests mechanisms for sharing your writing with others in a non-threatening and constructive way to help you develop your writing

Many students think there is an 'academic style' which is appropriate for tertiary level writing. This is partly right; but such writing is largely dependent on the conventions of particular disciplines; and it does not necessarily include long technical terms. Sometimes you do need to make use of particular terminology to convey a precise meaning, but such terminology can easily degenerate into jargon if used carelessly or to impress. When in doubt, opt for simplicity. The main aim of academic writing is to communicate what you want to say to someone, and the basic need to be lucid and direct applies as much to scholarly writing as to any other.

There is no one perfect academic style of writing. Each student will assimilate and present ideas in an individual way. The forms and conventions must be followed but the way in which you use these forms will be your own (see 'The discipline area', Chapter 8). You are not expected to be an expert or renowned author in your field, and it is preferable when writing essays or reports to express your own honest, carefully considered response, rather than paraphrasing or plagiarising other people's words and opinions or indulging your prejudices (see Appendix, 'Discrimination').

You have your own way of using words when you speak and, while you may not be a Shakespeare, you probably have your own style of writing. Use it in your academic writing. If your style includes irony, metaphor, an occasional flash of wit, use them unless they meet with strong disapproval from the people who assess your work.

From time to time I feel a need, sharp as thirst in summer, to note and to describe. And then I take up my pen again and attempt the perilous and elusive task of seizing and pinning down, under its flexible double-pointed nib, the many-hued, fugitive, thrilling adjective ... The attack does not last long; it is but the itching of an old scar.

Colette

The process of writing

Unless you are writing purely for yourself, writing is communicating. This involves thinking about the genre in which you write and about the person or people who read your writing. You are trying not only to express your thoughts fluently, accurately and creatively, but to do so in a certain style and way that your reader will understand. To do this you must be clear about what you want to say and why, and you will draw on any language, experiences and beliefs that you and your readers share.

> Find a subject you care about and which you in your heart feel others should care about. It is this genuine caring, and not your games with language, which will be the most compelling and seductive element in your style.
>
> *Kurt Vonnegut*

Writing is a process that involves both a creative and a critical dimension and it is important to work on both of these in developing and improving your writing. The creative phase is the process of turning the thoughts, ideas, inspirations or dreams in your head into written words; and the critical phase is when you reflect on, constructively criticise and edit these outpourings. Your instruments for either phase can be pen and paper, typewriter and paper, or computer screen—which of these instruments you use and how you use them will depend on your personal preferences and your finances.

The **creative phase** of writing involves thinking, reflecting and imagining as much as putting words on paper or tapping out sentences on a typewriter or computer screen. This writing phase at times involves transcribing words from inside your head according to a plan or presenting them in a required structure or genre. But the writing process can also stimulate new thoughts and directions to which you respond in writing as you write. As you write you can uncover areas of seemingly forgotten knowledge, or unanswered questions about the content of your work can suddenly become clear. So the process of writing can in itself be a learning process. Sometimes the creative phase of writing flows easily, while at other times the words just will not come. At these times it can be a good idea to put your work aside and come back to it later, or to write about whatever else it is that you have on your mind. Sometimes, especially when there are deadlines to meet, you need to struggle on in the hope that the flow will come.

The **critical or editing phase** of the writing process is very different from the creative. In fact the two phases are incompatible and it is difficult, if not impossible, to both create and edit simultaneously. It is claimed that the creative facility resides in one hemisphere of our brain and the critical in the other and that our brains are not capable of creating and criticising simultaneously. If this is so, it makes sense to separate these two processes in your writing. Do you procrastinate about writing because you don't know where to start writing on a topic? Do you feel that every sentence you write must be perfect? You perhaps sit for a long time over one sentence or paragraph. When you create try not to edit. Think about having two hats: a creative one and an editing one, which you change as required. You write fluently and complete most of an assignment, or you may write for only a short time and cover only a section or even a paragraph of a total piece of work. The main thing to remember is not to stop the creative process by editing or criticising as you go. Write, let it flow (see 'Freewriting') and when your creativity is spent or you are written dry only then go back and reflect and edit.

> Word processing, ... with its 'soft' stage in the activity of writing, encourages the writer rapidly to string together the basic thrust of what is to be said. Thorough acquaintance with the word processor invites a kind of compositional free association. At a later point, the user assumes he or she can return to the text and expand, delete, and reorganize. To some degree such a compositional strategy may be used with a pencil and paper or a typewriter. But there is almost inevitably a care-full habit of mind which comes into play with these instruments because of the time and energy involved in composing and reformulating with them. Typewriter and pencil impose, even at the opening stage of composition, the value of economy. Working on a word processor displaces the sense of care in the activity of writing. The manipulative power of the technology encourages the writer to become full-of-care only at a later phase. Word processing, in sum, makes second nature for the writer a sense of the flexibility of the text. The technology enhances the writer's sense of the possibility and importance of reformulation; this means many organizational and developmental elements of composition become focal interests only after the primary associational stage of writing.
>
> *Phil Mullins*

Once you have finished with the creative process of writing, do you put your work aside and not look at it again? Do you hand in the first draft of your assignments to your teacher without redrafting them? If so you are not fully developing your writing, as an essential part of the writer's craft is learning to edit your work. It may be useful to recognise that experienced writers often sit for hours over a page of work, or write several drafts and edit ruthlessly before producing the final one. Rarely is a writer entirely happy with even the final version. This chapter and the two which follow provide help with editing.

Does writing usually come easily to you? Do you enjoy putting ideas, thoughts, feelings on paper? Do you enjoy playing with different writing styles? If you enjoy writing and you write frequently, then you already have a enormous advantage when it comes to writing for academic purposes. You probably also have worked out an effective range of approaches to your writing—sometimes waiting till the ideas settle in your mind before beginning, perhaps writing a detailed plan and using that, or maybe just sitting down and beginning to write. Keep in mind that the many genres of informal writing differ significantly from those of academic writing, but that if you like to write you have the major advantages of a positive attitude, a fluency with written language and practice with the craft of writing.

Do you lack confidence in your writing because your ability to write was undermined by severe criticism? Do you have difficulty with writing because you think that what you write falls short of the standards expected by a teacher? Perhaps you think your vocabulary is limited, or you find that your writing seems to deteriorate when you are writing about material or concepts that you find difficult. Remember that when you are grappling with new and complex concepts and trying to present them according to unfamiliar conventions, your writing may not be as clear as when you write about material you understand in depth; and you may find it easy to write in one discipline area but difficult in another.

Developing your writing, including your formal academic writing, is a continuing process. You need to learn to vary elements of your style according to the discipline and the genre in which you are writing, and according to the topic, your audience and your purpose for writing. One way to do this is to experiment with different ways of writing.

Experiment with different writing methods

Free writing

> Free writing is the best way to learn—in practice, not just in theory—to separate the producing process from the revising process. Freewriting exercises are push-ups in withholding judgement as you produce so that afterwards you can judge better.
>
> *Peter Elbow*

When you free write, you write without attending to a plan and without editing as you write. The process of writing is the stimulus that helps you discover the focus and approach of what you want to say and how you want to say it. Free writing can help bring out ideas and words which are lying dormant or jumbled in your head and give them coherence. This method is particularly valuable if you freeze up when you have to write or if you have a mental block when writing an assignment (see 'Free writing', Chapter 12).

Sit quietly for 10–15 minutes while you write down the thoughts that flow through your mind. Don't stop to select, organise or edit what you are writing, and don't worry about details such as spelling and punctuation. If your mind suddenly flashes elsewhere, explore that sidetrack. Don't stop writing. If you can't think of anything to say, write 'I don't have anything to say' over and over until a thought hits you.

Practice in this way can develop your writing—try free writing about your dreams or problems, about people or events. Incorporate this method into the initial stages of an essay or seminar paper. To help break the habit of always editing as you write, try free writing directly by using a personal computer, or by speaking your thoughts onto a tape recorder and then transcribing them. Once you have the words on the page or screen you can look at them critically and begin the editing process.

Structured writing

> ... creativity has much more to do with mastering a genre and then adjusting it to meet one's own purposes that with writing stories ninety percent of the time one puts pen to paper. It is surely creativity of this more general and practical kind that schools need to foster in young writers.
>
> *Jim Martin*

Sometimes you need to write according to a plan because you are required to write in a specific genre or format. Using a plan is the writing method frequently taught and expected in formal education, and you are likely to use it when writing a report, an essay, an article for a paper or a business letter. However, even if you are working closely to an overall plan as you express your ideas and information in words, try not to edit as you write. Once your ideas are sorted out on paper, you can always go back and find the precise phrase you want.

Write often

> Learning to write again is ... not a tightening up process. It is not a matter of learning lots of techniques. It is learning to relax one's muscles and one's brain.
>
> *Brian's Wife Jenny's Mum*

One of the most effective ways to improve your writing is to write, write, write—and then write some more. Make writing an integral part of your life, and write regularly and for extended periods. Play with words and write in as many forms and styles as you can. Write informally about yourself and your life and write about your academic work—your lectures, readings, discussions and ideas. If your writing is to improve, from time to time re-read your informal work, because as with your formal writing it is important to cast a critical eye over your creative endeavours. Assess your strengths so you can build on them, and work on your weaknesses. This section of the chapter offers you suggestions to develop your informal writing.

Letters, articles, poems and other forms

> I am not urging you to write a novel ... although I would not be sorry if you wrote one, provided you genuinely cared about something. A petition to the mayor about a pothole in front of your house or a love letter to the girl next door will do.
>
> *Kurt Vonnegut*

Do you write letters to family and friends, turn out business letters and reports as part of your job, keep a journal, write an occasional poem or short story, or send 'letters to the editor'? Many people who write in these forms don't see themselves as able to write because they are not producing a book or because writing is not a major part of their job. But regular practice in a variety of writing forms can help you discover and develop your writing.

If you haven't thought of letters, articles or poems as part of your writing, try experimenting with:

- writing letters occasionally instead of 'phoning your friends, and keeping copies of your letters
- capturing an experience or playing with words in poems, lyrics, short stories or dialogue
- writing a letter to the editor of your local paper if you feel strongly about an issue, or
- writing an article for the newsletter of a community group in which you are active.

If you are accustomed to writing letters, poems, articles or dialogue you could occasionally use these familiar forms in your assignments (but first check that this is permitted as your teacher may wish you to concentrate on learning how to write in a certain genre). For example:

- an essay comparing Freud with Jung could take the form of an exchange of letters setting out the basis of the disagreement between the two men
- an assignment on evolution could be written as a dialogue between Bishop Samuel Wilberforce and Thomas Huxley, or
- a preface or introduction to an essay may be written as a poem or a personal letter.

Keeping a personal journal/diary

> I never travel without my diary. One should always have something
> sensational to read in the train.
>
> *Oscar Wilde*

If you have ever kept a diary, what did you record in it? As a teenager,
did you record those major events in a small notebook that you kept
hidden, or did your entries read something like, 'Got up early this
morning. School was okay except I got into trouble on the way home.
Watched TV.'? When travelling, have you ever kept a diary as a record
of places and events? During periods of emotional trauma, have you
written pages and pages that you destroyed afterwards? For some people,
the thought of keeping a diary or journal conjures up images of
monotonously recording facts and details, or pouring out secret feelings
on paper. A journal can be these, but it can also be much more.

Why keep a journal?

In some courses you may be required to keep a working journal or log,
and if so the content, format and style should be specified. For example, field journals in natural history or ecology courses can have strict
rules on what to include and how to structure both the original field
notes and the journal entries that follow. If you don't have to keep a
specific course log, keeping a personal working journal as part of your
learning and writing can help you become aware of the experiences,
enthusiasms and biases you bring to your learning. In this journal you
can record your inspirations, thoughts and questions about your formal
learning and about lectures, reading and discussions in a way which helps
you understand who you are as a learner. Since keeping a journal also
provides an opportunity to experiment with and explore different writing
styles without being judged, it can have a positive impact on your
formal writing.

What is a journal?

A journal is a place where you write for yourself. As such, it is a place
where you can be as honest as possible with yourself, where your thoughts
and ideas won't be judged by others, where you collect what interests
you, and where you are free to write as you like. You may use a journal
to make an occasional entry, or write intensively for a couple of months
and then let it lapse. You might write in a journal daily to describe the
events, experience, feelings, people and ideas from each day.

Keeping The Daily Log

Think back to how you felt when you awakened in the morning. Describe
the mood, the sensations—physical, mental.

Do you have the feeling that you were dreaming during the night? What was the general atmosphere of those dreams? How much of them can you remember and write down?

What was your mood as the day started? How did the morning unfold?

What thoughts kept coming into your mind without your deliberately thinking them? Worries, hopes, fantasies? What emotions? Angers, loves?

What events took place with people, works, groups?

Did unusual situations occur, situations of intensity, crisis, joy?

How does the day proceed? Note the rhythms of the day as you move from the morning to the afternoon, into the evening. Does the quality of your feelings, your mood, your emotions change?

Recapitulate your experiences of the day—all the occurrences that you can perceive both within your mind and on the outside of your life.

Write these without judgement: nothing to be proud of, nothing to be ashamed of; no praise, no blame.

Now feel the day as a whole. Write a few adjectives and a metaphor for how the day feels to you.

Ira Progoff

A journal might be about yourself:

- your dreams, daydreams and fantasies, descriptions of the circumstances in your life that connect with these, and discussion of them
- your emotions
- how your body feels
- your reflections, thoughts and reminiscences on your past, and
- your ideas, theories or inspirations.

It might be about your world:

- descriptions of a particular situation or event
- observations about people, and
- comments on public happenings or issues.

It could include items such as:

- poems, short stories, song lyrics which you write or collect
- important letters to you or copies of letters from you
- clippings from newspapers or magazines and your comments on them, and
- notes on books, lectures, movies or television programmes.

If you write about your private life and thoughts in your journal, do you worry that other people might read it? You don't have to write about personal matters, but if you do, be careful not to leave your journal where it might be found. You can use symbols instead of names and places, or write as if describing a fantasy or a dream that makes sense only to you.

A format

You can keep your journal entries chronologically or organise them into sections. A looseleaf format enables you to organise or reshuffle your writing into sections, to easily remove pages you want to share, and to elaborate on entries started long ago. You can also carry a couple of pages in your pocket or bag, in the glove box of your car, or attached to your clipboard, and write when the impulse moves you.

> Never have I seen as clearly as tonight that my diary-writing is a vice ... I glided into my bedroom, closed the curtains, threw a log into the fire, lit a cigarette, pulled the diary out of its last hiding place under by dressing table, threw it on the ivory silk quilt, and prepared for bed. I had the feeling that this is the way an opium smoker prepares for his opium pipe. For this is the moment when I relive my life in terms of a dream, a myth, an endless story.
>
> *Anais Nin*

If you are already an avid journal writer, you will understand how Anais Nin feels about writing in her diary. If you haven't already done so, read the diaries of some well-known diarists such as Anais Nin or Charles Darwin to enrich your own journal writing. If keeping a journal is not a part of your life and you think you would find it valuable, set aside a regular time so that you can enjoy writing it.

Share your writing

> The essential human act at the heart of writing is the act of giving ... This central act of giving is curiously neglected in most writing instruction. Otherwise people would have shared their writing—just given it to another human being for the sake of mutual pleasure—as often as they gave it to a teacher for evaluation and advice. For most people, however, the experience of just sharing what they have written is rare.
>
> *Peter Elbow*

Do you ever write solely for yourself, or for one or two close friends?
If you write letters, short stories or poems, do you share these with friends?

Writing alone is a traditional method of producing assignments, sitting for hours at your desk with the aid of innumerable cups of black coffee the night before the assignment is due and never discussing your thoughts and ideas with anyone. And usually only your teacher reads your formal assignments, so you receive only one person's perception and evaluation of what and how you write.

Most students do not share their written work or their ideas about how they will approach a written assignment with anyone else. Before you start any sustained writing, it can help you clarify what you want to put on paper if you talk about your ideas to someone else. This is useful when you are beginning to formulate ideas on a topic or when thinking how you intend to present your work. It is not necessary to talk to someone who is familiar with your area, although the feedback will be more valuable if you can find another student from your course or discipline. If you cannot find such a student it can help to explain your ideas to a friend or member of your family who will listen carefully—or even to express them aloud to the family pet. But the ideal is to find someone taking similiar courses with whom you can share a mutual exchange of ideas and comments on written work. A working relationship such as this is invaluable, and from it you can both learn and improve your written work.

Contrary to what many students believe, talking to other students about your work and receiving their assistance with writing is not cheating. Cheating is when you take other people's ideas and use them as your own, or if they write parts of your work for you (See 'Plagiarism', Chapter 12).

While developing your writing is largely a matter of writing and receiving feedback on it, analysing well-written models of other people's work can give you insights into a genre. Just as reading published diaries will give you ideas for the format and content of your journal writing, other students' essays or reports can inform your own academic work. So when required to write a report or an essay in a subject, you could usefully ask your teacher for copies of previous students' work on another subject and ask for comments on why they meet the teacher's expectations or the course objectives. Take these points into consideration when you are editing and rewriting your own work.

Comments from others on your writing can be extremely useful. Have one or two friends read your writing and respond to it, or tell your teachers that you want to improve your writing and ask for detailed feedback on your work. Perhaps you would like to share what you write with a wider audience but feel unsure of the criticism you might receive. If you work on your writing with a friend or a group of people who feel as you do, sharing your work and actually writing in their company is likely to give you confidence in developing your writing style.

Why join a writing group?

1 Actually writing in the same place as other people who share a common writing purpose can provide a new stimulus for what to write about and how to write.

2 If other people read or listen to what you have written and each comments on it immediately, you receive a variety of feedback which

you can question and discuss. If this feedback is positive and is accompanied by useful suggestions, you won't be devastated by criticism and you will have some ideas on how to change your writing.

3 As each member of the group will have his or her own way of expressing themselves, listening to or reading other people's work gives you access to a variety of different styles and approaches to each subject.

4 After some time, giving feedback on other people's work and receiving comments on your writing can help you evolve your own writing objectives and standards.

Setting up a writing group

1 Find people with whom you share a purpose in writing, such as writing assignments for a course, making journal entries, or putting together a student magazine.

2 Keep the group small enough for each person to take part, yet have sufficient people to provide variety and depth in feedback.

3 Attend regularly, and after the first few meetings don't admit new members. People who get to know each other feel more comfortable about sharing their writing.

4 Agree on the length and frequency of meetings according to the size and purpose of the group.

5 Between meetings, do any necessary rewriting or preparation for the next meeting.

6 If group members bring a piece of writing to be discussed, provide copies for everyone to make discussion easier.

7 The group might decide to write for a short time during meetings. You might:

- free write on a set topic (as described earlier in this chapter)
- practise a particular style (such as narrative or expository) or form (such as a dialogue or a scientific report), or
- focus on a specific subject, such as the theory of evolution or a piece of music.

8 While there should be no compulsion for people to share their writing, allow each member the opportunity to present his or her work. In some sessions the group might discuss everyone's work, while in others it may concentrate on the writing of one or two people.

9 Allow time for each piece of work to be read with care, perhaps both silently and aloud.

10 Feedback should be constructive, emphasising strengths rather than weaknesses. Initially negative criticism which points out weaknesses should be avoided because it can undermine a beginning writer's

confidence which the group is aiming to build. Destructive criticism is always taboo. When negative criticism is given, suggest how to make changes. Give feedback by responding to the piece spontaneously, or according to agreed-upon criteria such as those set out in the next two chapters.

Whether you write on your own or with other people depends on your purpose and subject. You could make journal entries with a group of other students in a course, write a report with one other person, or write poetry by yourself. Trying alternatives to find out which ones you enjoy is one way of discovering and exploring your writing voice.

ೕ ೕ ೕ

A writer does not just sit down and instantly write a great book. She spends time practising the craft of writing and puts in many hours on the individual book. Writing has become part of her daily life as well as a talent which delights readers. You may not be a world-famous author, but writing frequently and experimenting with a variety of forms and styles can help you develop your writing and give you pleasure as a writer. And as a great writer refines her skills and thrives on the response of both her fellow writers and her readers, so can you polish and enjoy your writing if you share it with others.

Further reading

Casewit, Curtis W. 1982. *The Diary: A Complete Guide to Journal Writing*. Angus Communciations, Texas.

Darwin, Charles. 1972. *The Voyage of the Beagle*. Bantam Books, New York.

Elbow, Peter. 1973. *Writing Without Teachers*. Oxford University Press, New York.

Elbow, Peter. 1981. *Writing with Power*. Oxford University Press, Melbourne.

Holly, Mary Louise. 1984. *Keeping a Personal-professional Journal*. Deakin University Press, Victoria.

Progoff, Ira. 1975. *At a Journal Workshop: The Basic Text and Guide for Using the Intensive Journal*. Dialogue House Library, New York.

Rainer, Tristine. 1980. *The New Diary: How to use a Journal for Self Guidance and Expanded Creativity*. Angus and Robertson, Sydney.

Stuhlmann, Gunther (ed.). 1974. *The Journals of Anais Nin*. Vols. I-IV, Quartet Books, London.

12

Writing Essays

... I always try to write on the principle of the iceberg. There is seven-eighths of it under water for every part that shows.

Ernest Hemingway

Writing an essay is more than putting words on paper—defining your purpose, analysing your topic, and carrying out your research are integral to what and how you write. Each activity requires careful thought as you integrate your purpose with what is expected of you (see 'Your teacher's purposes', Chapter 6), and as you bring together your ideas and the information you find. Each activity can also have its own pleasures—discovering new information, turning ideas on a topic over in your mind, talking about them with other people or trying them out in different combinations and sequences. When you have more or less analysed and researched a topic you can begin to focus on the task of writing the essay as a whole.

This chapter looks at the processes involved in producing written work. Although primarily concerned with writing, the ideas in the chapter can also be used in producing other written assignments and oral or audiovisual work, as these often rely on a written outline or script.

The processes outlined are intended as a framework from which you can develop your essay writing. This framework can help you understand written comments on your work, or can be used as a basis for discussing your essays with a teacher or a group of students. When writing an essay you may use the entire chapter, or you might prefer to use parts of it to help with specific problems such as planning an essay or writing coherent paragraphs.

However, the framework offered is useful only if you write frequently and if you receive a lot of feedback from others. Each essay is not an isolated end in itself—what you learn from writing one can help you with the next, even if the content and format of each differ and each is in a different discipline. Improving your writing takes time and practice and your writing may seem worse before you notice any improvement—it takes time to change old habits and develop and refine new methods. Saying exactly what you want and in the style you want is easier if you have confidence in your writing abilities (see Chapter 11).

Before you start writing

As a result of your thinking and research, perhaps you have written sentences or paragraphs which capture thoughts you want to use. You should also have notes from your research and a written definition which reflects the theme of your essay.

Your definition of the topic

An essay develops from how you have analysed the topic which you arrive at as a result of research (see 'Your revised definition', Chapter 6). This definition should do the following.

- Make clear your purposes for the essay. Ask yourself, 'Why am I writing an essay in the first place?' 'For what purpose was this piece of work set?' 'What is my purpose for writing this particular essay, and for choosing this topic?'
- State the theme/thesis/argument of your essay. Ask yourself 'What position will I take on the topic?' or 'What case will I argue?'

- Propose a possible structure which indicates the main points in your definition of the topic and how they are connected. Ask 'Exactly what is my topic?', 'Do I have a specific clear title for it?', 'What are my main points for the topic?', 'How might I order these main points so that they reflect my theme/thesis/argument?', 'What information or reasons or examples will I use to support my theme/thesis/argument?' and 'Which directive words (see Table 6.1) are relevant to my essay?'
- Indicate how you will approach your assignment. 'How will I handle the subjectivity of my work?', 'How many of my own ideas will I include?'

Your readers

> I wish thee as much pleasure in the reading, as I had in the writing.
>
> *Francis Quarles*

Before you start writing the whole essay, think about your readers. Is your teacher the only one who will read your essay? Are you writing a paper to be read or listened to by a group of students? Is there a possibility your paper will be published in a collection of student work or elsewhere? If you are uncertain of the level at which to pitch your writing, a good rule of thumb to use is to write for another student who is taking the course but does not have an in-depth understanding of your topic. To communicate effectively:

- have clear in your mind a theme that you think is worth presenting
- keep in mind your purpose for presenting it
- be aware that you are communicating with someone
- take care to say exactly what you want to, and
- say it simply and succinctly.

Writing your rough draft

> We would be given an assignment. I would take one look at it and think, 'That's the end of that. I won't be there next week so I won't have to worry about it.' After two harrowing days, when I kept thinking, 'Will I, won't I?' I'd sit down to look at it.
>
> *Brian's Wife Jenny's Mum*

For each essay you write, start with a rough draft, or more than one draft if your definition of the topic changes as you write and if you have the time. Your final draft will then be a matter of editing your last rough draft.

When you write the rough draft of an essay, your main concern should be the *structure* or framework of your topic and the *clear expression* of your ideas. You may be expected to fit your material into a particular format (for example, see Chapter 13), but even so you still need to organise the material within the sections of that format and to express yourself clearly.

Whether or not you are using a set format, concentrate on saying what you want, in the order you want, and as accurately as you can. When you are in the creative phase of trying to express your ideas, don't worry about organisation or niceties of style or about having the precise word. And don't become bogged down with concerns about perfect spelling or being absolutely correct and detailed in conventions such as footnoting. Be as precise and detailed as you need to be to express your ideas clearly and fully, and leave the perfecting formalities to your final draft.

Most professional writers produce several drafts of a work before arriving at a final version. Many students, however, sit down with pen and paper and expect to start writing the first sentence and to write straight through to the end, producing a more or less complete essay in one draft. This is not the way to produce a satisfactory essay—any method of writing relies on thoughtful research and time to mull over the topic before writing, and any method should lead you to a rough draft which has three clear sections, an introduction, a body and a conclusion. (How these sections should be organised and written is outlined in 'Writing to a plan'. Once your draft is produced, use the checklist of questions in 'Working with your rough draft'.)

Writing methods

Working from your definition of the topic, you can produce your rough draft by free writing, working from a detailed plan, or a combination of these two methods. Any of these methods can be effective.

Free writing

In free writing you use the act of writing to clarify your thoughts, without editing them as you write. Free writing can help start you on your writing and you will often be surprised how much knowledge of the topic you have (see 'Free writing', Chapter 11).

If you have a mental block when writing essays, particularly when starting to write, it may be because you don't feel confident about your writing or about your knowledge of a topic, or how to organise your information, or because you are anxious about your study, or have other pressures in your life (see 'Your emotions', Chapter 1). If you do block, but you have to or want to write, sit down at your computer or at your desk with lots of paper and a pen or pencil. Don't worry about notes or plans or references. Start writing or typing *anything on your topic* that comes to mind and write *continuously* for about ten minutes. If you can't think of what to write, write about why you can't think of what to write, or about the thoughts which are coming between you and the topic. When the time is up, look over what you have written. Some of it may be useful later or may stimulate new thoughts. This free writing activity is often enough to shift a mental block and to stop you procrastinating, but if it doesn't you may need to leave your work for a few hours or days, or longer if possible. And remember that even for skilled writers, sometimes writing refuses to flow smoothly.

> The writer wandered to the water cooler, washed his hands, looked up the weather report, made some unnecessary phone calls, looked at his tongue in the mirror for symptoms of fatal disease and, when he had at last exhausted methods of killing time, went to his typewriter.
>
> *Russell Baker*

You can also use free writing to *produce an entire essay* in draft form. Review your ideas and notes on the topic but don't plan what to write. Write a first draft of all or part of the essay *without editing as you write*. Then look at what you have written and quickly sum up the themes of your writing in one statement. Write a second version, again without editing and repeat the looking over and summing up process. If your topic is still unclear in your mind, write a third draft. When you have a draft that pleases you, use it as the basis for your final one, and so proceed with your editing. Be prepared, however, to throw away much of what you have written. Using this process may sound time consuming but it isn't any more so than other methods. Allow the same time as you usually would for writing an essay.

Writing to a plan
When writing more or less to a plan, the plan structures and limits what you write and prevents you going off on tangents. A plan includes:

* your purpose
* your theme/thesis/argument
* your approach
* an introduction and conclusion
* the order of your main points and how you intend to link these
* the balance between each of your main points, and
* your supporting points.

Don't be surprised if you don't follow your plan exactly. As you write, the process of expressing your ideas can stimulate new thoughts and directions and lead you to see familiar ones in new ways. Actually expressing your ideas with clarity involves searching for and choosing words, phrases and sentences, so part of the structuring can only be done as you write. Integrating new ideas into your plan and making choices as you write can further clarify what you want to say and can lead you to revise your plan. Hopefully such revisions will only be minor at this stage of your work.

Other writing methods

Two extreme ways of producing the rough draft of an essay are completely free writing it from your written definition, but without a plan, or writing exactly to a detailed plan. Between these two lie many alternatives, of which the following are a few.

- Use a plan and, with your notes and references in front of you, edit your thoughts and words as you write and use free writing whenever you are stuck. You could:
  - begin with the introduction and write in the order you planned, right through to the conclusion, or
  - write the body of the essay first, and then the introduction and conclusion, or
  - begin writing the section where your ideas are clearest, and proceed section by section until you have written the one which is least clear to you.
- Make a plan and then with your notes and references put aside, free write your rough draft. If you don't understand a section well enough to write about it or if you need a quote or item of information, turn to your notes and references to refresh your memory—and then close them before you start writing again. When you finish writing your draft, check your work against your notes for completeness and for references you could cite.

> It took me two hours to write this. I bit my finger-nails, cut my toenails, had a snack, crunched an apple and generally procrastinated. But I did it!
>   *Brian's Wife Jenny's Mum*

The parts of your essay

No matter which method you use to produce an essay, your rough draft should finish up with the following parts.

The introduction

The introduction outlines *what you are going to say*. It should make clear your definition of the topic and make your reader want to read on. You might:

- ask a question you will attempt to answer
- state a case you will argue
- outline your theme or thesis

- pose a hypothesis you will test and report on
- outline your reasons for focusing on specific aspects of a general topic
- give selected data to establish an issue as worth writing about, or
- use a quote which conveys the key ideas you will discuss.

Any terms or words which are central to your topic should be defined in the introduction or early on in the body of the essay.

The body of your essay

Here you *say what you want to*. You should order your main points effectively and make this order clear to your reader, present each main point as fully and accurately as necessary and write coherent paragraphs, and you need to keep a balance between your main points.

1 *Ordering main points* After the introduction, your theme, thesis, or argument should be developed clearly and logically throughout the essay and restated in the conclusion. The following suggestions may help you decide on the order in which to develop material.

- Refer back to your purposes and definition.
- If you have decided on your main points, ask yourself why you chose these and how they are connected to each other. In the moon topic, shown in Table 12.1, you might have chosen the three points because they reflect significantly different aspects of the topic. Does an understanding of one point depend on explaining another point first? In the moon example you might have decided to put the point about general beliefs first as a background for scientific theories and popular myths.
- If you have several main points from which you will choose as you write, write each point out as a separate section of your essay. See what links emerge from what you have written and re-write your final points as necessary to clarify the links and develop an ordered whole.
- As you write, use a separate page for each paragraph. When you come to order your whole essay, you can add or delete paragraphs and arrange them in the order which seems most logical.

Your reader needs to know how you have structured your essay. To convey this, use subheadings (if allowed) and pointers such as 'Having discussed idea X, I now want to examine ...' or 'However ...'. Include a plan or a detailed table of contents. Remember that to make clear the order of the main points in your essay and to indicate the links between them, they need to be clear in your mind.

> 'Then you should say what you mean,' the March Hare went on.
> 'I do,' Alice hastily replied; 'at least—at least I mean what I say—that's the same thing, you know.'
>
> *Lewis Carroll*

Table 12.1 A sample essay plan

You are writing on the topic 'Examine the theory that the moon is made of green cheese'. After thought and research you decide it is likely that the moon is made of green cheese. You think that the most important and interesting aspects of the topic are the beliefs for and against the question, scientists' attitudes to the relevant theories and evidence, and popular myths about the green cheesiness or otherwise of the moon. You define the topic accordingly. The following model is a basic one you could use to structure your essay.

Topic: **Examine the theory that the moon is made of green cheese.**

Introduction
Argument: That the moon is made of green cheese.

    (a) Beliefs for and against
    (b) Scientists' attitudes
    (c) Popular myths

What you are going to say

Main Point (a)

General beliefs for and against

1 In Greek times

2 In 19th-century industrial Europe

3 In mid-20th Century

Brief summary of these beliefs

Main Point (b)

Scientist' attitudes

1 Geology of the Mice Age.

2 Properties of green cheese

3 Causes of craters on the moon

4 Discoveries of astronauts

Personal evaluation of these attitudes

Main Point (c)

Popular myths

1 Mice on the moon

2 The Green Cheese Revivalist Movement

Personal comments on these myths

Saying it

Conclusion

That the moon is made of green cheese

(a) Beliefs for and against
(b) Scientists' attitudes
(c) Popular myths

Personal conclusions and a further hypothesis

What you said

2 *Presenting main points fully and accurately* Saying what you want to also entails presenting each of your main points fully and accurately. To support the major points of your essay you might explain a point further, give reasons for a statement, cite statistics or facts, or use examples or quotes.

Don't expect your reader to be a mind reader. Remember that you have been researching and thinking about the topic recently, so a sentence you write which conveys a whole collection of ideas to you may not do so to your reader. Don't skim over points which need explanation. Don't assume that your reader automatically knows who or what Alcibiades is, or precisely what you mean when you use terms such as 'instinct', 'good' or 'Western society'. When you make general statements, support them with reasons or examples.

Even if your teacher is the only person to read your finished work, check if you are expected to write without assuming his or her knowledge of the topic so that you demonstrate your own knowledge fully. If you are in doubt about the level of writing to aim at, imagine that you are writing for a reasonably intelligent student just about to begin the course and with an interest in your topic. This helps to avoid pitfalls such as writing on the implications of Hegel's ideas without actually describing the ideas because you assume that your teacher knows what they are.

Each main point should consist of one or more **paragraphs**.[1] Each paragraph should contain one key idea or cover one aspect relevant to the main point. This idea or aspect is frequently set out in a key sentence, which may come anywhere in a paragraph or may be implied by the total content of the paragraph rather than stated explicitly. Each of the other **sentences** in the paragraph should explain or illustrate the point which the paragraph is making, but each should also have a purpose of its own.

Stop for a moment and think about what you just read. Now look at the next paragraph. What is its main point? Is there an explicit key sentence? How does each of the sentences in the paragraph relate to the point of the paragraph?

A paragraph should be coherent, so that your reader is led smoothly from one sentence to another and understands the connection between them. For example, if the paragraph uses a central metaphor, each sentence may echo and expand that metaphor. Words and phrases such as 'similarly', 'because', 'besides', 'in contrast', 'meanwhile', 'therefore' or 'for instance' help to indicate the links between sentences (see Table 12.2). If a paragraph is not coherent, your reader will be faced with bewildering jumps of thought, events out of sequence, or facts illogically arranged.

> Just as the sentence contains one idea in all its fullness, so the paragraph
> should embrace a distinct episode; and as sentences should follow one

another in harmonious sequence, so paragraphs must fit into one another like the automatic couplings of railway carriages.

Winston Churchill

Table 12.2 Transitional words and phrases

These are words and phrases which show relationships between two ideas or facts. They indicate:

Addition

in addition, again, also, and, besides, finally, first, further, last, moreover, second, too, next

Cause and effect

accordingly, as a result, consequently, hence, otherwise, therefore, thus

Comparison

similarly, likewise

Contrast

in contrast, although, and yet, but, however, nevertheless, on the other hand, on the contrary

Examples or special features

for example, for instance, in other words, in illustration, in this case, in particular, specifically

Summary

in brief, in conclusion, in short, on the whole, to conclude, to summarise, to sum up

Connections in time

after a short time, afterwards, as long as, as soon as, at last, at length, at that time, at the same time, before, earlier, of late, immediately, in the meantime, lately, later, meanwhile, presently, shortly, since, soon, temporarily, thereafter, until, when, while.

---

3 *Balancing main points* Decide if all your main points should have equal weighting within the essay. In the moon topic (Table 12.1), you might decide to look more closely at the scientists' attitudes and research, or you might devote more space to the popular myths because they are controversial.

Even with the most careful planning, as you actually write you may find that you need to devote more of the total essay to a point to explain it fully, to give less emphasis to a point, or to delete a point which no longer seems essential to your approach.

Some essays have a strict word length requirement. What do you do if you discover part-way through your essay that it will be too long if you present all the points you have planned to cover? You may need to reduce the number of points you cover, or to eliminate repetitive sections. Conversely, does your essay look as though it will fall short of the length required? If so, check that your plan hasn't been too skimpy on the number of points you cover, and check that you have supported each of your main points thoroughly.

When in doubt about whether or not to include or omit material, refer back to your purposes for the essay and your definition of the topic, and ask yourself if the material fits with these. Learning to discard material is an essential but often difficult part of writing—you may have to force yourself to do it.

> Have the guts to cut ... If a sentence, no matter how excellent, does not illuminate your subject in some new and useful way, scratch it out.
>
> *Kurt Vonnegut*

The conclusion

This draws together *what you have said* in the body of your essay. It should sum up and reflect your main points and your approach to the topic, and should be related to the introduction. You might suggest a question or hypothesis which arose directly from your conclusions, but you should not introduce a main point or a statement which needs detailed explanation. As well as drawing together what you have said the conclusion serves to round off your essay—don't make it so abrupt that your reader is surprised that the essay is finished.

> There are two things I am confident I can do very well; one is an introduction to any literary work, stating what it is to contain, and how it should be executed in the most perfect manner; the other is a conclusion, shewing from various causes why the execution has not been equal to what the author promised to himself and to the public.
>
> *Samuel Johnson*

Working with your rough draft

Working with your rough draft is essentially a checking and rewriting stage, since by now you should have a clear idea of the purposes, content, structure and basic writing style of your essay. Part of your work with the rough draft will probably be remedying oversights. For example, you may need to find full details for bibliography entries, or check on the precise wording of a quote or exact data for part of a graph. What else do you check for at this stage?

Purposes

- Does the essay reflect your purposes in:
  - undertaking an essay in the first place
  - doing this particular essay

- choosing this particular topic, and
- selecting your theme and focus within the topic?
- Does the essay reflect the purposes for which the essay was set?
- Have you checked that you have met all requirements for the essay?

Theme/thesis/argument

- Does the essay have a theme, thesis or argument?
- Have you clearly stated this?
- Do the main points support your theme?

Content

- Is your topic clearly defined?
- Does your title reflect this definition accurately?
- Is all your material relevant to your definition?
- What are the main points of your essay?
- Are your main points presented as clearly and fully as necessary?
- Have you included reasons or evidence or examples to support each of your main points?
- Have you clearly defined any central terms?
- Are quotations and examples which you have used integral to your essay?
- Do you have too much or too little material for the length of your essay?
- Have you sometimes unnecessarily repeated what you said previously?

Structure

- What is the structure of your essay?
- Does your structure logically and effectively develop your theme/thesis/argument and definition of the topic?
- Have you clearly indicated to your reader the stages by which you develop your theme?
- Does your introduction accurately outline your definition of the topic, state your theme and seduce your reader?
- Is there a balance between your main points?
- Have you linked your main points clearly?
- Does each paragraph within your main points contain only one key idea, and is this idea clearly relevant to the main point it is supporting?
- Have you clearly connected your paragraphs?
- Does your conclusion:
  - reflect the material and theme presented in the essay
  - relate to your introduction
  - finish smoothly, and
  - suggest any further areas or questions to be followed up without introducing any major new ideas?
- If you are expected to organise your material within a particular format, have you done so?

Approach

* Have you acknowledged your beliefs and attitudes and commented on how they affect your interpretation of the material?
* Have you been too biased in your selection of material?
* If allowed, have you incorporated your own ideas which develop the theme, and have you supported these ideas?

Style

* Have you expressed your ideas clearly and simply?
* Is your writing style your own?
* Have you incorporated any formal style requirements into your writing?

> Reheating a piece of writing after it has cooled, tempering it, and sharpening it is enjoyable—if you know how. Otherwise it may turn out worse, brittle and misshapen.
>
> *Ken Macrorie*

 za za za

If you have thoughtfully researched, planned and written your essay, you are less likely to have to make major revisions to your rough draft. However, sometimes when you re-read your draft you are struck with a new idea about the structure or content, or you suddenly see a major flaw in what you have written. If you have sufficient time, you may want to re-work an initial rough draft substantially. Be prepared for this, but realise that at some stage you have to stop working on your essay and let it stand as it is, warts and all. If you are writing your essay at the last minute, you are unlikely to have the time for detailed rewriting. In this case, the amount of work depends on how clearly you really knew what you wanted to say before you started writing.

When you have finished writing and working on your rough draft, you have done most of the work on your essay. Wherever possible, write a rough draft, work on it and put it aside for at least a few days before you write the final one. You might discuss it with others, or have someone else read it and comment. You may want to change a phrase, add a word, rewrite a sentence or a paragraph. In any case, give yourself time to stand back from what you have written, time to reflect on your whole essay before you finally sit down and edit it.

Editing your final draft

In the final draft, you edit what you have written to polish your writing style and to complete details of formalities such as punctuation or footnotes.

- Often a good essay is difficult to read because of inadequate **proof-reading**. (Chapter 14 is designed to help you check details such as presentation, writing conventions and spelling.) Using a spelling or grammar checker on your computer is no substitute for thorough proof reading.
- Improving your **writing style** involves imagination as well as hard work (see Chapter 11). When polishing your writing in an essay, check carefully for points such as unnecessary repetition, inaccurate use of words of whose meaning you are uncertain, and ambiguous use of 'it', 'this', 'they', 'them'. Reading your essay aloud (particularly to someone else) is an effective way of checking for these items.

Evaluating your essay

Ask yourself:

What were my purposes for the essay?
How well have I achieved these?
How would I change what I researched, planned and wrote if I repeated the essay? Why?
Has working on my essay led me to any ideas or questions I might follow up?

You should be the first person to evaluate the strengths and weaknesses of what you write. You will provide your readers with a basis for constructive criticism if you include your written evaluation (as well as your plan or detailed table of contents) with your essay.

The next stage is up to **your readers**. If your essays are usually read only by your teacher and the teacher provides helpful feedback, you will be encouraged to write more even if you have difficulties to overcome. If your teacher provides only curt or cursory comments on your writing, find one or more other people who will spend time and care commenting on your work. If such help is not possible, you can discover a new perspective in your writing by reading your work aloud to a tape recorder and listening to it. Even if you have comments from other people, learning to evaluate your own work is part of the craft of writing.

If your way of writing essays or reports is criticised explicitly because it does not conform to the accepted conventions of your discipline at tertiary level, you may need to learn how to write in the appropriate genres and to adapt to what is expected. Find out from your teacher why your written work does not meet the requirements and read the relevant sections in this book.

The more useful the feedback you receive on an essay, the more you can evolve your own style and craft as a writer. Think carefully about any comments you are given and discuss them with your reader to learn more about your strengths and weaknesses as a writer. Remember that for your writing, yours is the final evaluation. (See Chapter 15 for more on evaluating your own work.)

≈ ≈ ≈

Hopefully, writing an essay is not a postscript to research, or a duty that you scribble through at the last minute. If you think of essay writing as a craft to be practised and as part of all the writing you do, you will understand that it can reward you for the time, care and imagination you put into it in ways which are more satisfying than achieving a good grade.

Further reading

Bate, Douglas. 1979. *Essay Method and English Expression.* Harcourt Brace Jovanovich, Australia.

Bate, Douglas, & Sharpe, Peter. 1990. *Student Writer's Handbook: How to Write Better Essays.* Harcourt Brace Jovanovich, Sydney

Becker, Howard S. 1986. *Writing for Social Scientists: How to Start and Finish Your Thesis, Book or Article.* The University of Chicago Press, Chicago.

Clanchy, John, & Ballard, Brigid. 1991. *Essay Writing for Students.* 2nd edn, Longman Cheshire, Melbourne.

Lovell, David W., & Moore, Rhonda D. 1992. *Essay Writing and Style Guide for Politics and the Social Sciences.* Australian Political Studies Association, Australian Defence Academy, Canberra.

Murphy, Eamon. 1985. *You Can Write: A Do-it-yourself Manual.* Longman Cheshire, Melbourne.

Taylor, Gordon. 1989. *The Student's Writing Guide for the Arts and Social Sciences.* Cambridge University Press, Melbourne.

Notes

[1] A paragraph may vary in length from one sentence to many (and such variety makes more interesting reading). As a *very approximate* rule of thumb for assignments, each paragraph averages about 100 words. Thus in a 2000-word assignment, you would have approximately twenty paragraphs, which you might divide up with two each for an introduction and conclusion, and an average of four or five paragraphs to make points which support each of three or four main points. Thinking of your assignment in this way can help you understand how many main points you can make fully and clearly.

13

Writing Scientific Reports

Some of the worst (articles in scientific journals) are produced by the kind of author who consciously pretends to a 'scientific scholarly' style. He [*sic*] takes what should be lively, inspiring and beautiful, and in an attempt to make it seem dignified, chokes it to death with stately abstract nouns; next, in the name of scientific impartiality, he [*sic*] fits it with a complete set of passive constructions to drain away any remaining life's blood or excitement; then he [*sic*] embalms the remains in molasses of polysyllable, wraps the corpse in an impenetrable veil of vogue words, and buries the stiff old mummy with such pomp and circumstance in the most distinguished journal that will take it. Considered either as a piece of scholarly work or as a vehicle of communication, the product is appalling. The question is, does it matter?

F. Peter Woodford

Yes, it does matter—whether your report is published in a scientific journal or is a course requirement. Communicating your findings and observations in a report is an integral part of science, and communicating clearly is interwoven with thinking clearly. Unless your reports are clearly thought out and written, your practical work—no matter how good—is of limited value.

What do you bring to an experiment or field trip which affects the quality of your written report? Your knowledge of a subject—of underlying theory and specific detail—is obviously important and can be improved with preliminary reading. Your care in observation (see 'Observation', Chapter 7), your practical skills, and your expertise in using research techniques also affect the standard of your scientific work and writing.

Your purposes

Another facet which is basic to good research and report writing is an awareness of your purposes. Some of your purposes are very specific—to test a particular hypothesis, to observe a certain phenomenon. However, you also need to think about why you are doing the research in the first place. And as one of your purposes is to communicate your findings, think about who will read the report. You might:

- write a report on a routine laboratory session for your teacher, where both carrying out the practical work and writing about it are exercises in using a meticulous scientific method, or
- write a public report for a government department or the popular press or as part of your work in an interdisciplinary course; readers of such reports need emphasis on general ideas without too much scientific detail or too many bland descriptions.

Each individual research project and its report has a different purpose. Keeping your purposes and your readers in mind when researching gives you a basic framework for clear report writing.

This chapter looks at basic principles of writing highly structured reports. It is mostly concerned with reports based on gathering primary data from laboratory experiments and fieldwork, and less concerned with reporting on secondary data gathered from reports of other people's research (see 'Identifying primary and secondary sources', Chapter 7).

How you use the chapter depends on the detail in your laboratory manuals, and on the number of practical sessions you have each week, and on the extent to which you design your research. For example:

- if your laboratory manual describes in great detail the experiments you are to carry out, focus on planning the experiment and use each section of the chapter as you write your report
- if you have to write up three laboratory sessions each week, you could use this chapter to help you write any difficult sections, and

• if your research is substantially your own, the sections on writing styles and conventions may be particularly valuable.

Beginning a report

Is 'writing up' something you see as a task to be done after the 'real work' of an experiment or fieldwork is over? In practice, the process of writing can help you to clarify your thoughts and stimulate new ideas, so write at all stages of laboratory and fieldwork rather than leaving this activity to the end.

Your laboratory or field notebook

> ... a lab notebook. Everything gets written down, formally, so that you know at all times where you are, where you have been, where you are going and where you want to get. In scientific work and electronics technology this is necessary because otherwise the problems get so complex you get lost in them and confused and forget what you know and what you don't know and have to give up ... Sometimes just the act of writing down the problems straightens out your head as to what they really are.
>
> *Robert M. Pirsig*

Begin writing for a report during your practical work as you record methods and results, and immediately afterwards while the work is still fresh in your mind. This helps you think critically about what you are doing, and can lead you to repeat an experiment while it is still set up, or to fill in gaps in your field observations. Your notes should be a complete and chronological record of what you did and when, including calculations and diagrams of apparatus.

As you carry out and record research, your results are usually in the form of numbers. For example, if you are interested in how long it takes a one-celled animal to divide, you would measure the time from one division to the next with a number of these animals and then derive the average time. The results would be a set of numbers called *data*. In the early stages of analysing data, ordering them in tables or graphs can help you see patterns emerging in your results. Include in your notebook a brief discussion of your main results or observations.

Write the name of each of the sections of your report on separate pages of your notebook and record your ideas, observations and results under the appropriate heading. Don't worry at this stage about your writing style or the order of material within a section—concentrate on putting ideas and information down as clearly and concisely as possible.

Planning your writing

- Before you start writing your whole report plan *what* you are going to say and how you are going to say it—this is where your sheets of paper for the various sections are useful. Discussing your work with others—teachers, students, friends—gives you practice in explaining your ideas and results and helps clarify what you want to say and how.
- Consider also *how* you might write your report. You could tackle it in stages, so that you start by writing up Materials and Methods, drafting the Conclusions, and planning your Discussion, and you edit each section as it is written. Another method is to write the whole paper at once, concentrating on conveying your ideas and information accurately, and then editing what you have written.
- *When* you write your report probably depends on when it is due and your overall workload, but the earlier you begin writing, the more time you will have to set your completed report aside and think about it (see 'Writing to a plan', Chapter 12).

As you write your report

A scientific or technical report usually follows a highly structured format, and is expected to follow certain conventions in data presentation and writing style.

Format

Think about your report as a whole, rather than as an assortment of sections. However, each section should by itself convey intelligible information to your reader.

When considering the sections which make up a report, it is important to realise that there is *more than one format* for reports. For example:

- biomedical reports often consist of an Introduction, Materials and Methods, Results and Discussion
- reports in descriptive field sciences are likely to include an Introduction, Materials and Methods, Geographical Context, Analysis of Data, Results, and
- more theoretical papers may consist of an Introduction, Theoretical Analysis, Applications, and Conclusions.

In a first-year student report, you are probably given a title, expected to write a one or two-sentence introduction, and to describe the materials and methods as in the laboratory manual. Most of your own effort on the report is spent on your results and discussion sections. Occasionally reports require a cover page, a table of contents or illustrations or preface, and they may include recommendations, appendices and acknowledgements. It is not unusual for two sections, such as the Results and Discussion, or the Conclusions and Recommendations, to be combined when this makes sense.

It is *the purpose of each section* of a report which is important. Even if you are told which sections to use in your report, think about the function of each section in the whole report.

The following descriptions of report sections include some points which apply more to articles for publication than to conventional student reports. These points are mentioned because they relate to the purpose of a section, and as such need to be thought about early in your report writing career.

1 The title or 'What is the specific problem or the specific question being asked?'

Your title should attract a potential reader and should be short and specific, for example 'Resources and Environmental Management: Fundamental Concepts and Definitions', or 'Numerical Data Bases for Australian Science and Technology'. Use a subtitle if a fuller description is necessary, and for the sake of brevity omit words such as 'a', 'the', and 'on' where possible.

The title should state the problem posed or the question asked and indicate how this problem or question was approached; but a title is not a summary of your report. On the page headed 'Title' in your notebook, list key words and write the title before you write your full report. Check it for accuracy afterwards and ask yourself, 'Do the results and discussions actually answer the particular question or problem set out in the title?'

2 The synopsis or abstract or 'What are my main findings?'

Your synopsis or abstract is a précis of the content of your report, and is meant to be read in conjunction with the title. A synopsis should enable your reader to decide whether to read the whole report, so it should be intelligible by itself and should not be full of technical jargon. To help you clarify your ideas and plan your material, it may be useful to write the synopsis before the rest of your report. After the whole report is written, revise the synopsis to ensure that it presents the essential content of your report in a balanced manner.

A synopsis differs from a *summary*, the latter being a review included at the end of a report to help your readers understand your conclusions or recommendations. Such a summary includes more detail than a synopsis and may contain tables and figures.

3 The introduction or 'What did I do, and why?'

In Part One of formal scientific method, which is the statement of the
problem, the main skill is in stating absolutely no more than you are positive
you know. It is much better to enter a statement 'Solve Problem: Why
doesn't cycle work?' which sounds dumb but is correct, than it is to enter
a statement 'Solve Problem: What is wrong with the electrical system?'
when you don't absolutely *know* the trouble is in the electrical system.
What you should state is 'Solve Problem: What is wrong with cycle?' and
then state as the first entry of Part Two: 'Hypothesis Number One: The
trouble is in the electrical system'.

Robert M. Pirsig

The introduction should state the specific problem or question under
consideration, perhaps as an enlargement of the title.

- State clearly the purpose and scope of your work. If you are testing an
  hypothesis, introduce the relevant theoretical background.
- Discuss selected research studies which, when taken together, show
  that your work is logical and worthwhile within its field. Don't cite a
  large number of studies in the introduction. Either refer to any papers
  which review the relevant research literature or, if you want to discuss
  a large body of research literature, add a separate section after the
  introduction or a review which is separate from your report.
- Explain any unusual or complicated theoretical aspects of the subject
  which aren't covered by the literature, particularly if your readers
  include people without a strong background in the field.
- State the assumptions and limitations of your work, and define any
  technical terms as you introduce them.
- Paraphrase your conclusions if necessary, but without attempting to
  provide a review of these or of your results.

4 The materials and methods or 'How did I go about what I did?'

This section describes what you did in the order in which you did it, *so
that a reader with experience in the same field could repeat the experiment or
observations*. Strike a balance between being concise and giving sufficient
detail. To this end, a diagram of apparatus used can be preferable to a
long written description of the same apparatus.

- Broadly outline the overall experimental design or theoretical approach
  of your research, unless this is obvious from your introduction.
- Describe the subjects used (where applicable).
- List the apparatus used.
- Refer to any preliminary experiments and any changes of techniques
  you have made.
- State the conditions and procedures of the experiment and obser-
  vations.

- Describe sampling and control devices used.
- Describe measurement techniques used.
- Include your reasons for choosing a particular method if there were alternatives.

5 The results 'What did I observe or find?'

The purpose of this section is to present in a logical order a statement of your findings and observations. These should be supplemented with tables or graphs derived from an analysis of data recorded (see 'Data presentation' p. 188). In a student practical report, present your results accurately but don't simply provide large amounts of raw data—you are expected to show that you have thought about the raw data and translated them into an appropriate format. Your results are usually presented in relation to your hypothesis, and provide the building material for the discussion and conclusions.

If you can fully report the results in a few words or figures or in a simple table or graph, the Results section should be coherent on its own. If your results led to further experiments which produced further results (and so on), you might want to combine your results and discussion sections.

- Any raw data, or data to more decimal places than appropriate for the summaries in your results, should be placed in an appendix.
- State the number of results obtained, and your reasons for omitting any of these from this section.
- Give the results which support your conclusions (or lack thereof), but be careful that your selection doesn't distort the results in order to reach a particular conclusion.

6 The discussion or 'How have I interpreted the results and what are my answers to the specific question asked?'

> I am appalled by the frequent publication of papers that describe most minutely what experiments were done, and how, but with no hint of why, or what they mean. Cast thy data upon the waters, the authors seem to think, and they will come back interpreted.
>
> *F. Peter Woodford*

In some student practical reports you are only required to discuss whether your hypothesis is tenable or whether you have answered the question asked. Nevertheless, the discussion is the heart of your report and the section where you have the greatest opportunity for creative analysis. Your aim here is to interpret your results; show their significance in relation to your introduction; explain how the results add to what is already known; and discuss your work in relation to the theory underlying similiar studies.

- Discuss the precision of your results. Refer to or take them as read, rather than summarising them.
- Explain any irregularities, shortcomings or unexpected results. Note that these discrepancies, rather than being a problem, can often alert you to significant findings.
- Compare your results with the findings of studies that you mentioned in your introduction. To do this satisfactorily, check the original studies to find out exactly what other researchers did, how they did it, and the conclusions they drew, then report these findings accurately.
- Give theoretical explanations for the data discussed.
- Avoid any obviously subjective judgements, such as talking about 'excellent results' or 'highly useful data'.

The points in your discussion should be logically argued and developed, but the section should not be too discursive. Use subheadings to help your reader follow the stages of your argument unless your discussion is brief. The reader should be able to judge the validity of your conclusions from the information in the discussion.

7 The conclusions or 'What conclusions can justifiably be drawn?'

> The TV scientist who mutters sadly, 'The experiment is a failure; we have failed to achieve what we had hoped for,' is suffering mainly from a bad scriptwriter. The experiment is never a failure solely because it fails to achieve predicted results. An experiment is a failure only when it also fails adequately to test the hypothesis in question, when the data it produces don't prove anything one way or another.
>
> *Robert M. Pirsig*

State succinctly the conclusions which can justifiably be drawn from your work, and indicate their significance. If your results are inconclusive (for example, after a short student practical session), say so, give reasons for this, and suggest improvements or further work to be done. Don't present another summary of your results.

8 The references or 'Which studies did I cite?'

Your list of references should be in alphabetical order, and should consist only of reports or studies cited in your report, not literature consulted. When citing from references which report on other people's experiments, each reference should be checked if possible to ensure that any errors in citing the original experiment are not repeated (see 'Conventions' and 'Questions and mistakes').

ðŸ‚ ðŸ‚ ðŸ‚

Many student reports are intended to teach a scientific method and subject material, as well as to provide an exercise in writing. In this case you will be faced with the often-conflicting aims of showing your teacher how much you know about a subject, while including only necessary detail as expected in a professional report. When confronted with this dilemma, don't rehash textbook material on basic theory, and don't bury your discussion and conclusions under a mass of detail. Do talk about the problem with your teacher for suggestions on how the different aims can be reconciled or which one should have priority. When deciding what to include and what to omit, remember that in professional reports the readers usually know less about the subject than the author, while the reverse is presumably true of the readers and writers of student reports. However, don't assume that because your teacher knows a subject you should not explain it fully and clearly. Your teacher needs to know that you understand the basic principles of a subject.

Data presentation

Your data must be ordered, presented in a clear format, and interpreted, or your readers won't be able to make sense of them. How you order and present your data depends on a host of factors, but the guiding principle is always clarity. To achieve clarity, data are usually presented in tables and graphs, accompanied by an explanatory text.

Why use tables or graphs?

Use tables or graphs if they enable your reader to understand the data more clearly. Use them if, for example, they present data more concisely than words could, or if they enable your reader to visualise the relationships within your data. Use them at the beginning and end of your analysis of results to show the relationship between variables in a graphic form. Don't use tables or graphs simply for the sake of having them in the report.

How will you present data?

This depends on the information you have to convey. For example, don't use graphs if you have data for an insufficient number of points. Think about whether the relationships within your data can be displayed most effectively in a graph or in a table. Consider which form of presentation might be appropriate for your data when it is simple and when it is complex, when it is new and when it is repetitive.

Ordering data There is more than one way of ordering your data within a table or graph. If your reader has sufficient knowledge of the type of data you are presenting, you can arrange your information so that the patterns and exceptions are easily seen. If you can't assume your reader has this knowledge, supply a sentence or two interpreting the information presented. The patterns and exceptions should then be clear after your reader has read the interpretation. To achieve this clarity, think carefully about the ordering of your data, rather than putting it down in the first format which comes to mind. For example, when presenting tables these are some points to consider:

- Decide to what degree of accuracy you will present your figures. Depending on the purpose of your tables and the precision of your experiment, you may be able to round off your figures without losing any vital information. Your reader may do this anyhow to understand your table easily.
- Consider whether to present your data primarily in columns so that your reader's eye is led down the page, or in rows across the page. Which form makes it easier to see the patterns and exceptions in the data presented? In which form will the table fit most easily on the page?
- Decide whether to include aids such as averages, columns or rows, totals, maxima or minima, or percentages to help your reader interpret your data.
- Think about how to set out and space your material, for example where and how to divide columns of figures from each other.

Amount of information There is a limit to the amount of information you can convey in one table or graph. Often it is better to opt for several small tables or graphs rather than for one large complex one. This allows you to place each one close to the relevant text, and helps your reader focus on one or two aspects of your data at a time.

Labelling To label your graphs or tables:

- number them in consecutive order
- give each one a title which is precise but concise, and a legend to explain the elements it contains
- specify the units used in the headings for columns and rows, so that each entry in the column or row need be a number only, and
- indicate units and magnitudes clearly on the axes of a graph.

Table 13.1 A sample table

	Private Sector		Education		Public Sector	
	1972	1976	1972	1976	1972	1976
Arts & Social Sciences	35.1	31.2	38.3	41.5	26.5	27.2
Science	23.2	29.1	42.2	38.1	34.6	32.8
Engineering	42.6	58.2	5.0	4.4	52.5	37.4

First full-time employment of new graduates by subject and sector (Graduate Careers Council): as % of all those in subject group securing full-time employment.

Source: Graduate Careers Council of Australia (1972–76), 'First Destinations of University Graduates' cited by Stuart Macdonald, 'Unemployed Among Qualified Scientists and Engineers in Australia', in *Search*, vol. 10, no. 6, June 1979, p. 227.

Note that the author has:
- given figures to one decimal place
- presented the data as percentages rather than as raw data
- arranged the data primarily in columns
- presented the 'sector' headings at the top of the table and the 'subject' headings at the side
- arranged the data into three 'sectors' rather than putting together all the 1972 figures and all the 1976 figures, and
- given an explanatory title for the table.

Presenting data in tables and graphs is an integral part of communicating your findings from practical work. In student practical sessions you may have little latitude to opt for different forms of data presentation. But when you design experiments yourself, have someone who knows your subject look at your initial data presentation to see what it conveys to them, and try different formats and ordering of your data to see which one conveys most precisely what you want to say. Data presentation is a complex skill, and this section touches on only a few of the basic points. To learn how to convey information as concisely and unambiguously as possible, find people who are skilled in the use of data presentation techniques, and work with them on the results of your own experiments.

Writing styles and conventions

... execrable writing ... is the product of shoddy thinking, or careless condescension, or of pretentiousness.

F. Peter Woodford

Your writing style in scientific and technical reports is likely to be shaped by conventions about what 'scientific' thinking is. For example, you are usually expected to avoid using 'I' or 'we' when describing what you did or found because scientists are supposed to be impartial observers. Become familiar with the range of techniques available and practise these often so that they become part of your writing repertoire. Whatever conventions and style you choose, use them to help you report your findings more clearly, rather than to impress your reader or hide ignorance. The principles which underlie all successful communication also apply to scientific writing. Be lucid and unambiguous, and ask yourself:

'Exactly what do I want to say?'
'Why do I want to say it?'
'How can I say it most effectively?', and
'To whom am I saying it?'

Style

Reports should describe concisely what happened in an experiment or in field work—they should not be written in a narrative or story-telling style. Events are usually presented in chronological order, and arguments should develop logically, step by step. Write most of your report in prose, and be careful of over-using formulae and other abbreviations when the information they convey could easily be expressed in words.

Language

The language you use should not be too technical or too elementary. Your level of writing should be aimed at whoever will read your report and you should:

- define any new words or mathematical symbols when you first use them
- use technical terms accurately, for example, 'constantly' and 'efficient', and avoid careless use of words which can have a technical meaning, such as 'parameter' or 'factor'
- use chemical and pharmacological names rather than unfamiliar trade names
- write scientific names, proper names, numerical data, equations and formulae correctly, and
- opt for familiar, short or concrete words rather than unfamiliar, long or abstract ones.

I am a Bear of Very Little Brain, and long words Bother me.
A.A. Milne

Conventions

Check with your teacher which conventions you are expected to follow in a report. Some examples follow.

- Are you expected to use passive tense rather than active? For example, are you expected to write 'pH4 is needed by the enzyme' (passive) instead of 'the enzyme needed pH4' (active)? Using the passive tense does not in itself make your writing more scholarly, and active tenses generally make your writing more direct.
- Are you required to use past tense when describing your methods and reporting your results? Are you expected to use the present tense when stating facts which are generally agreed upon?
- Are some numbers to be written in words and some in figures? How are times and dates to be recorded?
- Will you number your report sections and sub-sections consecutively as in '2.1.1.', '2.1.2.', '2.1.3' etc.?

To cite *references*, it is customary to use the author's name and the year of publication in the body of your text, rather than using footnotes. For example:

'According to Brown (1959) ...'

'Recent studies (Black, 1975; White, 1976) show that...'

'After a thorough training, 'The student can no longer write; he pontificates' (Woodford, 1967).'

For references you cite but have not seen in the original:

'The mouse ran up the clock (Green, cited by Blue, 1971)...'

If you refer frequently to other research literature, the text may become so cluttered with bracketed references that it is difficult to read. In this case list all references at the end of the text (alphabetically or in order of appearance) and number each item. To cite one of these references, quote the number of that reference in your text. For example:

'The mouse ran up the clock [31]'

or

'The mouse ran up the clock (31)'.

Grammar, spelling, punctuation

If poor grammar, spelling and punctuation prevent you communicating clearly, work on these with the help of a good reference text on the subject (see Further reading for this chapter, and 'Grammar, spelling and punctuation', Chapter 14). Find a patient friend who's proficient in these skills and willing to proofread your work.

Sentences and paragraphs

Keep your sentences short and simple if in doubt about their length. Construct your paragraphs so that each one contains one idea (see 'The body of your assignment', Chapter 13). If you have trouble writing coherent sentences and paragraphs, work with someone who will help you improve these skills. Read and analyse plenty of well-written articles to get the feel of effective writing—*Science* and *Nature* are good sources of these.

۰   ۶۰ ۶۰ ۶۰

When your report is finished, set it aside if you have the time, so that you can come back to it with something of the approach of a person reading it for the first time. While it is set aside, think about what you have written and make occasional corrections—but allow yourself some distance from it before you prepare your final version.

Editing the report

Check through the **contents** of your report. If some of your report seems irrelevant or too detailed, prune it ruthlessly. See if you have covered all the points in 'As you write'. Have you:

* recorded all experimental information such as strength of solutions, ambient temperature, specification of instruments?
* put units against all your measurements and results?
* defined all symbols?
* checked your calculations?
* compared your results with expected or established results, and
* dated your work?

Look at your **writing style**. Be prepared to replace an inappropriate word and to re-write a clumsy sentence or paragraph. Proofread your report for mistakes or omissions in details such as spelling, grammar and punctuation, or ask someone else to read your work to point out incorrect details and to suggest ways in which you can polish your writing style. When you have edited the content and style of your report, write or type a clean, legible copy (see 'Presentation', Chapter 13).

Writing a scientific report involves putting words on paper, but it also involves thinking about and planning what you want to say as you take notes during an experiment or fieldwork, as you begin to draft your whole report, and when working on your final draft. As you try to express exactly what you want to say, the process of writing itself can set off new ideas and make you look again at old ones. And remember, writing is you communicating about your work to your reader.

Questions and mistakes

Many students see experiments and practical work as exercises to be gone through to find the Right answers. Yet any real learning for you as an individual follows from the questions you ask for information, *because you* want to know. Following procedures laid down by someone else to answer a question asked by someone else inevitably leads to someone else's answers. You can learn from someone else's answers—but only if their answers have a connection with your questions (see Chapter 4).

You interpret the results of an experiment according to the hypothesis being tested, and according to what you expected to find. The way a question is asked, a problem stated or an hypothesis worded influences the results you are likely to come up with. Even researchers who start with the same hypothesis and arrive at similiar results can and do interpret those results to reach considerably different conclusions. Their results and conclusions are then interpreted by other researchers in the light of their own hypotheses and findings and opinions. To discover how scientific research has developed in an area, and just how shaky 'facts' can be, take a paper on a specific topic, and read through the originals of any studies cited in that paper. Read these original studies carefully, and compare their actual findings with the way in which these findings have been cited in the later paper. It is not uncommon to find noticeable discrepancies between the two.

> School books even more rarely tell us how thinkers of the past have gone about trying to answer their own questions, and still more rarely, what mistakes they made along the way. A graduate student in Psychology suggested one day to a noted professor in that field that there should be a publication in which psychologists would write about their mistakes, the hunches that had not worked out, the experiments that had not proved what they meant to prove; or didn't prove anything. The professor agreed that such a publication would teach students a great deal about the doing of psychology. But, he said, there was no use even thinking about such a publication, because no-one with a reputation to defend would ever put anything in it. So we find it hard to find most of our mistakes because we are so rarely told how the do-ers of the past came to make and later find theirs.
>
> *John Holt*

If, at the end of an experiment or fieldwork, you have not found the answers you expected, if your results are inconclusive or point to other answers, don't automatically think you have failed. Think about what you did and try to discover *why* your results were inconclusive or unexpected. If you made a mistake, acknowledge it. If your work could be improved, suggest how this might be done. If you discover related questions, or areas to be explored for a more complete answer, suggest these as part of your report. Don't try to hide your unexpected or inconclusive results, or distort them to produce the Right answers. You can learn much by analysing your mistakes.

ᶻᵃ ᶻᵃ ᶻᵃ

You can learn as much from writing a report of observations made in the laboratory or field as you can from doing the practical work about which you write. The challenge of trying to describe your work accurately, logically and lucidly for someone else to read and understand should make you think about what you actually did. In serious research, describing your work helps you think about how to design and conduct experiments or a set of observations, and about the nature of the disciplines in which you are working and writing. What do you think science is all about? Or technology? Your answers to these questions will shape and be shaped by the reports you write about your scientific and technical work.

Further reading

Bailey, R.F. 1984. *A Survival Kit for Writing English*. 2nd edn, Longman Cheshire, Melbourne.

Barrass, Robert. 1978. *Scientists Must Write: A Guide to Better Writing for Scientists, Engineers and Students*. Chapman and Hall, London.

Booth, Vernon. 1979. *Writing a Scientific Paper*. 4th edn, The Biochemical Society, London.

Cooper, Bruce M. 1964. *Writing Technical Reports*. Penguin Books, Harmondsworth.

Lewis, John. 1982. *The Usborne Pocket Calculator Book*. Davies, Helen (ed.). Usborne Publishing, London.

Lindsay, David. 1984. *A Guide to Scientific Writing*. Longman Cheshire, Melbourne.

O'Connor, M., & Woodford, F.P. 1978. *Writing Scientific Papers in English: An ELSE-Ciba Foundation Guide for Authors*. Pitman Medical, London.

Pauley, Steven E. 1979. *Technical Report Writing Today*. 2nd edn, Houghton Mifflin Company, Boston.

14

Using Conventions

'... besides that's not a regular rule; you invented it just now.'
'It's the oldest rule in the book,' said the King.
'Then it ought to be Number One,' said Alice.

Lewis Carroll

When using conventions in your written assignments it is useful to understand their **purposes** rather than simply following rules. For example, the standard conventions used by most Western publishers serve as a shorthand to make writing and reading easier. Much of this shorthand has its origins in the reporting of scientific research where the reader needs to be able to follow up references to understand or evaluate a report fully.

If citing a reference or paraphrasing an idea in a piece of writing, acknowledge your source. It may seem unimportant and pedantic to give full details of the reference. For example:

Savage, Jo. 1979. *The Film 'Fangs'*. Wolf Publications, Alaska. p. 54.

However, if you omit any of this information (for example, if you refer only to 'Savage's book on the movie *Fangs*'), your reader has to ask for further information to know how recent the book is, who the author is, the book's title, where the book was published, and precisely where in the book to find the reference.

Individual academic disciplines and publications and individual teachers frequently adopt their own variations of the standard conventions. The essential elements are the same but the conventions of the format used vary. Whichever format you use, be *consistent* and *accurate*. Check with a teacher about the conventions you are expected to follow in a discipline, programme, course or assignment, and find out the teacher's personal preferences in these matters.

> Either stick to tradition or see that your inventions be consistent.
>
> *Horace*

But don't let the punctilious observance of correct conventions become the focus of your writing. *Use* them as necessary to help you communicate more clearly—and if in doubt about which one to use or whether to use them at all, rely on your common sense to convey clearly and accurately to your reader what you want to say.

> This chapter outlines why and how to use quotations, references and bibliographies and is based on the conventions set out in the Australian Government's *Style Manual* (although these conventions are universally recognised).[1] The chapter also looks at the question of plagiarism, and at some conventions for presenting an assignment.

All of the examples in the chapter are taken from material written about the sea, a place where human conventions are subservient to nature.

Quotations

> I might repeat to myself, slowly and soothingly, a list of quotations beautiful from minds profound; if I can remember any of the damn things.
>
> *Dorothy Parker*

Why use quotations?

Quotations can be useful:

- to express a thought or concept succinctly
- to illustrate a point you want to make
- to convey the flavour of a work, or
- when analysing the quotation in depth.

How to present quotations

Long quotations

These should be set apart from the main body of your writing so that they are easily identified. If a quote is longer than about twenty words or two complete sentences, introduce the quotation with a colon. Identify it by using one or more of the following:

* miss a line above and below the quotation
* indent from the left
* use single-spaced typescript when the rest of the text is double-spaced
* reference the information as required.

For example:

* ... In his book *Sailing to the Reefs*, Bernard Moitessier (1971, p.83) discusses the motivation behind single-handed sailing:

  And it is, I believe, this need not simply for novelty, but for physical and spiritual cleanliness which drives the lone sailor towards other shores; there, his body and mind are freed from their terrestrial ties and bondage, and can regain their essence and integrity in the natural elements which the ancients deified.

  This description captures the spirituality of the experience ...

* A familiar children's poem describes an unusual sea voyage:

  The Owl and the Pussy-Cat went to sea
  In a beautiful pea-green boat,
  They took some honey, and plenty of money,
  Wrapped up in a five-pound note.[2]

Short quotations

These are usually part of your text and are enclosed by quotation marks. For example:

Truly immersed in the experience, 'one forgets oneself, one forgets everything, seeing only the play of the boat with the sea, the play of the sea around the boat...' (Moitessier, 1975, p.52) as the present takes priority over all else.

If quoting a couple of lines of poetry within your text, you need not set them apart and can indicate the division between the lines with an oblique. For example:

The single-handed sailor knows the power of being 'Alone, alone, all, all, alone, / Alone on a wide, wide sea!'[3]

Paraphrasing and plagiarism

With just enough of learning to misquote.
Lord Byron

When you paraphrase, you re-express another person's thoughts in your own words and acknowledge their source. You plagiarise if you take someone else's thoughts and writings and present them as your own. Plagiarism also has a cultural basis in that modern writers and researchers in the Western tradition expect to be fully acknowledged if their ideas or their work are referred to in any way. Failure to acknowledge or cite another person's work is called plagiarism and is treated very seriously in universities and colleges.

Plagiarism often results in an unsatisfactory piece of work because, for example, your writing style differs awkwardly from that of the plagiarised piece, or the section you have copied is not exactly relevant to your overall theme. You may not know that it is unacceptable to copy from a source without acknowledgement, and may inadvertently include in your own work phrases, sentences or paragraphs from another source. More extreme forms of plagiarism (cheating or stealing) occur when a student copies, with or without minor changes, an entire article or chapter, or another student's essay.

In most instances, teachers are familiar with the relevant source material and can easily diagnose a case of plagiarism. Otherwise, they may ask another teacher to read your work, make a thorough search for the original source, or discuss the paper with you. If plagiarism is confirmed, there are several possible courses of action for a teacher. You may be asked to write another paper, the piece of work could be failed, or work completed out of class might be disregarded and you may be expected to sit for an exam. Sometimes official disciplinary action is taken and in serious cases a student may be expelled from the institution. In any case, reading the work of a student who has plagiarised someone else's words and ideas is a disheartening experience for a teacher.

Lies were such small things, like stones that you pitched into the water. The stones disappeared, but the water rippled out into ever widening circles that you couldn't ever catch and put back.

Ivy Baker

How to avoid plagiarising

• You may be tempted to plagiarise if you are not confident about your knowledge of a subject or your writing ability, or because you feel pressured by work. If so, talk about these difficulties with someone who can help you (and use any relevant sections of this book) rather than resorting to plagiarism and being confronted with the same problems later on.

- When taking notes from material, read a section, put the reference aside and express the idea in your own words (see 'Notetaking and/or underlining', Chapter 8). If you copy any words exactly, put them in quotation marks; or if you want to use another writer's words or ideas, clearly identify the beginning and end of paraphrasing. In both cases note the page reference.
- When writing, put quotes in quotation marks or indent longer quotes. For quotes or paraphrases, use footnotes, endnotes or textual references to acknowledge the source. You can indicate clearly where a paraphrase begins by acknowledging the author immediately before in your text, for example, 'Humphries says...'. If you take an opinion from someone else, don't disguise it by using the passive tense, such as 'It has been said that...'. If you use factual information, for example statistics that are not common knowledge, acknowledge the source.

References

Why include references?

References are used:

- to give the source of a quotation or paraphrase so that your reader can locate this item if they want to
- to give the source of authority for a 'fact' which a reader might question as true, or
- to make a cross reference to another part of your text.

How to reference material

Textual references

These author–date references enable a reader to continue reading your text smoothly, and may be used in conjunction with footnotes or endnotes which comment on your text. They are the accepted form of referencing in scientific reports and have become more acceptable in the social sciences and humanities. These references give the author's surname and the year of publication, and need to include page numbers for quotes or for references to a specific item in a source. For example:

> Bernard Moitessier (1975, p. 4) describes sailboats as living creatures.

> Sailboats are sometimes described as living creatures (Moitessier 1975, p. 4).

Textual references are brief so they are used to refer to a work already under discussion and they must be complemented by providing full details of the item in a bibliography.

- If bibliography items are numbered, refer simply to the number of the item and the relevant pages in that item. For example:

  Sometimes sailboats are described as living creatures (2:4).

- If an author has more than one publication in a year, distinguish these with letters after the year, for example:

  1978a and 1978b.

- If work by more than one author is cited, present them as follows:

  (Moitessier 1975; Letcher 1974), or

  Moitessier (1975) and Letcher (1974).

- If a work has two or three authors, the format used is:

  (Pardey & Pardey 1979), or

  Pardey & Pardey (1979).

Footnotes

These allow for more information on the same page about your source. As well as being used to acknowledge a source in detail, a footnote may comment on or support what you have written in your main text.[4]

Footnotes appear on the same page as the reference. A number follows after the quotation or paraphrase you are referencing and is repeated at the foot of the page.[5] Footnotes may be numbered consecutively throughout your text or numbered separately for each page or chapter.

The first time you acknowledge a particular book in a footnote give whichever of the following details are available and applicable, so that your reader can locate the work if they want to:

- the author/editor's name (surname last)
- the year of publication
- the title of the book (underlined or italicised)
- the translator/illustrator/reviser's name
- the publication details (edition, publisher, place), and
- the page reference. For example:

  Francis Chichester, 1967, *Gipsy Moth Circles the World*, Hodder and Stoughton, London, p. 67.

- For immediately consecutive footnotes referring to the same source, in the second footnote use the author's surname and the page numbers. For example:

  1 David Lewis, 1969, *Children of Three Oceans*, Collins, London, p. 60.

  2 Lewis, p. 66.

- If there is more than one item by the same author, give the author's name in each case and follow it with the title and page numbers of the individual item.
- If there is more than one author with the same surname, give forenames also.

Endnotes

These serve the same purposes as footnotes. If too much space would be taken up in your text with numerous, lengthy or complicated footnotes, use endnotes. They can be easier for your reader to refer to and are easier to lay out in the final draft of an assignment, especially if this is being typed. However, as with footnotes, if you have too many endnotes in relation to the length of your assignment, consider whether the assignment is adequately planned.

When compiling endnotes, all reference notes that would have appeared as footnotes are collected at the end of your assignment. Number these references consecutively throughout your text, and apply the same rules of abbreviation to them as to footnotes. It's useful for your reader if endnotes can be detached from your text for easier reference, and if they are headed 'References' to distinguish them instantly from a bibliography.

Table 14.1 Abbreviations and contractions

app.	—	appendix
bk, bks	—	book (s)
©	—	copyright
c. (*circa*)	—	about a certain date [as in '*c.* 1901']
ch., chs (or chap., chaps)	—	chapter(s)
col., cols	—	column(s)
diss.	—	dissertation
ed., eds	—	editor(s)
edn	—	edition
et al. (*et alii*)	—	'and others' [used when a book has several authors, as in 'P. March *et al.*'].
et seq. (*et sequentes*)	—	'and following' [as in 'pp. 64 *et seq.*']
f., ff.	—	'and the following' [to refer to page numbers as in 'pp. 30 ff.']
facsim.	—	facsimile [that is, an exact copy of writing, printing, picture]
fol., fols	—	folio(s)

front.	—	frontispiece
ibid. (*ibidem*)	—	'in the same work' [as previously cited]
ill., ills	—	illustrator(s)
loc. cit. (*loco citato*)	—	'in the same place (already) cited' [that is, in the same passage referred to in a recent reference note]
ms, mss	—	manuscript(s)
n., nn.	—	note(s) [as 'p. 56, n. 3' or 'p. 56 n.']
n.d.	—	no date [of publication]
n.p.	—	no place [of publication]
op. cit. (*opere citato*)	—	in the work [recently] cited
p., pp.	—	page(s)
passim	—	'throughout the work' [rather than on specific pages]
q.v., qq.v. (*quod vide*)	—	'which see' [used in cross referencing]
rev.	—	revised [by], reviser
[*sic*]	—	'thus so' [to guarantee exact quotation when the reader might doubt this]
trans., tr.	—	translator, -ion, -ed
v., vv.	—	verse(s)
viz. (*videlicet*)	—	'namely', 'in other words' [usually after words or statements about to be elaborated]
vol., vols	—	volume(s)

Bibliographies

Why include a bibliography?

A bibliography is designed:

* to provide full details of the works mentioned in textual references
* to provide a complete or selected list of the sources you consulted in preparation for writing an assignment, and
* to provide annotations, that is, brief commentaries on your sources.[6]

If you have used fully detailed footnotes or endnotes and if these cover all your sources, you may not need to provide a bibliography. However, it is useful for your reader to see all of your sources listed together, and you will usually be expected to prepare a bibliography for all assignments whether written, oral, taped or audiovisual.

How to present a bibliography

Book entry

The basic format for these entries in a bibliography is:

- author or editor's name (surname first)
- year of publication
- title (underlined or italicised)
- the translator, illustrator or reviser's name
- publication details.

For example:

> Colgate, Stephen. 1978. *Fundamentals of Sailing, Cruising and Racing*. W.W. Norton and Company, New York.

An article, chapter, or anthology item

The basic format for such entries in a bibliography is:

- author or editor's name (surname first, followed by forename or initials)
- year of publication
- title of article, chapter or item, enclosed by inverted commas
- author or editor of the book in which the chapter or item is found
- title (underlined or italicised) of the periodical, book, anthology or newspaper from which the item was taken
- publication details of periodical or book, and
- page numbers of article, chapter or item.

For example:

> Burke, K.M. 1979. 'A Dream in Ice and Snow'. *Cruising World*. Newport, Rhode Island, vol. 5, no. 1, January, pp. 60-63.
>
> Crealock, W.I.B. 1955. *The Far Side of the Moon*. Cloud of Islands. David McKay Company, New York.

Additional points

- Publication details are as follows:
  - periodical: place (if overseas), volume number, issue number (if pages are numbered afresh for each issue), date
  - book: edition (if not the first edition), place, publisher, date.
- If there is more than one entry for an author, list these entries in chronological order of publication.
- Entries may be classified into groups according to topic or the nature of the material, for example:
  - 'Primary Sources' and 'Secondary Sources'
  - 'Books' and 'Articles'
  - 'Items from Newspapers' and 'Personal Conversations'.

- The heading of a bibliography should indicate its scope, for example, 'Selected Bibliography', 'Brief Annotated Bibliography' or 'A General Bibliography'.

Table 14.2 Bibliography entries

Books
One author
 Van Dorn, William G. 1974. *Oceanography and Seamanship.* Dodd, Mead and Company, New York.

Two authors
 Pardey, L., & Pardey, L. 1979. *Seraphyn's European Adventures.* W.W. Norton and Company, New York.

Three or more authors
 Pariser, E.L. *et al.* 1978. *Fish Protein Concentrate: Panacea for Protein Malnutrition?* M.I.T. Press, Boston, Mass.

Repeat entry by same author
 Letcher, John S. Jr. 1974. *Self Steering for Sailing Craft.* International Marine Publishing Company, Camden, Maine.
 —— 1977. *Self-Contained Celestial Navigation with H.O. 208.* International Marine Publishing Company, Camden, Maine.

Author and translator
 Moitessier, Bernard. 1975. *The Long Way.* Trans. William Rodarmor. Doubleday and Company, New York.

Editor
 Kemp, Peter (ed.). 1976. *The Oxford Companion to Ships and the Sea.* Oxford University Press, London.

Unknown author
 The Voyage of Governor Phillip to Botany Bay. 1790. London.

Corporate author
 Naval Training Command. 1972. *A Navigational Compendium.* 2nd edn, Government Printing Office, Washington, D.C.

Article (unsigned) from reference book
 'Oceanography'. 1968. *Encyclopedia of the Sciences.* 2nd edn, Sill, W.B., & Hoss, N. (eds), Grosset & Dunlop, New York.

Excerpt from book not read in original but seen reproduced in another book
 Robertson, Dougal. 1973. 'Sunk by a Whale' in *Survive the Savage Sea.* Elek Books, London. In Stevenson, Ralph (ed.). 1978. *Small Boats and Big Seas: A Hundred Years of Yachting.* David McKay Company, New York.

Table 14.2 Bibliography entries *continued*

Chapter of a book where both are by the same author

Crealock, W.I.B. 1955. 'Stainless Steel and Panties', *Cloud of Islands*. David McKay Company, New York.

Article from edited book (author and editor different)

Fuller, R. Buckminster. 1970. 'Formula for a Floating City' in Dunstan, M.J., & Garian, P.J. (eds). *Worlds in the Making.* Prentice-Hall, New Jersey.

Journals, newspapers

Article from journal

Lundberg, Madeleine. 1979. 'Eugenie Clark: Shark Tamer'. *Ms.* VIII, 2 August, pp. 12-21.

Article from newspaper

Heydon, Neville. 1980. 'Right Port for Jan'. *The Mercury.* Hobart, 14 February, p. 1.

Oral information

Information from a lecture

Macbeth, J.W. 1991. 'Participant Research: Ocean Cruisers, a Study of a Deviant Subculture'. Lecture, Murdoch University, 4 June.

Information from a television or radio programme

'Voyage to the Ice'. 1978. Australian Broadcasting Commission, Sydney, 27 September.

Personal conversation

Driscoll, John. 1978. Personal conversation with author.

Interview

Fletcher, Dorothy. 1978. Interviewed by Jim Macbeth, 9 September.

The finishing touches

You are expected to present your work clearly and to use correct grammar, spelling and punctuation in writing assignments and reports. Check with a teacher and with reference books if you are uncertain about the conventions you are expected to follow in these matters.

Grammar, spelling and punctuation

'He has got no good red blood in his body,' said Sir James.
'No. Somebody put a drop under a magnifying-glass, and it was all semi-colons and parentheses,' said Mrs. Cadwallader.

George Eliot

A sound knowledge of grammar helps you write more fluently and is an important part of the writer's craft. Your ideas have less impact if your

Differences between bibliographies and reference notes

Bibliographies	Reference Notes
Surname followed by forename or initials	Surname follows the forename or initials
Alphabetical listing by surname of author/editor	Consecutive listing as the notes first appear in the text
Items need not be numbered	Each item numbered
Subtitle and series information given (where applicable)	Subtitle and series information often omitted
May be annotated	No annotation
Page reference for articles but not for entire books or journal issues	Page references for each item
Full stops used to separate certain sections	Commas used to separate sections

grammar, spelling and punctuation are poor, since your reader frequently has to re-read what you have written to clarify what you meant to say. To improve these skills, consult books and ask for help from other people. You may have to learn by heart the correct forms and usages, but if you can discover underlying reasons for a particular rule you remember the correct version more easily. Read your work aloud to yourself (possibly into a tape recorder) and check the grammar and punctuation of any sections which don't flow smoothly. If you use a computer, use the spell checker facility of your word processing program, and if is possible develop your own dictionary for your computer. If English is not your first language and you have trouble with grammar and punctuation, ask for help from a language adviser.

'I struggle through the alphabet as if it had been a bramble bush; getting considerably worried and scratched by every letter.'

Charles Dickens

Presentation

The purpose of presenting work clearly is to help your reader.

• Legible writing saves your reader from eye strain and irritation. Assignments should be typed, printed or clearly written in ink. When hand writing, take care with details such as dotting your 'i's accurately or forming your 'r's clearly, as these make your writing surprisingly easier to read. If your handwriting is atrocious, persuade a friend to write or type your assignments for you, or learn to type yourself.

- Keep a copy in case your reader happens to lose your assignment. If you use a computer, save your work on disk.
- Do not overcrowd each page. If your work is typed or printed from a computer, leave space on the sides and at the top and bottom. A wide left hand margin (at least 4 cm) enables your reader to write full and detailed comments.
- For easy identification, provide a cover sheet giving your name, the assignment title, course, teacher's name, and date on which the assignment is due and the date of submission. The cover sheet may also include an abstract or synopsis (see 'Synopsis', Chapter 13).
- Number the pages.
- Write or type on only one side of the paper, particularly if you write in ink or on lightweight paper. However, as this is environmentally wasteful, if you wish to save paper explain this to your teacher.
- Secure all pages firmly together. Any appendices to which the reader will refer frequently should be detachable (for example, endnotes or tables of results).
- To help your reader understand the structure of a long assignment you may decide to provide a contents page. This could be accompanied by a list of any diagrams, graphs or appendices.

> No publication, whatever its nature, should be expected to follow slavishly any set of rules—by whomsoever prescribed—if to do so would have an adverse effect on the text as a whole. What counts above all is consistency of approach and treatment; and for that reason, discretion, sensitivity and sheer common sense should always prevail in writing and editing.
>
> *Australian Government Publication Service*

ᔛ ᔛ ᔛ

Use conventions to help you say what you want to as lucidly as possible. Don't worry about the correct form of academic conventions so much that they prevent you from writing effectively. Become familiar with the basic conventions and their purposes, check which forms to follow for a particular piece of work, and then rely on your common sense to convey what you want to say to a reader. If you have trouble with using any convention, find yourself an efficient proofreader and work at overcoming your difficulties.

Bibliography (for textual references)

Letcher, John S. Jr. 1974. *Self Steering for Sailing Craft.* International Marine Publishing Company, Camden, Maine.

Moitessier, B. 1971. *Sailing to the Reefs*. Translated by Rene Hague. Hollis and Carter, London.

Moitessier, B. 1975. *The Long Way*. Translated by W. Rodamor. Granada, London.

Pardey, L. & Pardey, L. 1979. *Seraphyn's European Adventures*. W.W. Norton and Company, New York.

Further reading

Australian Government Publishing Service. 1988. *Style Manual: For Authors, Editors and Printers of Australian Government Publications*. 4th edn, AGPS, Canberra.

Bate, Douglas, & Sharpe, Peter. 1990. *Student Writer's Handbook: How to Write Better Essays*. Harcourt Brace Jovanovich, Sydney.

Bailey, R.F. 1984. *A Survival Kit for Writing English*. 2nd edn, Longman Cheshire, Melbourne.

Bullock, Alan, Stallybrass, Oliver, & Trombley, Stephen. 1988. *The Fontana Dictionary of Modern Thought*. Fontana Press, Glasgow.

Collins. 1987. *Cobuild English Language Dictionary*. Collins, London and Glasgow.

Gibaldi, Joseph, & Achtert, Walter S. 1988. *The MLA Handbook for Writers of Research Papers, Theses, and Dissertations*. 3rd edn, Modern Language Association of America, New York.

Landau, Sidney I., & Bogus, Ronald J. 1987. *The Doubleday Roget's Thesaurus in Dictionary Form*. Doubleday, Sydney.

Murray-Smith, Stephen. 1990. *Right Words: A Guide to English Usage in Australia*. Penguin, Ringwood.

Roget, P.M. 1962. *Thesaurus of English Words and Phrases*. Revised by Dutch, Robert A. Longman, London.

Turabian, Kate L. 1987. *A Manual for Writers of Term Papers, Theses, and Dissertations*. 5th edn, The University of Chicago Press, Chicago.

Whitaker-Wilson, C. 1975. *Punctuation*. Sun Books, Melbourne.

Notes

[1] A variety of conventions have been used in this book to provide examples for you to follow. The quotations, for example, use an endnote system (See 'Sources') whereas in this chapter textual references have been used. Some of the endnotes in this chapter could easily have been presented as footnotes.

[2] Edward Lear. 1943. *Nonsense Omnibus*. Frederick Warne and Company, London, p. 251.

[3] Ernest Hartley Coleridge (ed.), 1912, *The Poems of Samuel Taylor Coleridge*, Oxford University Press, London, p. 196.

[4] Lengthy footnotes suggest that your essay has not been planned with sufficient care, and they break from the flow of the text for your reader. In such cases, ask yourself if the footnote information is really necessary. If it is, consider whether the information should be incorporated into the assignment or placed as an appendix to the text.

[5] The quotation or paraphrase may be a word or phrase, a sentence or a paragraph.

[6] A bibliography can also be a self-contained work which gives an exhaustive list of works on a topic.

15

Learning from Evaluation

"...BUT I ONLY GAVE MYSELF A C."

If you want to learn to speak Italian, you learn more quickly if you live among Italians. You can evaluate your pronunciation constantly by comparing it with what you hear, and you receive instant feedback when you practise your new language skills.

If you want to take a more effective part in discussion groups, you need frequent practice in talking and listening in groups. At the same time, you need to think about your strengths and weaknesses as a group member, and how to improve. You can then evaluate your participation and make more use of any feedback you receive from other people in a group.

In both these instances, evaluation and feedback are fundamental to your learning. Part of the evaluation you need to do for yourself, for example, to compare your pronunciation or evaluate your group participation. On the basis of what you want to learn you appraise your learning so that your goals and your strengths and weaknesses emerge more clearly. You may discover, for example, that you want to learn more colloquial Italian so you can take part in day-to-day conversations, or you may decide that in discussions you need to practise listening carefully to other people. These discoveries provide you with further criteria for evaluating what you learn—and so the learning process continues.

This chapter emphasises that evaluation—whether your own or other people's—should help rather than hinder the process of your learning. The chapter looks at the purposes of evaluation, at who evaluates your learning and how this is carried out by feedback and recorded assessment. In conclusion, we list some of the assumptions underlying the evaluation of your formal learning.

In your formal learning you both give and receive responses. If a friend asks for helpful comments on an essay, what sort of comments might you make? You could respond with the first thoughts that come into your head. You might write down your reactions in detail, confine yourself to a few pithy statements at the end of the essay, or discuss your comments with your friend. If you do discuss your comments, you will probably modify some of your criticisms as you come to understand more clearly what your friend was trying to achieve. And if you don't already realise it, you will soon come to know that your responses are subjective— they come from your preferences and beliefs which arise from your personal experiences of learning in particular cultures. Do you believe that you know how 'good' essays should be written? If you judge your friend's work according to a particular model of what is desirable in essay writing, you need to explain this model so that your friend can accept or reject it. Your comments will be more useful if you make it clear that you are giving personal reactions to the work.

When you are in a situation where your understanding of a topic is to be assessed, how would you prefer to prove what you know? What would you submit: writing you have done, other people's comments on your work, your own evaluation? Could this evidence adequately demonstrate what you have learnt? You might want to discuss what you know with the people assessing you, or to take an exam on the topic. What particular aspects of your learning would you want to be tested? Who do you think could best assess these? Answering these questions involves thinking about your reasons for learning. These reflections in turn might lead you to ask if you wanted or needed someone else to assess your knowledge at all, and to ask 'What are the purposes of evaluation?'

Why evaluation?

Your objectives

One explicit purpose attributed to formal evaluation is to help you learn further, to help you progress towards your objectives (see 'Why remember?', Chapter 5). Being able to ask for and use evaluation and feedback requires that you think about your purposes for undertaking an assignment or a course, about why you want to learn. Think about *what* you want to learn, and ask yourself *how* and *when* you want to learn. These questions are often too complex to answer fully, but unless you are content mostly to follow the goals other people set for you, you need to consider them seriously. Your purposes will probably evolve further during your learning, so re-formulate them as this happens. If your objectives are clear, you can use them as criteria to evaluate whether, what and how well you are learning.

You are likely to modify your abilities or behaviour or ideas according to the responses and evaluation you receive when you try to communicate and practise what you are learning. These changes may be slight, for instance when you learn how to pronounce a word more accurately; or they may be a new cornerstone in your learning, for instance if you gain a significant new insight into how people behave in groups. The feedback you have received then becomes an integral part of learning according to your objectives. (This contrasts, for example, with an exam at the end of a course which tests your knowledge according to others' objectives and from which you gain no feedback.)

However, sometimes you don't have enough experience and knowledge to make use of the information in a response you are given, and at other times you reject feedback because it 'feels wrong' or doesn't fit with your knowledge or beliefs. Being able to use other people's responses to your learning depends on being ready for them.

Proving your knowledge

A schoolgirl answered the question 'In what countries are elephants found?'
'Elephants are very large and intelligent animals, and are seldom lost.'
James Agate

Another explicit purpose of formal evaluation is proving your knowledge to satisfy *other people's objectives*. These people are usually teachers who directly assess your work, and they also include academic and administrative committees within a university or college, professional bodies, and prospective employers. Their objectives are grounded in particular cultural expectations of higher education.

When you begin a programme, course, or assignment, the objectives your teachers have planned for it should be clearly formulated. These objectives should preferably be set down in writing so you can refer to them, and you should be able to discuss them with your teachers and other students. When teachers don't set out clear objectives, this may be because they are unaware of them beforehand and/or because they have not thought them through in detail. Teachers may also choose to conceal their aims. For example, early in a course you may be given a written assignment to introduce you to a basic area of knowledge and at the same time to diagnose your writing abilities. To test you more 'effectively' you may not be told about the second objective.

Like you, teachers often develop new objectives as a programme or course progresses, perhaps as implicit purposes become obvious or in response to the particular group of students taking the course. As new objectives emerge, they should be discussed with you. To decide whether or not you accept your teachers' objectives, be clear about your own.

Teachers often use their evaluation to judge if you are ready to move on to what they consider more difficult material. This use of evaluation is important in subjects which teach a sequence of physical skills, where a thorough knowledge of the preliminary steps is necessary to cope with the more demanding ones. This sequential model is often applied to intellectual learning, and sequences are constructed according to particular models of a body of knowledge. For example, unless you understand and can do what a teacher defines as elementary grammar, you are not permitted to move to more advanced language courses. These sequences are not essential for you to learn a subject—they are not inherent in the material. You *can* take structured courses in Italian which formally evaluate your learning at various stages; but you *can* learn Italian by living in Italy and immersing yourself in the language.

> ... reading, unlike dancing, is not a muscular act, and it is a serious mistake to treat it like one. The dance master [*sic*] must stretch and strengthen the student's muscles so that the student may make the next movement, and without injury. But one cannot injure oneself with a difficult thought.
>
> *John Holt*

Who evaluates your learning?

> It is much more difficult to judge oneself than to judge others.
> *A. de Saint-Exupèry*

Who gives you feedback on your learning?
Who formally assesses your work?

You should be the first person to evaluate your work. Make your evaluation more than a passing reflection or a casual comment to a friend. Compare what you have learnt with your objectives and with the aims of a programme, course or assignment. Other people can help you reach your objectives by evaluating your learning with these objectives in mind. However, you should know your objectives, abilities and previous learning best, so by these criteria you are the best person to decide how well you are learning. If when you hand in an assignment you also submit a written evaluation of the piece, your teacher is more able to provide you with comments to help further your learning.

A discussion or study group to which you belong can give you feedback on work such as an essay plan or a seminar presentation (see 'Share your writing', Chapter 11). The group may formally assess some or all of your work. This alternative to more traditional assessment requires thorough planning to work well, but people in groups which undertake this collective responsibility gain a great deal from their involvement in each other's learning. If you are willing to have your biases and assumptions challenged you may actively seek comments from a group with a diversity of ideas.

An adviser whom you seek out to be your sounding board can provide you with help ranging from correcting spelling errors in a report to giving a detailed critique of a major assignment. This adviser might be a sympathetic teacher, a learning counsellor, a language adviser, a student who has previously taken the course, or a friend.

A teacher with whom you work in a course is usually responsible for formally assessing your work, sometimes in collaboration with you or other teaching staff. The amount of informal feedback teachers give you varies according to their teaching styles—and to your willingness to ask for comments.

> I wrote my name at the top of the page. I wrote down the number of the question '1'. After much reflection, I put a bracket around it thus '(1)'. But thereafter I could not think of anything connected with it that was either relevant or true... It was from these slender indications of scholarship that Mr Welldon drew the conclusion that I was worthy to pass into Harrow. It is very much to his credit.
>
> *Winston Churchill*

Ideally the person who comments on your ideas and work should be someone you find stimulating as a teacher. They should also be someone you respect, whether or not they share many of your assumptions and beliefs. Your commentator also needs to be easily accessible. Your official teacher may be difficult to find or talk to, or may give you little or no feedback on your work. Make an appointment, go with a clear question or idea to discuss, and ask for comments on particular aspects of your work (see 'Approaching teachers', Chapter 3). If your attempts don't change the situation, find another person or group of people with whom you can discuss your learning. If your teacher is the person who formally assesses your work, you still need to be prepared to approach her or him if you want to discuss or question an assessment you are given.

How is your learning evaluated?

Your own evaluation

A written evaluation of your own work enables you to look at your learning in relation to what an assignment, course or programme has given you and what you have put into it. Of course your life cannot be neatly segmented as if it was an orange, and in a self-evaluation for a particular subject or piece of work you inevitably comment on the relevance of other work or other courses on your approach to studying, or your informal learning.

This may sound like a lot of writing. In fact self-evaluations can vary in length from a couple of paragraphs about a specific assignment to several typewritten pages about a course to three months of diary entries about your tertiary study. The guidelines in Table 15.1 were used by students preparing a written self-evaluation for a half-hour discussion with their teacher at the end of a course. They may suggest to you some ideas for evaluating your own learning.

Build up a learning portfolio during your formal education. This can give you a sense of how your learning develops, and can serve as a file from which to choose material when applying for entry to a particular course, an honours or postgraduate programme, or a future job.

What might you include in a learning portfolio?

- Items you have written about yourself as a learner—your aims, your questions, your enthusiasms (see 'Why keep a journal?', Chapter 11). Your self-evaluations are an important part of this.
- Individual pieces of work you have completed, along with comments and assessments by yourself or others.
- Any material connected with you as a learner, material such as drawings you have done in response to an idea, items of information you want to follow up, articles which have been particularly significant for you.
- Descriptions of your involvement in a paid job or voluntary work which is an important part of your learning.

> His [sic] '*noteworthy contribution*' is an essential step demonstrating a student's readiness for a degree. This may be a work of art, a research finding, or a community service. It will be intended to show that the candidate for a degree is more than a consumer of what earlier scholars, creative artists, and social leaders have given to him [sic].
>
> *University Without Walls*

Table 15.1 A self evaluation

Imagine you are writing for someone you will meet in the future. This unknown person wants to know about you and your work during the course.

- What were your goals when you started the course?
- What strengths did you feel you possessed?
- What were your weaknesses?
- How did you apply your strengths?
- How did you try to overcome your weaknesses?
- What work did you accomplish in quality and quantity (for example, in assignments or for tutorials)?
- How much recommended reading did you do for the course and for tutorials?
- What reading did you do beyond recommended readings (author, title, and any comments)?
- What ideas came from your 'outside' reading, and how did they relate to the course?
- What do you feel you learned:
  - about tutorials
  - about university or college
  - about yourself
  - about improving your ability to learn, and
  - about directions you want to pursue in future learning?

A self-evaluation should not be a compilation of your real or imagined shortcomings, or a prosaic listing of the number of books read and lectures attended. Write about your strengths as well as your weaknesses. Evaluate your learning so that if you read the evaluation again in a couple of years' time it would tell you about this one aspect of yourself. Your evaluation is not a formal course assignment to be judged, and will be next-to-worthless if you are not honest with and about yourself.

Other people's evaluations

Imagine what you would do in one of the following situations, and discuss this with friends if you can.

- You have spent two weeks carefully preparing and writing an assignment. When it is returned at the end of a tutorial, you skim through the pages and find the only comment on the final page—'C+. Satisfactory work'. You would like to ask the tutor for further comment but don't feel as if you know him well enough. What do you do?
- If asked to record an assessment of a friend's essay in an official student file, on what would you base your assessment? How would you record it?

- You are in your first year at university or college, and don't have to enrol in a particular programme until you have completed several first-year courses. You are told that all first year courses will be assessed only on a Pass/Fail basis. How does this assessment method affect your choice of courses?

The two most common methods used by individual teachers when evaluating your learning are:
- making an assessment which is to be recorded on your official student file, usually as a percentage, a letter grade or a Pass/Fail, and
- giving you feedback in the form of comments which are not officially recorded.

1 Unrecorded feedback

A person giving you feedback on your learning should give you constructive comments on both the strengths and the weaknesses as they perceive them, rather than merely demonstrating your seeming inadequacies or rating your work according to apparently 'objective' criteria. You may not be ready to understand and use all such comments, but you should be able to find them when you need them and you should be able to decide how detailed any responses need to be. Ask for the feedback you want—you can't expect a teacher to know this exactly. If possible, ask for feedback from the person you think might give you the most useful responses for a specific piece of work.

What form might feedback and comments take? Ideally this depends mostly on what you need. In formal education, the comments might be written or oral. They might be given ad hoc, or structured according to specific criteria or the requirements of situations such as a seminar. They might be part of a required individual consultation with your teacher at the end of a course, or given when an assignment is returned to you.

Feedback needs to be given in a way you understand. For example, if you ask for an idea to be clarified, you need an explanation which gives you more information but doesn't overwhelm you with detail, or if you have used a word inaccurately, you need to see it in different contexts so that you understand its correct meaning.

Feedback is most useful if given immediately or when you want it. For example:

- if a friend shows you how to throw a frisbee after you have made several unsuccessful attempts
- if a teacher gives you useful hints when you are attempting to remember the proof of a theorem, or

- if you ask for comments and discussion on a tutorial paper immediately after delivering it.

When a batch of work is due your teacher should have set aside time for commenting in some detail on each piece submitted; your responsibility is to hand the work in on time. Ask your teacher when your work will probably be available. If it hasn't been returned by this time, ask again when you can expect it back. It is particularly important to ask for prompt comments if you need them to proceed with your next assignment, or if you are an external student for whom the return of work is already slow because of mailing time.

2 Recorded assessment

> For most of the students, the competitive grade has come to be the essence. The naive teacher points to the beauty of the subject and the ingenuity of the research; the shrewd student asks if he is responsible for that on the final exam.
>
> *Paul Goodman*

Assessment may include formal, structured comments, but more usually it consists of a letter grade, a percentage or a pass/fail mark. The effect of *grades and percentages* on students' learning is controversial. Some people argue that grades and percentages enable student performances to be ranked more efficiently and objectively and that future employees will look only at grades and ignore comments. However, others argue that grading creates pressures which hinder learning, and that at least some aspects of student learning (such as tutorial participation or introductory courses) should not be graded. Some educational theorists argue that students should have a substantial input into any recorded assessment of their own learning.

Recorded assessment may be based on *continuous assessment* and/or on a major *final* paper or exam (see 'Exams', Chapter 5). 'Continuous assessment' refers to frequent cumulative assessments of your learning by methods such as weekly tests, regular seminar papers, monthly assignments or a combination of these. It may be used on its own or in combination with a major final assessment.

Educators debate the value of both forms of assessment. Continuous assessment provides you with regular feedback often on different types of work; but it can limit your freedom to pursue topics in depth and in your own way. However, if your work is assessed only or mostly at the end of a course, you may receive little feedback on your learning during a course, you have no formal indication of your progress until the end, and it is difficult to convey your total understanding of a subject in one final assessment.

Criteria and standards

When other people evaluate your learning, they usually do so in comparison with certain *criteria*. These include:

* your previous knowledge or work in an area
* the work of other students on a topic or subject area
* specific standards which have been decided on by one or more of the teachers involved in a course
* the educational/cultural models and preferences of an individual teacher who directly assesses your work, and
* the requirements of professional organisations.

As well as academic standards, the evaluation of your work is shaped by *administrative requirements*. These may include demands for assessment methods which require minimum staff time or for results which can be recorded in a particular computer format. They may reflect a desire to conform to practices in other institutions and the implicit expectations of employers and professional organisations.

For each programme, course or assignment, you need to know *how you are to be assessed* and the standard you are expected to reach to pass or achieve a particular grade or percentage.

You need to know as early as possible:

* what work you are expected to complete, and when
* whether you must pass each assignment in a course (or each course in a programme), or whether you can fail one or two of the individual assignments/courses and still gain an overall pass
* whether results are given as a Pass/Fail, a grade, a percentage and/or comments
* who assesses your work
* what degree of choice you have in the four previous points
* whether you are able or expected to contribute to the assessment of your work, and
* whether you can appeal against or record a dissent from an assessment in your official file and if so how.

The *academic criteria* used to arrive at a recorded assessment should reflect the objectives of an institution, a programme, a course and an assignment (see 'Expectations of academic assignments', Chapter 6). For example, if you are explicitly expected to display knowledge about a particular topic or to write cogently, the assessment criteria should explicitly take account of this. Such criteria should be available to you so that you can check them against your objectives, so that you know what is expected of you, and so that you can plan your work schedule ahead of time.

... students have to play an academic game to succeed. The rules of this game are determined by personal and organisational requirements of the course as they see them. These perceived requirements frequently conflict with aims explicitly stated by teachers. Teachers say they want students to have critical minds, but they feel threatened if they do. Teachers say they like students to write thoughtful answers in examinations, but they award marks on the basis on regurgitated 'facts'.

Donald A. Bligh et al.

Recorded assessment based on other people's aims inevitably means that you have to do a certain amount of guessing about what you are expected to learn. And when you are also required to compete with other students in your guessing, it is only fair that the rules of this guessing game are made as *explicit* as possible. This is particularly important where teachers have more than one criterion for assessment. For example, an assignment may be graded according to the content you select and your use of quotations and general writing style. If the result is recorded by a single letter grade, the letter you are given can't tell you how well you have done on each of the criteria. Neither does it indicate how your teacher averaged or added up your performance for each criterion to arrive at a single grade. To learn from evaluation it is vital that you know explicitly why your teacher chose the particular letter grade, and that you receive comments or grades for each of the criteria involved. If recorded assessments are to mean anything useful to you, they must be accompanied by detailed comments. Hopefully, recorded assessments are formalities which follow on from the comments you are given, but this seems rarely to be the case. Why?

The criteria used in assessment may be explicitly set out, widely accepted and clearly defined in an individual teacher's mind, but this doesn't make the use of these criteria objective. In practice, the individual teacher adopts some of the cultural and discipline-based guidelines used for evaluating learning in an area and combines these with a personal preference for certain academic conventions. And when applying these methods and criteria to your work, a teacher arrives at a result partly because of the feeling that your work evokes at the time. All students are familiar with the game of trying to uncover the subjective approaches that each teacher brings to assessment—and with the hope that their particular piece of work appears at the most favourable place in the pile of assignments to be marked.

After some years it began to happen that I would find myself in the middle of writing a comment and begin to wonder whether it could really be trusted, whether it was really useful. Perhaps I was telling someone about his flowery and wordy diction. His diction was indeed wordy and would be called flowery. But I began to wonder if this was *why* I was complaining about it. I sometimes found myself suspecting it was something else I couldn't put my finger on that bothered me but floweriness was more available. If I were in a different mood or the paper were in a different place in the stack, perhaps I wouldn't have made the comment I did.

Peter Elbow

Some underlying assumptions

When assessing your work, individual teachers bring to the evaluation process many assumptions which are integral to a particular educational system (see 'Tertiary institutions and you', Chapter 3). Since these assumptions are often not made explicit, it may not seem necessary or desirable for you to understand or question them. However, understanding the assumptions underlying evaluation in your culture can demystify the evaluation process; and questioning the assumptions can help you use evaluation for your learning purposes instead of blindly following someone else's. What are some of these assumptions?

Students should be evaluated by formal institutions

I look upon social and professional life as a continuous examination ... In ordinary scholastic examinations marks are allotted in stated proportions to various specified subjects ... The world in the same way, but almost unconsciously, allots marks to men [*sic*]. It gives them for originality of conception, for enterprise, for activity and energy ... and much besides of general value, as well as for more specially professional merits ... Those who have gained most of these tacit marks are ranked, by the common judgement of the leaders of opinion, as the fore-most men [*sic*] of their day.

F. Galton

In our society, compulsory education in primary and secondary schools is seen as inevitable and desirable. As part of this belief, it is assumed that one of the purposes of formal education is to evaluate and grade students according to the knowledge they are judged to have acquired and the characteristics they are deemed to have displayed. Teachers, for example, may define a child as 'hyperactive', 'promising', 'lazy', 'a problem child', 'a tomboy', or 'too sensitive', or a child may be placed in stream A or stream E, in a 'professional' or 'academic excellence' class.

In universities and colleges, evaluation and grading is continued in a specialised way. Tertiary education is often seen in itself as desirable in terms of intellectual and social status, if not always in terms of usefulness, and this is reflected in approaches to evaluation. Where and what you study has a further effect on this status. Are you attending a technical college or a newly-created or an old-established university? Are you training as a surgeon or a primary school teacher or an accountant? Are you planning to do postgraduate work, or are you studying for a diploma? Courses such as veterinary science or geology may be seen as 'relevant', or as 'mundane' and 'too job-oriented'. Subjects such as politics and literature are sometimes seen as 'real' and 'people-oriented', and sometimes as 'airy-fairy'. The area in which you enrol is often taken as an indicator of your status.

> 'I've been to a day-school, too,' said Alice. 'You needn't be so proud as all that.'
> 'With extras?' asked the Mock Turtle, a little anxiously.
> 'Yes,' said Alice: 'we learned French and music.'
> 'And washing?' said the Mock Turtle.
> 'Certainly not!' said Alice indignantly.
> 'Ah! Then yours wasn't a really good school,' said the Mock Turtle in a tone of great relief.
>
> *Lewis Carroll*

Evaluation is best done by teachers

In universities and colleges, it is usually assumed that people who have researched and published in a subject can also teach that subject, whether or not they are trained as teachers. It is further assumed that teachers can and should evaluate students' learning in the subject. Correspondingly, any evaluation you as a student make of your own formal learning is usually seen as less satisfactory than a teacher's, or your evaluation is ignored altogether.

Who decides what is worth learning and why and how this learning is to be evaluated? These decisions are made by an individual teacher, a group of teachers, administrators, other educational institutions or—at a fundamental level—society in general. An individual teacher may decide if you deserve to pass a course which leads to your becoming a doctor; but that teacher is mostly making that decision on behalf of other people. Those people include a professional medical association which sets down standards for doctors, patients who expect certain skills in doctors, and government bodies which make decisions about the number of doctors needed.

Learning can be reliably graded

Along with the assumption that teachers are the best people to evaluate your learning goes the assumption that there are reliable methods which teachers can administer to grade learning, methods such as examinations and tests, essays and reports. Many people disagree about the value of these methods, but they are used frequently because they are familiar and because they produce qualifiable 'results'. Too little consideration is given to whether the methods test what they are supposed to, or to alternatives such as self-evaluation or collective assessment. Very little thought is given to whether learning can or should be graded at all.

Evaluation can be objective

> Objectivity, in short, has the logical status of a myth: it builds up one sense of reality rather than others. It is a myth whose attainment and maintenance demands of its subjects a rigorous and continued asceticism ...
>
> *Michael Novak*

It is impossible for any human to be objective, yet humans make decisions about the purposes, methods and criteria of evaluation and often assume that they are being objective. In practice their decisions are based on an array of beliefs and assumptions such as what 'education' can be, what type of student is being assessed, what a university or college should be, which knowledge is valuable, and whether such knowledge can or should be evaluated.

The criteria by which your learning is evaluated may appear to you to be objective. These criteria are often taken for granted, and most people who use them arrive at results they believe to be valid. These criteria appear even more objective when they are elaborated in a system of precedents and percentages, examinations and 'weighted averages', 'full-time equivalent students' and confidential files. How else, it is argued, is a teacher or employer to know the 'good' students unless students have mostly As or firsts on an official record, unless a student has produced a thesis on an acceptable topic, or has completed all the work set for a course? It is easier and more economical in the short term to deal with the results of a system than with complex individuals. But problems arise when evaluation is claimed to be purely objective, or if the stated bases of evaluation differ from what students see as the real bases. As a student you need the opportunity to disagree with subjective assessments of your learning and to have an impact on these assessments.

Some teachers help with this because they acknowledge and attempt to spell out the assumptions, criteria, biases and beliefs by which they evaluate your learning. They don't assume that a practice which has 'always' been carried out, or which is used 'everywhere else' or is 'efficient' is thereby the best and only valid system. These teachers don't attempt to judge your work by immutable standards of what Physics or History is all about. You as a student then have the opportunity to accept, reject or negotiate these teachers' decisions about your work according to your own reasons and needs for learning.

Academic failure is always deserved

What if a piece of your knowledge is formally assessed and you are told that you don't know what you were expected to know—if you are given an E, or a Fail, or 45%? Many students assume that there is little they can do. If you care about that particular area of knowledge, you would probably try to find out what it is that you apparently don't know. You might ask yourself if you agree with the assessment. How would you decide? You could ask for the explicit criteria on which the assessment was based, but even then it could be difficult to decide if you agree unless you are dealing with a tangible physical skill like the ability to walk a straight line. What if you find that you disagree with the criteria? Do you challenge them?

Whatever you do, you will undoubtedly have to handle the implanted idea that you don't know. Do you fight it? Probably not, because teachers are people who know. Do you question a Fail on a university or college paper? Only if you have considerable confidence in your ability to write, to think and to understand, and if you are not overawed by the authority of teachers and institutions. Can you learn from a Fail, apart from the unhappy fact that you have been classed as a failure? If you expected to pass or if you have to pass, you might try to find out why you failed and use this to help you pass. Otherwise you probably accept the verdict, and try again or drop out.

This is the power of evaluation in formal education—that those who lose accept that they deserve to lose. Why? Because all of us are taught from our first day at school that there are experts who know—doctors, judges, priests, scientists, football heroes and test pilots. And teachers are the experts who know when students should pass and when they should fail. We all know that we should learn and to do so we have to go to school and then on to university or college if we want to learn some more. And teachers know what we should learn and when and how and why. As students, our job is to try to find our way through the maze of formal education, to discover the Right way to learn. We develop our own likes and dislikes among individual teachers and subjects, but we don't question the basic rules of the competition.

> School is ... a training for later life not because it teaches the 3 Rs (more or less), but because it instills the essential cultural nightmare fear of failure, envy of success, and absurdity ...
>
> *Jules Henry*

ᐁᐁ ᐁᐁ ᐁᐁ

To have been accepted as a student in a tertiary education institution means that you are accepted as a potential winner. The chances are high that as a new student you accepted most of the assumptions, purposes and criteria by which the decision was made. Whether you continue to accept any or all of them is one of the most fundamental decisions you can make as a tertiary student, and depends on how much you question and think about what learning is for you.

What are your assumptions about learning and formal education? What do you want to learn?
How do you want to learn?
Why do you want to learn?

Further reading

Boud, David. 1986. *Implementing Student Self Assessment.* Higher Educational and Research Development Society of Australasia Green Guide. HERDSA, University of New South Wales.

Lindsey, Crawford W. 1988. *Teaching Students to Teach Themselves.* Kogan Page, London. Chapters 8 and 9.

Rowntree, Derek. 1977. *Assessing Students: How Shall We Know Them?* Harper and Row, London.

Appendix

Discrimination: Sexist Language and Attitudes

Focus on discrimination has been concerned mostly with stereotypes based on sex, sexual preference, disability or race. Some other stereotypes commonly perpetuated in our culture relate to a person's age, religion, politics, economic circumstances and occupation. Using language which depicts people according to stereotypes is undesirable for a couple of reasons.

1 It shows a lack of awareness of our biases and prejudices. We can never be totally objective and it is essential to our learning and communicating that we are as honest as possible about our particular forms of subjectivity.
2 It reveals insufficient thought and care about what we are communicating. Some manifestations of the shoddy use of language are unsupported generalisations, terms which are not defined clearly, and clichés.

- 'Australians are easy-going'. Does this apply to all, most, many or a few? Has this general statement been supported and explained?
- In 'a neurotic woman' or 'the average Italian', 'neurotic' and 'average' are both terms which have precise meanings in certain disciplines. Has their meaning been defined?

- The phrase 'a career woman' is sometimes used to describe a woman seriously interested in her work, or 'a dole bludger' to describe someone who is unemployed. Why have these clichés been used?

In this appendix we look at sexist language and attitudes as an example of discrimination.

Avoiding sexist language

Sexist language is based on stereotypes which assume that being biologically male or female implies a whole range of associated characteristics. Occasionally it is relevant to describe a woman as petite or a man as husky, or to describe a female person as someone's wife or mother; but all too often adjectives such as these form part of a description in which they are irrelevant.

> 'Janet Smith, a petite brunette, has just become the first woman truck driver for the company.'

> 'Henry Jones, a husky ex-footballer, today graduated as a male nurse.'

One useful test for sexist language is to substitute mention of a woman where a man is mentioned and vice versa. Would you write 'Fred Smith, a tall redhead who is married to a typist, was today awarded his second gold medal'? How do you react to reading 'The stockbroker should at all times protect her clients' interests'?

Pronouns—'he'? 'him'? 'his'?

'He' is commonly used to refer to both females and males; for example, 'The best time to teach a child maths is when he is about two years old'. This convention limits our view of reality. Studies have shown that children literally think of a male when they read or hear the word 'he', and many people who argue for the use of 'he' as a convenient shorthand to include both sexes object to the suggestion that 'she' might serve the same purpose. There are alternatives to using only 'he', 'him', and 'his'.

- Re-word to eliminate unnecessary gender pronouns:

> This monograph is for a teacher concerned with improving communication with students ... The intention of the authors is to share experiences so that a reader may find some of them helpful in teaching situations.

- Change from singular to plural:

> This monograph is for teachers concerned with improving their communication with their students ... The intention of the authors

is to share experiences with teachers who may find some of them helpful in their own situations.

- Replace the masculine pronoun with 'he or she', 'him or her', 'her or his', or with 'he/she', or 's/he', or with 'one' or 'you'.

'Man'?

The word 'man' has an ambiguous double usage—to refer to a male person and to describe humanity in general. As with the use of 'he', the word 'man' creates a male image. When we read of 'man the hunter' we visualise a male adult and forget about the women (and children and elderly people) who are supposedly part of the total picture.

Instead of:	Consider:
man or mankind	humanity, human beings, people, the human race, men and women
manpower	human resources, human energy, workers, workforce
the man in the street	a typical person, the average person, lay person
manmade	synthetic, artificial, manufactured, constructed
chairman	chairperson, the chair, leader, co-ordinator, convenor.

Apples are apples and oranges are oranges; but apples *and* oranges are fruit.

Without Bias

'A man's job'? 'Woman's work'?

Our language is based on assumptions, frequently outdated, about the occupations of women and men (for example, nurses are assumed to be female and doctors male). Women are categorised primarily as mothers and wives, despite the high proportion of women who are in the paid workforce. We read newspaper headlines such as 'Rebel mum of three suicides in cell' to describe the prison death of a prominent political activist and journalist; or 'Dr Samuel Keep, a leading physician, and his wife Margaret' is used to introduce two doctors who are married. Women should be treated as people in their own right, and women in traditionally masculine fields (or men in traditionally feminine fields) should not be singled out.

Instead of:	Consider:
'Anna Clarke, career girl' to describe a woman who takes her work seriously	describing the woman's occupation 'Anna Clarke, teacher' or 'Anna Clarke, engineer'
terms such as 'male secretary', 'lady executive' or 'woman doctor'	the terms 'secretary', 'executive' or 'doctor' to apply to both men and women
workmen	worker, labourer, employee or staff member
author or authoress	author
waiter or waitress	steward or attendant
the lady of the house, housewife, cleaning lady, cleaning women	the consumer, home maker housekeeper, domestic help, cleaner.

Names

Different attitudes of men and women are reflected in the inconsistent use of forenames and surnames, for example, 'Peter Braithwaite and Miss Smith', 'Braithwaite and Janet Smith'. The use of titles also reveals attitudes, for example, 'Dr White and Alison Black' (instead of 'Dr Black'). One of the most common examples of discrimination by title is that the title 'Mr' refers to both married and single men while the terms 'Mrs' and 'Miss' are used for women, thus assuming that marital status should be an important part of a woman's identity, but not a man's.

Instead of:	Consider:
Peter Braithwaite and Miss Smith	Mr Braithwaite and Ms Smith, or Peter Braithwaite and Janet Smith
'Dr Tom Jones and Ms Margot Thomas recently published a book on marine biology. Margot is now doing further research on this topic. Dr Jones is acting as her assistant.'	'Dr Tom Jones and Ms Margot Thomas recently published a book on marine biology. Ms Thomas is now doing further research on this topic. Dr Jones is acting as her assistant.'

Put-downs

Patronising descriptions of women are unnecessary and are often clichés.

Instead of:	Consider:
the girls, the ladies, the fair sex, the weaker sex	the women
the missus, the wife, the little lady, the better half	wife (or refer to the woman concerned by her name)
chicks, birds, girls	girls (for the younger women), women
libbers	feminists, liberationists

- Issues that seriously concern women should not be considered as trivial or funny, for example, the use of 'Ms', discrimination in employment, or rape.
- Jokes which are based on stereotypes of both women and men are offensive to many people, for example, jokes about incompetent women drivers, frustrated spinsters, gossiping housewives, men-hating 'women's libbers', hen-pecked husbands, helpless house-husbands, effeminate males.
- Referring to 'men and ladies' instead of 'men and women' or 'ladies and gentlemen' is discriminatory.
- Don't always refer to 'men and women' or 'he and she'; use 'women and men' or 'she and he' as well.
- Avoid talking about 'man and wife'; instead use 'partners', 'husband and wife', 'a man and a woman' or 'a couple'.

Identity

'Who's she?' they asked
and straight away
I answered back,
'She's Brian's wife'.
Why say it so?
Why not just say
'She's Josephine'?
A rose by any name
should smell as sweet.
But Josephine's a sweeter name
by far, than
'Brian's wife'
or 'Jenny's mum'
or 'Noelene's friend'.
    Brian's Wife Jenny's Mum

Male and female characteristics

- Unless it is relevant to describe a person's physical or sexual attributes, omit them. Women are often described as blonde or brunette, curvaceous or slim, or men as tall, dark or handsome when such a description is unnecessary.
- Instead of assuming that only women can be gentle, compassionate, sensitive and only men can be decisive, logical, assertive, strong, or adventurous, think of these qualities as human rather than sex-based. Similarly, avoid the assumption that only women are passive, helpless or emotional and only men are insensitive, angry or ruthless.
- Women who don't comply with the stereotype of a passive female and men who don't conform to the image of an aggressive male are often described in a negative way.

Instead of:	Consider:
a pushy woman	a powerful woman
a gossiping woman	a talkative woman
an effeminate man	a gentle man
an hysterical woman	a woman who is upset
an aggressive woman	an assertive woman

Avoiding sexist attitudes

Sexist language is a subtly pervasive yet tangible way of perpetuating stereotypes. Sexist attitudes are equally pervasive and subtle. The following are some instances of sexist attitudes which you are likely to find in written material.

- **The 'invisible woman'** attitude occurs when women as part of a group of people or society are ignored or rarely included in writings about that group or society. For example:
    - in writings on human evolution, where only hunting societies and the activities of male *homo sapiens* are considered, with little or no reference to the female of the species
    - in sociology, where there has until recently been a dearth of studies of housework as work in itself, rather than as part of a woman's role as a wife/mother
    - in children's books, where the majority of characters in stories and illustrations are male, and
    - in anthologies, where most or all of the writers represented are male.

- **The 'token woman'** position is seen when individual women are described because they are unusual but the majority of women are still ignored. For example in history texts, which include descriptions of the life of a woman who is prominent as a social reformer (such as Elizabeth Fry) or a pioneer in a traditionally male field (such as Elizabeth Blackwell), but which neglect the 'ordinary' female contemporaries of these women.
- **The 'patronised woman'** approach occurs when a special section is allocated to women without a corresponding section for men. For example, a book index which has an entry under 'Women' but none under 'Men'.
- **Stereotypes** of women and men are common. For example:
  - in sociology texts which assume that women are wives and mothers and that men are breadwinners, and
  - in career information brochures which assume that women are nurses and men are doctors, or that females have no serious work interests.

Instances of these attitudes can also be found when discrimination is based on grounds other than sex. For example, the 'invisible' ethnic group; the invisibility of people in poverty; the 'token' black or 'working-class' representative; the patronised handicapped person or religious sect; stereotypes of homosexuals or of elderly people or of socialists.

≈ ≈ ≈

In writing, reading and speaking, being aware of discriminatory attitudes or language in ourselves and in others requires that we question and evaluate what is communicated. The discriminatory thought patterns of many academic disciplines need to be redressed, but these changes are not just exercises to be followed in the interests of scholarly rigour. They are changes which involve an awareness of the biases we bring to our learning, changes in who we are and how we see the other human beings with whom we live. Such changes can only be achieved by consistent and conscious effort because our discriminatory attitudes and language are part of who we have learned to be.

Further reading

Curriculum Development Centre. 1975. *Guidelines for Writers*. CDC, Canberra.

Hill, Robert. (n.d.) *Understanding Inequality* in Lovat, Terry (ed). People, Culture and Change. Social Science Press, Wentworth Falls.

International Association of Business Communicators. 1977. *Without Bias: A Guidebook for Nondiscriminatory Communication*. IABC, San Francisco.

Lakoff, Robin. 1975. *Language and Woman's Place*. Harper and Row, New York.

McGraw-Hill Book Company. 1974. *Guidelines for Equal Treatment of the Sexes*. McGraw-Hill, New York.

Miller, C., & Swift, K. 1981. *The Handbook of Non-Sexist Writing for Writers, Editors and Speakers*. Women's Press. London.

Poynton, Cate. 1985. *Language and Gender: Making the Difference*. Deakin University Press, Geelong, Victoria.

Random House. 1976. *Random House Guidelines for Multi-Ethnic/Nonsexist Survey*. Random House, New York.

Quotation Sources

1 You

3   Gay Gaer Luce, 1973, *Body Time: The Natural Rhythms of the Body*, Paladin, St. Albans, England, p. 177.

3   Evelyn Waugh, 1928, *Decline and Fall*, Chapman and Hall, London, p. 143.

4   Virginia Woolf, 1929, *A Room of One's Own*, Harcourt, Brace and World, New York, p. 18.

5   Gayle Olinekova, 1982, Go For It, Simon and Schuster, New York, p. 142

6   Fred Morgan, 1972, *Here and Now II: An Approach to Writing Through Perception*, Harcourt Brace Jovanovich, New York, p. 3.

6   Liz Carpenter, 1977, in 'The All-American Complaint 'If I Only Had the Time...' ', *Ms*, January,p. 48.

7   Marie Bashkirtseff, quoted in Jean Webster, 1912, *Daddy-Long-Legs*, Scholastic Inc., Apple Paperbacks, New York, p. 75.

8   Michel Foucault, quoted in Rux Martin, 1988, 'Truth, power, self: an interview with Michel Foucault', October 25, 1982. In Luther H. Martin *et al.* (eds), *Technologies of the Self: a seminar with Michel Foucault*, The University of Massachusetts Press, Massachusetts, p. 14.

10   Sidney B. Simon *et al.*, 1972, V*alues Clarification: A Handbook of Practical Strategies for Teachers and Students*, Hart Publishing, New York, pp. 13-14.

11   Jean Webster, 1912, *Daddy-Long-Legs*, Scholastic Inc., Apple Paperbacks, New York, p. 22.

11   Eight-year old girl, in Hazel Edwards (ed.), 1975, *Women Returning to Study*, Primary Education, Richmond, Victoria, p. 43.

13   Margaret Norton, in Allan Hall (ed.), *Worse Verse* from the 'Look!' pages of *The Sunday Times*, Times Newspapers, London, undated and not paginated.

14   William Shakespeare, *Hamlet*, Act I, Scene iii, p. 58.

2 Planning When and How You Study

15   Jerome K. Jerome, 1947, *The Idle Thoughts of an Idle Fellow*, J.W.Arrowsmith, Bristol, p. 51.

16   Western proverb.

17/18 Norton Juster, 1962, *The Phantom Tollbooth*, William Collins, London, p. 24.

18   Anon.

20   Edwin C. Bliss, 1977, *Getting Things Done: The ABCs of Time Management*, Macmillan, Melbourne, pp. 32–3.

21   Lewis Carroll, 1970, *The Annotated Alice: Alice's Adventures in Wonderland and Through the Looking-Glass*, revised edn, Penguin Middlesex p. 304.

22   Vivienne, in Hazel Edwards, p. 26.

24   Lewis Carroll, p. 322.

25   Barbara Sher, 1979, *Wishcraft: How to Get What you Really Want*, Ballantine Books, New York, p. 213.

3 Becoming an Independent Student

27   Ian Lowe, 1990, 'The dying of the light', *The Australian Universities Review*, vol 33, nos 1 and 2.

27   Harold Taylor, 1969, *Students Without Teachers*, McGraw-Hill, New York, p. xii.

29   Jean Webster, p. 79.

29   Lewis Carroll, p. 88.

30   Michael Deakin, 1973, *The Children on the Hill: The Story of an Extraordinary Family*, Quartet Books, London, p. 27.

32   F. R. Leavis quoted in J. Wyatt, 1990, *Commitment to Higher education: seven West European thinkers on the essence of the university, Max Horkheimer, Karl Jaspers, F.R Leavis, J.H. Newman, Jose Ortega y Gasset, Paul Tillich, Miguel de Unamuno*, Society for

Research into Higher Education and Open University Press, Buckinghamshire, p. 82

33 E. P. Thompson, 1967, 'Time, work-discipline and industrial capitalism', *Past and present: a journal of historical studies*, vol. 38, December, 56–97, p. 50.

34 Michel Foucault in Martin *et al.*, p. 9.

35 Jean Webster, p. 103.

38 Gwen Wesson (ed.), 1975, *Brian's Wife Jenny's Mum*, Dove Communications, Blackburn, Victoria, pp. 164–5.

4 Asking Your Own Questions

44 John Holt, 1977, *Instead of Education: Ways to Help People Do Things Better*, Penguin Books, Middlesex, p. 20.

45 Donald Sutherland, 1951, *Gertrude Stein: A Biography of her Work*, Yale University Press, New Haven, p. 203.

46 Bertrand Russell, 1964, quoted by G.M. Carstairs 'Concepts of Insanity in Different Cultures', in *The Listener*, LXXII, 1844, July 30, p. 160.

46 N.J. Berrill, 1958, *Man's Emerging Mind*, Dennis Dobson, London, p. 158.

46 Kurt Vonnegut Jr, 1971, *Cat's Cradle*, Victor Gollancz, London, p. 150.

47 Jules Feiffer, 1963, *Crawling Arnold*, Dramatists Play Service, New York, in J.M. and M.J. Cohen (eds.), *A Dictionary of Modern Quotations*, p. 72.

48 Dylan Thomas, 1954, *Quite Early One Morning*, New Directions Publishing, New York, quoted in Daniel G. Kozlovsky, *An Ecological and Evolutionary Ethic*, Prentice-Hall, Englewood Cliffs, New Jersey, p. 7.

49 Lewis Carroll, p. 251.

50 John Holt, *Instead of Education*, pp. 87–88.

50 John Holt, 1969, *How Children Fail*, Penguin Books, Middlesex, England, p. 166.

5 Learning and Remembering

53 Ogden Nash, 1972, 'Who Did Which? or Who Indeed?' in *I Wouldn't Have Missed It: Selected Poems of Ogden Nash*, Little, Brown and Co., Boston, p. 224.

54 Lewis Carroll, pp. 137–88.

55 Sam Keen, 1970, *To a Dancing God*, Harper and Row, New York, p. 32.

58 Lewis Carroll, p. 149.

59   Hermann Hesse, source unknown.

61   J Chaytor, 1945, *From Script to Print*, other details unknown.

61   Lewis Carroll, pp. 247–8.

63   Jorge Luis Borges, 1972, 'Funes, the Memorious', *A Personal Anthology*, Picador, London, p. 33.

65   Jean Webster, p. 82.

6 Analysing and Researching a Topic

67   Lewis Carroll, p. 137.

68   William Shakespeare, *Henry IV Pt I*, Scene iii, p. 41.

68   Norton Juster, 1962, The Phantom Tollbooth, Collins, England, p. 17.

69   Gunter Kress, 1990, 'Two Kinds of Power', *The English Magazine*, vol. 24, Autumn, p.4.

74   *Lewis Carroll, p. 269.*

75   Robert M. Pirsig, 1975, *Zen and the Art of Motorcycle Maintenance*, Bantam Books, New York, p. 166. Originally published by The Bodley Head, London.

75   Marshall McLuhan, 1969, interviewed by Eric Norden 'Playboy Interview: Marshall McLuhan', *Playboy*, March, p. 54.

78   Zoe Sofoulis, 1992, 'Serendipitous Ventures', *StarGuide: Study Techniques and Materials*, Murdoch University, Western Australia, p. 21.

78/9 David Hawkins, 1973, 'What it Means to Teach' in *Teachers College Record*, vol. 75, no. 1, September, p. 11.

81   Lewis Carroll, p. 86.

81   John Milton, in *The Oxford Dictionary of Quotations*, p. 352.

82   Idries Shah ('Rahimi'), 1974, *Thinkers of the East*, Penguin Books, Middlesex, England, p. 104.

83   Samuel Johnson, in *The Oxford Dictionary of Quotations*, p. 276.

7 Using Libraries and Other Information Sources

88   A Librarian, source unknown.

91   Edward Gibbon, in *The Oxford Dictionary of Quotations*, p. 224.

94   *University Without Walls: First Report*, Antioch College, Yellow Spring, Ohio, undated, p. 32.

97   Werner Heisenberg, 1959, *Physics and Philosophy: The Revolution in Modern Science*, Allen and Unwin, London, p. 75.

98   Joan Acker, Kate Barry, & Joke Esseveld, 1983, 'Objectivity and Truth: Problems in Doing Feminist Research', *Women's Studies International Forum*, vol. 6, no. 4, pp. 423–435

99   Edmund Carpenter, 1970, 'The New Languages', in Edmund Carpenter & Marshall McLuhan (eds), *Explorations in Communication: An Anthology*, Jonathan Cape, London, p. 163.

102 Ronald Firbank, 1961, 'The Flower Beneath the Foot', *The Complete Ronald Firbank*, Duckworth, London, p. 500.

102 Marshall McLuhan, 1967, from the film 'This is Marshall McLuhan: The Medium is the Massage', USA.

8 Reading

105 W. Somerset Maugham, 1967, *The Summing Up*, William Heinemann, London, p. 92.

106 Bronwyn Mellor, Annette Patterson & Marnie O'Neill, 1991, *Reading Fiction*, Chalkface Press, Scarborough, W.A. p. 21.

107 Doris Lessing, *Martha Quest*, 1970, A Plume Book, The New American Library, New York, p. 200.

111 John Holt, *Instead of Education*, pp. 74–75.

112 Doris Lessing, p. 28.

113 Lewis Carroll, p. 191

114 Francis Bacon, in *The Oxford Dictionary of Quotations*, p. 27.

117 Idries Shah, 1970, 'A Quality Must Have a Vehicle', *The Way of the Sufi*, Penguin Books, Middlesex, England, 1974, p. 61.

119 John M. Culkin, 'A Schoolman's Guide to Marshall McLuhan', *Saturday Review*, p. 301.

119 Bronwyn Mellor *et al.*, p.44.

121 Samuel Johnson, in *The Oxford Dictionary of Quotations*, p. 280.

122 Lewis Carroll, pp. 189-190.

123 Jean Webster, p. 36.

124 Lewis Carroll, p. 25.

9 Listening to Lectures

129 Samuel Johnson, source unknown.

129 Donald A. Bligh, 1972, *What's the Use of Lectures?* Penguin Education, Penguin Books, Middlesex, England, p. 61.

131 Lewis Carroll, p. 122.

131 Lewis Carroll, p 146.

135 Anon., in *A Dictionary of Modern Quotations*, p. 5.

136 Enrico Fermi, 1970, quoted in Anthony Smith, *The Body*, Penguin Books, Middlesex, England, p. 16.

10 Participating in Tutorials and Seminars

140 Samuel Johnson, in *The Oxford Dictionary of Quotations*, p.280.

144 Lewis Carroll, p. 235.

145 A student quoted in The Nuffield Foundation, 1976, *Small Group Teaching: Selected Papers*, Group for Research and Innovation in Higher Education, London, p. 123.

147 Lewis Carroll, p. 158.

147 Cicero, source unknown.

148 Anon.

149 A student quoted in The Nuffield Foundation, pp. 122–23.

150 *Brian's Wife Jenny's Mum*, Gwen Wesson, pp. 79-80.

11 Developing Your Writing

152 Erica Jong, 1975, 'The Artist as Housewife/The Housewife as Artist' in *Here Comes and Other Poems*, A Signet Book, The New American Library, New York, p. 255.

153/4 Colette, 1960, *The Vagabond*, trans. by Enid McLeod, Penguin Books, Middlesex, England, p. 13.

154 Kurt Vonnegut, 1980, 'How to Write With Style', advertisement in *Psychology Today*, September, p. 58.

155 Phil Mullins, 1988, 'The Fluid Word: Word Processing and its Mental Habits, *Thought*, vol. 63 no. 251, December.

156 Peter Elbow, 1981, *Writing with Power*, Oxford University Press, Melbourne, p. 14.

157 Jim R. Martin, 1985, F*actual Writing: Exploring and Challenging Social Reality*, Deakin University Press, Geelong, p. 15.

157 *Brian's Wife Jenny's Mum*, Gwen Wesson, p. 109

158 Kurt Vonnegut, 'How to Write With Style', p. 58.

159 Oscar Wilde, 1977, 'The Importance of Being Earnest', *The Portable Oscar Wilde*, Richard Aldington (ed.), Penguin Books, Middlesex, England, p. 481.

159/60 Ira Progoff, 'Intensive journal', unpublished handout from The Personal Growth and Creativity Program of Dialogue House Associates, 45 West Tenth St., New York, N.Y. 10011.

161 Anais Nin, 1966, *The Diary of Anais Nin* 1931–1934, Gunther Stuhlmann (ed.), A Harvest Book, New York, p. 89.

161 Peter Elbow, 1981, *Writing with Power*, Oxford University Press, Melbourne, p. 20–21.

12 Writing Assignments

165 Ernest Hemingway, 1965, interviewed by George Plimpton, *Writers at Work: The Paris Review Interviews*, Viking, New York. p. 235.

167 Francis Quarles, 1979, in *The Oxford Dictionary of Quotations*, 3rd edn, O.U.P., Oxford, p. 403

167 *Brian's Wife Jenny's Mum*, Gwen Wesson, p. 81.

169 Russell Baker, 1972, 'At Lunch' in Joseph Frank, *You*, Harcourt, Brace, Jovanovich, New York, p. 63.

170 Gwen Wesson, p. 1.20.

171 Lewis Carroll, p. 95.

173/4 Winston Churchill, 1958, *My Early Life*, School edn, Andrew Scotland (ed.), Odhams Press, London, p. 143.

175   Kurt Vonnegut, 'How to Write With Style', p. 58.

175   Samuel Johnson, in *The Oxford Dictionary of Quotations*, p. 274.

177   Ken Macrorie, 1968, *Writing to be Read*, Hayden Book Co., New York, p. 89.

13 Writing Scientific Reports

180   F. Peter Woodford, 1967, 'Sounder Thinking Through Clearer Writing', *Science*, 156, 3776, May, p. 743.

182   Robert M. Pirsig, p. 100.

185   Robert M. Pirsig, p. 101.

186   F. Peter Woodford, p. 744.

187   Robert M. Pirsig, p. 102.

190   F. Peter Woodford, p. 744.

191   A.A. Milne, 1926, *Winnie the Pooh*, Methuen and Co., London, p. 48.

194   John Holt, *Instead of Education*, p. 99-100.

14 Using Conventions

196   Lewis Carroll, p. 156.

197   Horace, 1936, 'The Art of Poetry', transl. by Edward Henry Blakeney in *The Complete Works*, Casper J. Kraemer, Jr. (ed.), The Modern Library, New York, p. 401.

197   Dorothy Parker, 1939, 'The Little Hours', in *Here Lies: The Collected Stories of Dorothy Parker*, Longmans, Green and Co., London, pp. 209-210.

199   Lord Byron, 1945, English Bards and Scotch Reviewers', 1.66, in *The Poetical Works of Lord Byron*, Oxford University Press, London, p. 114.

199   Ivy Baker, 1984, *If Wishes were Horses*, Bluegum, Angus and Robertson, Sydney, p. 32.

207   George Eliot, 1950, *Middlemarch*, The Zodiac Press, London, p. 70.

207   Charles Dickens, *Great Expectations*, Chapman and Hall, London, undated, p. 50.

208   Australian Government Publication Service, 1988. *Style Manual: For Authors, Editors and Printers of Australian Government Publications*, 4th edn, revised by J. Pitson, AGPS, Canberra.

15 Learning from Evaluation

213   James Agate, *A Dictionary of Modern Quotations*, p. 2.

214   John Holt, *Instead of Education*, p. 61.

214   Antoine de Saint-Exupèry, 1943, *The Little Prince*, Harcourt, Brace and World, New York, p. 39.

215   Winston Churchill, pp. 21-22.

216   *University Without Walls, First Report*, p. 35.

219   Paul Goodman, 1971, *Compulsory Miseducation*, Penguin Education, Penguin Books, Middlesex, England, p. 106.

221   Donald A. Bligh et al., 1975, *Teaching Students*, An Exeter University Teaching Service Production, Devon, England, p. 91.

221/2 Peter Elbow, p. 118.

222   F. Galton, 1896, *Hereditary Genius*, London Macmillan, pp. 49-50.

223   Lewis Carroll, p. 128.

224   Michael Novak, 1970, *The Experience of Nothingness*, Harper and Row, New York, p. 37.

225   Jules Henry, 1972, *Culture Against Man*, Penguin Books, Middlesex, England, p. 250.

Appendix   Discrimination: Sexist Language and Attitudes

229   International Association of Business Communicators, 1977, *Without Bias: A Guidebook for Nondiscriminatory Communication*, International Association of Business Communicators, San Francisco, p. 22.

231   Gwen Wesson, p. 26

Reference books

Teaching study skills

Ballard, Brigid & Clanchy, John. 1991. *Teaching Students from Overseas: A Brief Guide for Lecturers and Supervisors*. Longman Cheshire, Melbourne.

Fairbairn, Gavin J. & Winch, Christopher. 1991. *Reading, Writing and Reasoning: A Guide for Students*. The Society for Research into Higher Education and Open University Press, Buckingham.

Gibbs, G. 1981. *Teaching Students to Learn: A Student-Centred Approach*. The Open University Press, Milton Keynes.

Habeshaw, Trevor, Habeshaw, Sue, & Gibbs, Graham. 1989. *53 Interesting Ways of Helping Your students to Study*. 2nd edn, Technical and Educational Services Ltd, England. (See also the other seven volumes in this series for interesting ideas on teaching.)

Lindsey, Crawford W. 1988. *Teaching Students to Teach Themselves*. Kogan Page, London.

Main, Alex. 1980. *Encouraging Effective Learning: An Approach to Study Counselling*. Scottish Academic Press, Edinburgh.

Marshall, Lorraine (ed.). 1987. *Learning from Each Other: Proceedings of the 7th Language and Learning Skills Conference*. Murdoch University, Murdoch, Western Australia.

Marshall, Lorraine. 1991. *Learning Skills Tutors' Guide*. Murdoch University, Murdoch, Western Australia.

Marton, F., Hounsell, D. & Entwistle, N. (eds). 1984. *The Experience of Learning*. Scottish Academic Press, Edinburgh

Nightingale, Peggy. 1986. 'Improving Student Writing'. HERDSA Green Guide. University of New South Wales.

Nisbet, John & Shucksmith, Janet. 1986. *Learning Strategies*. Routledge & Kegan Paul, London.

Webb, Carolyn. 1991. 'Writing an Essay in the Humanities and Social Sciences' from Webb, Carolyn (ed.) *Writing Practice for University Students*. (series) Learning Assistance Centre, University of Sydney, Sydney.

Webb, Carolyn & Murison, E. 1991. 'Writing a Research Paper' from Webb, Carolyn. (ed.) *Writing Practice for University Students* (series) Learning Assistance Centre, University of Sydney, Sydney.

Index